KEYS TO CAREER SUCCESS

Carol Carter

Carol Ozee

Beth Bollinger

 Prentice Hall
Upper Saddle River, New Jersey 07458

Library of Congress Cataloging-in-Publication Data

Carter, Carol.
    Keys to career success / Carol Carter, Carol Ozee, Beth Bollinger.
      p. cm.
    Includes index.
    ISBN 0-13-834277-6
    1. Career development. I. Ozee, Carol. II. Bollinger, Beth.
    III. Title.
    HF5381.C368 1998
    650.14—dc21   97-11419
                                                              CIP

Acquisitions editor: Todd Rossell
Editorial/production supervision: Janet McGillicuddy
Managing production editor: Mary Carnis
Director of production/manufacturing: Bruce Johnson
Marketing manager: Frank Mortimer, Jr.
Prepress/manufacturing buyer: Marc Bove
Electronic page composition: KR Publishing Services
Chapter opening photos: Rick Singer Photography
Interior photos: Tan Pham
Interior design: HRS
Art director: Marianne Frasco
Cover art: Warren Gebert
Cover design: Bruce Kenselaar

©1998 by Prentice-Hall, Inc.
A Simon & Schuster Company
Upper Saddle River, New Jersey 07458

Printed in the United States of America

10 9 8 7 6 5 4 3 2 1

ISBN 0-13-834277-6

Prentice-Hall International (UK) Limited, *London*
Prentice-Hall of Australia Pty. Limited, *Sydney*
Prentice-Hall Canada Inc., *Toronto*
Prentice-Hall Hispanoamericana, S.A., *Mexico*
Prentice-Hall of India Private Limited, *New Delhi*
Prentice-Hall of Japan Inc., *Tokyo*
Simon & Schuster Asia Pte. Ltd., *Singapore*
Editora Prentice-Hall do Brasil, Ltda., *Rio de Janeiro*

*To people everywhere who, through their purpose
and their work, seek ways to improve themselves
and the world we live in.*

CONTENTS

PART 1 CAREER PLANNING AND DECISION MAKING

CHAPTER 1 Discovering Who You Are: Learning about Yourself   3

Exploring your personality traits and your values because the more you know about who you are and what you believe in, the better equipped you will be to choose a career path that's right for you.

CHAPTER 2 Assessing Your Interests and Abilities: Defining Your Passions   23

Exploring what interests and skills you already have and learning about where your talents lie, so that you can identify careers where you can excel and that you would enjoy.

CHAPTER **6**   Networking: How to Connect
with People   121

Teaching you to reach out to the people that you know
and learning how to build relationships throughout a lifetime.

CHAPTER **7**   Practical Experience: Internships, Co-Ops,
and Part-Time Jobs   145

Exploring options available in obtaining internships in
your chosen or related fields.

CHAPTER 11 Workplace 2000: How to Be Competitive
and Still Remain True to Yourself 247

Understanding how to deal with and excel in the workplace of the future while simultaneously learning to weigh
career, personal, and life priorities.

We wrote this book to help people focus on molding their career paths to fit the larger picture of their life goals, rather than just giving quick-fix answers on how to "land" a job. Certainly, students entering the workplace need to be concerned about making financial ends meet. We hope, however, that this book helps them not only to address their financial goals but also to develop and understand their personal and individual goals as well, especially as they relate to career development.

This first edition of KEYS TO CAREER SUCCESS retains the innovations and the tone of other KEYS TO SUCCESS books authored by Carol Carter, and has the following significant features:

Real People, Questions, and Answers: Featured in each chapter of this book are stories and advice from real people who have worked hard at building their own careers and can share their thoughts and ideas about career development. There are over 50 people—from accountants to marketers to teachers and lawyers—who unselfishly took their time to think through their own career paths and share with our readers the peaks, valleys, and lessons that they have experienced along the road of developing careers that mattered to them.

By reading these real life stories, students can learn from others' experiences rather than just read lectures on hypothetical career situations. Professors can point to career advice from *real people* in all different types of careers to explain the importance of career planning and skills development, rather than just expound about the importance of these areas without real life examples.

Skill Building End-of-Chapter Exercises: End-of-chapter exercises ask practical questions about career development and planning that help students to really prepare for their future. The exercises for each chapter are divided into three categories—Asking Questions and Getting Answers, Collaborative Learning and Team-Building Skills, and Long-Term Planning: Key to Your Personal Portfolio—that are designed specifically to teach students skills that they need in the workforce itself.

Success Skills Emphasized Throughout: Workplace skills such as communication, leadership, teamwork, problemsolving, decisionmaking, networking, creativity, tenacity, common sense smarts, ethics, independence, adaptability, and an overall positive attitude are discussed throughout. The text provides advice on how to juggle the "real world" workplace with personal life goals, and emphasizes the need to embrace technology and further education even after the career path has begun. This real-life emphasis on career development gives professors the opportunity to discuss how students can plan for their entire future (and not just the next few months). Included in the text is a discussion of how to plan for the unexpected and how to develop your own portfolio for future career moves.

Emphasis on Research and Networking: Two special features of KEYS TO CAREER SUCCESS are its unique, in-depth discussions of Researching and Ranking Companies (Chapter 5) and Networking (Chapter 6). These step-by-step guides are intended to take a lot of the mystery out of how to find a job. The Networking chapter in particular is an excellent tool for professors to help students think about how building relationships with people they like and respect can lead to positive career developments down the road.

This textbook touches a broad spectrum of areas, from discovering who you are to conducting career research, to learning how to present and prepare yourself for career opportunities and choices. We want this book to be a never-ending career reference that will stay on a student's bookshelf for a long time—not just for the duration of a semester-long class.

Carol Carter
Carol Ozee
Beth Bollinger

ACKNOWLEDGMENTS

In writing *Keys to Career Success*, we drew a great source of energy from many different people.

Pamela Zemper spent countless hours interviewing people about their career experiences. The result of Pam's efforts can be seen throughout this book in the stories these people shared. In addition, Pam drafted several career profiles as well as parts of the book. Pam also went through the entire text and made comments for improvement.

Our student editors, Kathleen Cole and Tim Short gave us valuable insights on the text—from a returning student's point of view and the perspective of a traditional college student. Jennifer Moe and Marisa Connell, students at Gonzaga University, also helped immensely in giving us feedback on drafts of the text. Both Kathleen and Marisa also helped in the mechanics of getting the book to the printer. Thanks, too, go to Raymona Baldwin and her professor Harry Hazel for allowing us to use the wonderful letter of recommendation he wrote for her. In the same vein, thanks to Jennifer Moe for giving us permission to use her application as an example of the whole "packet," and Lou R. Maxon, her former employer at Code Magazine, for letting us use his letter of recommendation as part of that packet.

The following people, all present or former instructors, gave us feedback on the text while it was still in draft form, helping us to make a lot of improvements: Rita Delude, Paige Terry, Nancy Kosmicke, Charlene Pearson, Jeff McIlroy, Celesia Snyder, Sharon Bollinger, Susan Casmier, Valerie DeAngelis, and Lillian Cole. Thanks to Jeff McIlroy for sharing his expertise and classroom strategies from UT Arlington.

Many thanks to the tireless people at Prentice Hall whose creativity and initiative made this book possible. Tricia Liscio, sales representative in Dallas, signed this project. Without her, the authors would never have met and this book would not have been written. Our editor, Todd Rossell, gave us direction, guidance and fast turn-around on key decisions. Our marketing manager, Frank Mortimer and our sales director, Karen Austin, provided market insight and worked hard to communicate our unique message. Our production editor, Janet McGillicuddy, was first-rate. She coached us and kept us focused on our goals and deadlines. Our special thanks also to the whole production team— Mary Carnis, Marianne Frasco and Kerry Reardon who worked with Janet to design and produce the book. Finally, we would like to thank the Career and Technology team, and especially Robin Baliszewski, Rit Dojny and Dave Garza and the sales and sales management staff of Prentice Hall, who are second to none. Our appreciation to Gary June, Director of Sales and to Jackie Fitzgerald, National Accounts Manager.

Many thanks to the faculty and administrators at De Vry Institute of Technology who encouraged us, especially Linda Dobbs-Willis who reviewed the book, giving excellent and most appreciated suggestions and insight from her career development teaching experiences. Also, thanks to Dr. Lory Hawkes, a published instructor, who was always there to answer questions, give advice, and bounce off new ideas; Dr. Sherry Berg who reviewed the draft and gave encouraging feedback; and Ann Rogers, who would drop whatever she was doing to read a sentence, a page, or even a chapter whenever English correctness was in doubt.

Also, special thanks go to Kimberlee Yates, Human Resource Consultant, for technical guidance; Vickye Schultz, Jerre Yoder, Tisha Hadley, Jennifer Auten, human resource professionals; and Curtis Yates and Ken Ozee who have a special knack for hiring the right people.

Thanks also go to the Casper Star-Tribune (and reporter Chris Tollefson), as well as The Wyoming Tribune-Eagle (and reporter Kurt Moeller) for their articles on Kathy Karpan.

Our friends and family were a great support and source of encouragement. At the beginning of any project, the end is not always easily in sight, so the support from those around us throughout this process has been especially important.

We are grateful to all the people who allowed us to photograph them. We also thank Rick Singer and Tan Pham, our photographers whose special vision really made the presentation of this book complete.

We want to give a special thank-you to all the people who allowed us to interview them and share their stories and ideas about career development—the students who ask the poignant questions at the end of each chapter, the people in our Career Profiles and all the people whose stories can be found throughout the text. Your experiences, insights and lessons teach us all and encourage us to seek out the best in ourselves and in others.

In writing this book, the authors have included the thoughts and experiences of many different people following many different career paths. The following is a list of those people and their careers (either present, past or future), as well as the page where you can find their input.

OCCUPATION	INDIVIDUAL	PAGE
Publishers Representative Attorney	Charlotte Morissey	3
Builder/Designer Business Editor	David Carter	3
Advertising Agent Receptionist	Amanda Morales	3
Criminal Defense Attorney	Oliver Loewy	5
Psychologist running consulting business in New York City	Bill Swan	6
Owner of copier company	Chakil Alexander	6
Assistant at copier company	Desmond Blevins	6
State employee analyzing state welfare programs	Jerelyn Burgess	11
Biological Engineer	Deborah Johnston	14
Legal Assistant	Glenda Rae	19
Electrical Engineer Photographer	Kathy Early	24
VP of computer company Owner of tutoring company	Katherine Minges-Albrecht	24, 250
Sales Manager	Jacob Stout	24, 252
Engineer Products Marketer	Rama Moorthy	28, 229
Hotel/conference manager	Kristen Shields	28
Information services analyst	Amy Gargas	37
Student of education	Patty Smith	42
Student aspiring to be sales manager or travel agency owner	Janice Holmes	45
Marketer researcher	Pam Rud	46
Bank executive Clothes manufacturer Operator of own seminar business	Lisa Aldisert	47, 235
Manager telecommunications	Ned Smith	55, 126

OCCUPATION	INDIVIDUAL	PAGE
Company employee striving to become CEO	Joe Jordan	56
Computer analyst striving to become manager	Mark D'Avila	69
Student choosing between career in human relations or finance	John Weaver	73
VP of marketing for MTV consumer products	Mark Kirschner	74, 250
Television reporter Intern at United Nations	Kathy Shannon	78, 152
Physician	Rebecca Parker	79, 234
Student of law enforcement	Roger Quick	79
Student of marketing with emphasis on fashion industry	Terry Bhola	79
Student of education Olympic hopeful	Brad Bauer	85, 223
Student of filmmaking	Hiipoi Kauahi	96
City administrator	Mike Patterson	97, 236
Student of business seeking job as administrative assistant	Julie Rhodes	104
Student becoming medical assistant	Naomi Shidake	117
Engineer in telecommunications industry	Jude Zemper	118
Insurance salesman	Dan Hoyt	123, 128
Laboratory technician	Rodney Ahart	125
Real estate agent	Virginia Cone	126
Recruiter for Deloitte & Touche	Kent Kirch	130
Student of marketing seeking to start own business	Afrika Higgins	142
Executive director of nonprofit organizations Business magazine owner	Shirley Kiser	143
News reporter	Patricia Farmer	146
Teacher of English as a second language	Thom Taylor	147
Student and housecleaner	Janice Lewis	148
Accountant	Pat Duncan	148, 230
Comic book editor	Rob Tokar	151, 233, 256

OCCUPATION	INDIVIDUAL	PAGE
Intern at Save the Children	Marcus McPherson	152
Claims investigator	Jamie Turner	152
Student of electrical engineering	Jeff Ellison	158
Staff specialist of INROADS, a nonprofit organization	Michael Fulton	159, 236
Auditor; university career counselor	Stacey Cloutier	168
Student of broadcast communications	Nicole Bauer	198
Executive recruiter	John Bringman	199
Employee of advertising agency	Cindy Parker	202, 257
Politician Lawyer Public relations	Kathy Karpan	224
Junior salesperson	Jasper Hutton	228
Nurse	Kelly Fox	230
Senior VP at Bell Helicopter	P.D. Shabay	230, 237, 244
Business owner Attorney	Herman Walker	235
Marketing representative/ Salesperson in engineering, firearms, and pharmaceuticals; Firearms instructor	Lisa Quigley	236
VP and district sales manager for Bank of America	Rick Benito	237
Interpreter	Lupe Caballero	243
Electrical engineer	Pat Mealey	251
News reporter/editor	Kerry Drake	257
Camera store owner	Camille Brooks	259
Economist	Sabrina Pabilonia	264
Regional sales manager	Michelle Larson	265

FROM OUR STUDENT EDITORS

KATHLEEN COLE: I decided to return to school after being out for a number of years. Even though the work I was doing was fulfilling, I had advanced as far as I could with my particular skills and credentials. Besides which, my earning potential had definitely hit a peak. After a difficult divorce forced me to take a realistic look at my life and future, I enrolled in college and began the process of creating a new and improved version of myself, with better skills and greater options.

When I was asked to be a student editor for *Keys to Career Success,* I jumped at the chance. If I had had these resources at my disposal, I certainly wouldn't have put so much time and effort into trying to figure these things out for myself. As it was, I had to learn by trial and error. My resume was far too long and contained way too much information. It looked like a small book. I also ended up changing majors twice because I just couldn't figure out which was the best path for me to take. If I'd had the self-assessment exams like the ones in this book or was able to read about others who'd had similar experiences as mine, I think my journey would have been easier.

That's why I want to encourage you to get the most out of this book. The tools are priceless. Whether you are beginning again, like me, or starting out fresh on your career path, this book will help you discover your options, increase your self-awareness, cue you into the latest technological resources, help you understand the necessity of being flexible, and inspire you to continue investing in your greatest asset—you. Enjoy!

TIM SHORT: As a senior in broadcasting at Washington State University, I am confident that I have many career paths and choices to consider in the coming months. When I enter the workforce I can only hope that I will find a job that will not only provide me with success, but one that I am interested in as well.

Keys to Career Success has helped me to assess what types of interests I have and what my abilities are. The Scans Report is a wonderful tool that has enabled me to gain a better understanding of where I belong in the workplace.

I have found that I lean towards jobs that are technical in nature. I enjoy figuring out how things work and then seeing them through to completion. That's why I've accepted a summer position as an electrical contractor. Of course, money is always a concern with any job, but finding work that you both enjoy and excel at is of paramount importance.

Keys to Career Success has helped me to formulate some ideas as to where I would like to go with my degree after graduation. I hope you find this book as enjoyable as I do. If you apply the information in this book, you will find it an invaluable tool in your search for a career and in your professional life.

ABOUT THE AUTHORS

CAROL J. CARTER

Carol Carter is Vice President and Director of Student Programs and Faculty Development at Prentice Hall. She has written *Majoring in the Rest of Your Life: Career Secrets for College Students* and *Majoring in High School*. She has also co-authored *Keys to Success*, *Graduating into the Nineties* and *The Career Tool Kit*. In 1992 Carol and other business people co-founded a non-profit organization called LifeSkills, Inc., to help high school students explore their goals, their career options, and the real world through part-time employment and internships.

CAROL OZEE

Carol Ozee has worked in the field of labor and human relations for over 20 years with companies such as General Dynamics and Computer Sciences Corporation. Designing and implementing classes and projects involving human relations is her specialty. Carol conceptualized and managed an ombudsman program for General Dynamics for almost 2,000 employees. With her leadership, over 1,500 complaints were resolved through the mediation system that she set up. Carol teaches at DeVry Institute in Irving, Texas and travels the country giving workshops on career development and human relations.

BETH M. BOLLINGER

Beth Bollinger is a litigation attorney in Spokane, Washington. Beth comes from a family of educators and has always been interested in the process and outcomes of education. Her own varied background includes time as a teacher and journalist. She has taught English in Japan, and has taught legal seminars on a variety of topics, including the admission in court of expert testimony on the Battered Spouse Syndrome. She has been a guest "judge" at law schools, assisting law students in preparing for their moot court and other law school competitions. Beth has lived around the nation and the world, and *Keys to Career Success* benefits from her diverse life experiences. She balances a hectic legal practice with her writing projects as she expands her commitment to helping others choose and develop careers.

KEYS TO END-OF-CHAPTER EXERCISES

These exercises are designed to help you work on the very skills that you need to succeed in your chosen career—communications, leadership, teamwork, problem-solving, decision making, and many more. You will explore the importance of these kinds of skills in Chapter 2 (when you evaluate the skills that you have or can develop), Chapter 7 (when you contemplate the importance of experience in developing your career), and Chapter 10 (when you study those business skills that are a necessary part of the workplace).

You also will *develop* these skills along the way, however, by participating in the end-of-chapter exercises. They are deliberately separated into three categories—"Asking Questions and Getting Answers," "Collaborative Learning and Team-Building Skills," and "Long-Term Thinking and Planning"—to teach you the following:

ASKING QUESTIONS AND GETTING ANSWERS

These exercises are designed to help you develop effective thinking skills. Why? Because that is the number one quality employers look for in people they hire.

> ➤ How do you ask questions?
> ➤ How do you create answers?
> ➤ How do you solve problems?
> ➤ How do you make decisions?

In every chapter, you will be reinforcing and improving your ability to think.

COLLABORATIVE LEARNING AND TEAM-BUILDING SKILLS

By working with each other on these exercises, you will learn to develop the art of

> ➤ Teamwork, one of the most important skills to have in today's workplace

To be a good team player, you need to develop the ability to

> ➤ work effectively with others to reach a common goal
> ➤ listen and respect the opinions of others
> ➤ communicate your own opinions clearly

An equally important lesson to learn from this section of exercises is

> ➤ Leadership, also crucial to succeeding in today's working world.

Leaders have the ability to

> ➤ Take responsibility with a group of people
> ➤ See something to completion
> ➤ Manage others well and with compassion

You may not be a leader or one of the leaders in every group exercise, but you will be able to take the lead in some. If you have any long-term interest in management, learning to be a leader will be essential.

Long-Term Thinking and Planning

This section of exercises helps teach you how to plan ahead and make goals that you can reach.

> ➤ How much time will it take for you to accomplish your goals?
> ➤ What are realistic goals for you?

By going through these exercises and making real-life plans for yourself and your future, you will get a sense of what planning and goal setting means in terms of your career success as well. They will teach you to have tenacity and drive to accomplish what you set out to do. This is exactly the kind of life lesson that will help you along your path to be successful on the job and in your life.

SUPPLEMENTS

INSTRUCTOR'S MANUAL

This is a complete package of course information, including: general tips for using this textbook; lecture outlines; overhead transparency masters; useful quotes; key terms; essay questions; explanation for end-of-chapter exercises; team building exercises for career development; classroom activities; movies summaries and questions; bibliographies; recruiter questionnaires; and sample resumes.

THEMES OF THE TIMES, PH NEW YORK TIMES SUPPLEMENT

This sixteen-page newspaper, containing articles published within the last year, teaches students about majors and career fields that they might wish to pursue.

ABC CAREER VIDEOS

There are ten videos from ABC news programs, including Nightline and 20/20, each relating to one of the chapters in the textbook. This supplement is accompanied by a Video Guide, which has a detailed summary of each video along with questions for class discussion or essay topics. This is an effective way to teach students through a medium they like, using real-world examples.

TRIPOD STUDENT WEB SITE

This innovative web site provides advice, insight, and information to students on thought-provoking and timely issues regarding college, career, work, finance, community, and social issues. This is a perfect opportunity to help students feel comfortable using the World Wide Web! Visit the site at tripod.com.

TRIPOD STUDENT MAGAZINE

This magazine, published each semester, is free to any student using this book, and contains tips to success for school, work, and personal development.

OTHER BOOKS BY CAROL CARTER

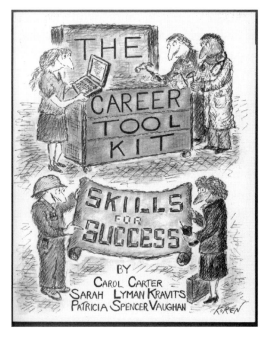

Part 1

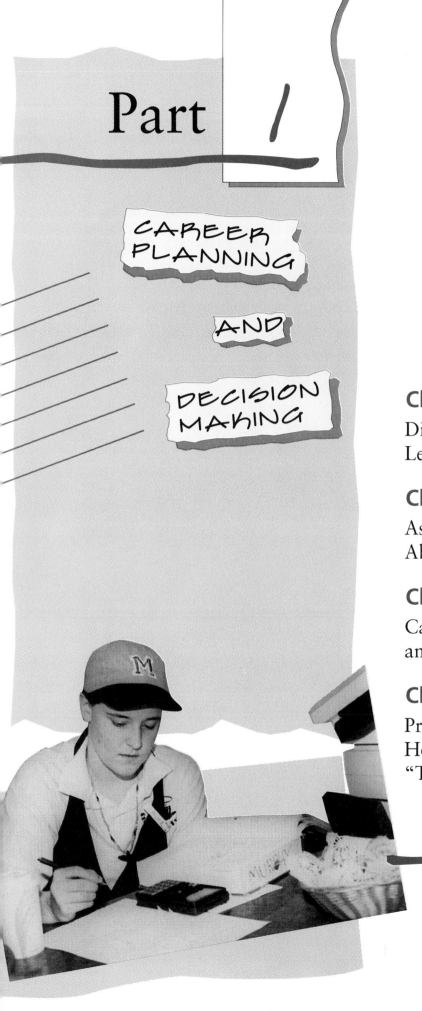

CAREER
PLANNING

AND

DECISION
MAKING

LEARN

1

Discovering Who You Are:

Learning about Yourself

Charlotte Morrissey graduated from law school at the University of Virginia, practiced law for three years, and then began to question why she was unhappy. After almost a year of analyzing who she is, thinking about her passions and fears, life goals, and ambitions, she decided that law was not for her. She loves people, books, and flexibility, so she decided to become a publisher's representative.

David Carter was the business editor for the *Arizona Daily Star* for several years until he discovered his passion for creating and designing homes. After a brief period of time exploring and developing his interests, he went into business for himself designing and building homes in Tucson's historic barrio. His new field of work combines his love of Mexican culture, his strict attention to detail, and his need to be his own boss, accountable to no one but himself.

Amanda Morales began working as a receptionist out of college. After answering the phones for over a year, she decided that she needed to be challenged more. She took a hard look at herself and her needs and decided to get a job at an advertising agency for roughly the same pay. Her new career affords her promotion opportunities, a rich and stimulating environment of creative minds, and the opportunity to assert herself and her ideas.

The key to self-discovery involves asking yourself lots of questions. You can't become educated about *any* subject without thorough and relentless questioning, especially when that subject is about yourself. The people in the examples figured out what was important to them—by asking themselves lots of questions—and listened to their inner voices about what they needed to do to feel passionate about their work.

The practical side of you may say that "discovering" who you are is not going to help you in the long run because it's not going to get you a paycheck. You may question how taking the time to explore your personality and values can have anything to do with your undeniably important priorities of paying bills and taking care of yourself and your family. You may feel that you can't "follow your passions" because your real interests will not prepare you for a job.

Certainly you have to take seriously the everyday, real-life problems of meeting budgetary concerns. The purpose of this chapter, however, is to help you do just that. You will see over and over in the examples throughout this book that people are most likely to be successful when they "follow their passions" and find a career that matches their personalities and interests. They earn money and enjoy their work. You can do both if you learn to listen to your heart as well as your head.

What Is Self-Discovery?

The first step in deciding what career best suits you is discovering who you are. For instance, a shy person probably would not want a job that involved constantly meeting new people. That person's personality just would not be suited for such a job. Conversely, an extrovert would probably go crazy in a laboratory out in the middle of nowhere where the only other living creatures are nocturnal hamsters. But what happens when the shy person also has an incredible talent for teaching or the extrovert has a special love for observational science? The purpose of this chapter is to help you figure out your personality and values to help you pioneer your own career path. Whether you are reading this book as a 55-year-old trying to figure out a new career or as an 18-year-old trying to get some ideas about what you might want to do, this book will help you answer some of your deepest questions and help to start you on the path to positive action.

Discovering who you are is simultaneously a straightforward but difficult task. It's straightforward because the information about who we are is contained within us. It seems difficult, though, because most of us are just a little too close to ourselves to have a realistic, objective view of who we are. The truth about ourselves can be scary because we are human; we have both positive and negative aspects. Don't be frightened by your weaknesses and don't be lulled into complacency by your strengths.

Commit yourself to the process of self-understanding. It is the first ray of enlightenment which can illuminate many personal and professional life choices.

So who are you, anyway?

WHAT ARE THE KEY ASPECTS OF YOUR PAST?

The tools that you bring to the workplace—your personality, your interests, your aptitudes and values, and your knowledge base—all are rooted in your background. Whether you are the third of three children, an only child, or an orphan, or whether you grew up in the city, the country, or the suburbs influences who you are today and in the future. As you explore the various sections of this chapter in discovering who you are, think about what role your background plays in your development as a person. Evaluate how your background has affected who you are. Do you have stereotypes about yourself from childhood that you want to challenge and change? Are you discovering that you were the family clown because you greatly value humor or because you were looking for a way to be different? How can you learn from your childhood experiences to understand yourself better? Think about how your past contributes to who you are today. For some, their past is a positive one overall, while others grew up with a lot of difficulties. Either way, evaluating your background can help you take a positive step toward achieving your own greatness.

Oliver Loewy, a public defender in New York City, knew early on that he would choose a career where he defended the rights of others, in part because of his heritage. "As far back as early elementary school, I felt there was a lot of unfairness in the way that a lot of people were treated, and I always wanted to do something about it." He believes that these feelings were "just my make-up, a personality trait," but that they also were fostered by his family's belief that it is important to help others. Most of Oliver's family on his father's side was killed during the Holocaust, and he remembers being raised on stories of that human tragedy. Oliver also recalls growing up with examples of helping other people. One story that affected him "was that my grandfather in Vienna instituted the first program in Vienna for poor children, where he got restaurants to serve hot meals to kids at schools rather than throwing the food out. At the same time, I heard about people eating bread with sawdust as supplements. That had a deep impact on me." Growing up in the 1960s, with social change as the center of the Democratic party, put Oliver's interest in helping others "in immediate context." Each of these elements of Oliver's background helped to mold what already seemed innate in his personality and value system—that is, a desire to help others.

Although Oliver's example is dramatic, each of us can examine our background to help put into perspective who we really are. We are made up of so many different parts, and we need to relish those parts in order to make them work to our advantage. In fact, sometimes the part of our background that we dislike the most can become a strength—both in our careers and in our lives. As difficult as it may be, try to look at *everything* in your background in the most positive light possible. Ask yourself, "How does this aspect of my childhood make me the person I am today?" "How can I use it to form a strength?"

WHAT ARE THE ASPECTS OF YOUR PERSONALITY?

Think of all the different labels we give to each other. If we meet someone at a party, we instantly want to know what they *do*. But a large part of being happy at what you do is understanding who you are and where your interests lie. Dr. William Swan is an example. Bill's father urged him to pursue a degree in engineering. As a result, when Bill went off to college for the first time he decided to major in engineering, but he quickly learned that he "hated it." Because he was unhappy with his choice, he did poorly in his classes and eventually dropped out of the engineering program. This doesn't sound like a beginning of a success story, but it is. When Bill started over, his first course in his new path was a class in psychology. He liked the topic and got an "A" in the class. He decided that this was a field where he would do well so he completed his bachelor's, master's and doctorate in psychology. Bill now owns a consulting firm that advises companies in a number of areas, including training managers on how to conduct interviews effectively. Bill is an excellent example of someone who chose not to give up but to regroup and evaluate his strengths instead, just as you are doing with this book.

There are many ways to identify *your* personality traits and, once identified, get them to work for you in your career and life. For instance, Chakil Alexander wanted to decide on a career. Chak brainstormed with friends and family as he tried to decide what career would best suit his personality. He spoke often with his parents about what type of career he should

choose. His parents pointed to Chakil's strengths—his ability to come up with creative ideas, his outgoing and public personality, and his tendency to think and act independently. Given his strengths, Chak's parents recommended that he open his own business and offered to help fund such a project. Chak talked to friends who agreed that it was an exciting idea that suited him well.

So Chakil took advantage of his parents' offer and decided to start his own copier company. He thought about his weaknesses, too, and decided he should hire an assistant who has an eye for detail—something Chak does not have. So he hired Desmond Blevins, who is a perfect match for Chakil because he is so thorough in accomplishing tasks that need to be done—writing good advertising proposals, sending thank-you cards, and putting together seminars for local businesses on how to improve their businesses. Like Chakil, Desmond is also an outgoing (though more private) person, so they are matched well there, too.

Chakil and Desmond have personalities which make them effective at what they are doing in their careers together. By correctly identifying some of the strengths of their personality traits, they are able to be stronger as a team.

Another way to identify your personality traits is to take a personality test. One caveat: be careful not to rely exclusively on the results of a personality test. Just as we can't pigeon-hole people from the same regions of the country (or the same ethnic or economic backgrounds), we can't assume that there is a finite number of personality types within which we all fit. These personality tests can help you understand yourself better, but they are still just *tests*, and you still are your own final judge of who you really are.

There are many personality tests which you can take to learn more about yourself. For instance, the *RIASEC theory* (created by John Holland) identifies six different categories of personalities (realistic, investigative, artistic, social, enterprising, and conventional) based on different interests. John Holland lists these categories in a circle, placing overlapping categories next to each other. Thus, an "artistic" personality has a lot in common with a "social" personality, and a "conventional" personality is connected to a "realistic" personality. Conversely, an "investigative" personality (for instance) is somewhat separated from an "enterprising" personality (since they are on opposite points in the circle).

The Holland test has people identify which three personality types they are the *most* like. It also has a discussion about what types of professions are most amenable to those three particular categories. The RIASEC categories are Realistic, Investigative, Artistic, Social, Enterprising, and Conventional. Your Holland "code" is the three categories that most reflect your personality (SEA, for example). Some adjectives that reflect these categories are:*

R REALISTIC	I INVESTIGATIVE	A ARTISTIC
practical	careful	emotional
conforming	introverted	expressive
persistent	curious	imaginative
stable	precise	disorderly
down-to-earth	independent	creative
rugged	achieving	impulsive
athletic	confident	flexible
frank	analytical	idealistic
self-reliant	intellectual	original

S SOCIAL	E ENTERPRISING	C CONVENTIONAL
helpful	energetic	conscientious
insightful	adventurous	efficient
kind	ambitious	organized
friendly	competitive	obedient
responsible	enthusiastic	dependable
understanding	driving	moderate
popular	powerful	orderly
cooperative	persuasive	persistent
tactful	assertive	detailed
flirtatious		thorough

*Adapted and reproduced by special permission of the publisher, Psychological Assessment Resources, Inc. Odessa, FL. 33556, from the *Self-directed Search* by John L. Holland, Ph.D. 1970, 1977, 1985, 1990, 1994 by PAR, Inc. Further reproduction is prohibited without permission from PAR, Inc. Self-directed Search materials can be purchased from PAR, Inc., at 1-800-331-8378.

Your career counselor or local community college should have the complete Self-Directed Search, as well as the Occupations Finder or Dictionary of Holland Occupational Codes which outline typical careers that work well with the various three-letter codes, and these materials can give you ideas of which careers match up best with your personal code. The possibilities are almost limitless.

Another well-known personality test is the *Myers-Briggs Type Indicator*, or MBTI®,* which places people in 16 personality categories, depending on whether they are extroverts or introverts, intuitive or sensing, thinkers or feelers, judgers or perceivers. Most career centers at community colleges or universities can give you this test and help you understand the results.

In lieu of the Myers-Briggs Type Indicator®, *People Types & Tiger Stripes* has published an exercise called "Thinking About Mental Habits." This exercise is reprinted as Figure 1-1. This exercise is NOT a type indicator, nor does it replicate the Myers-Briggs Type Indicator®, which is a validated instrument. The letters identifying "people types" are the same as Myers-Briggs, however. Because the Myers-Briggs Type Indicator® is a validated instrument with more detailed results, we recommend that you take the MBTI® if you can.

Figure 1-1 gives just a few descriptive phrases of personality patterns and, yes, there are times when we find ourselves in one of the other patterns. The combination of definitions helps you understand how different parts of your personality work together. For instance, someone testing as an "I" as well as an "F" may be excellent at coming up with new ideas of how to manage a large office with diverse personalities and be sympathetic to many different points of view. This type of person may be an effective supervisor, especially if he or she has as an assistant, someone who had the "down-to-earth" qualities of an "S" (or more detail-oriented) personality.

*®Myers-Briggs Type Indicator and MBTI are registered trademarks of Consulting Psychologists Press, Inc., Palo Alto, California.

FIGURE 1-1   EXERCISE: THINKING ABOUT MENTAL HABITS

Which Pattern describes you better, E or I?

E		I	
E	likes action and variety	I	likes quiet and time to consider things
E	likes to do mental work by talking to people	I	likes to do mental work privately before talking
E	acts quickly, sometimes without much reflection	I	may be slow to try something without understanding it first
E	likes to see how other people do a job and to see results	I	likes to understand the idea of a job and to work alone or with just a few people
E	wants to know what other people expect of him or her	I	wants to set his or her own standards

E's interest turns mostly outward to the world of action, people, and things. I's interest turns more often to the inner world of ideas and private things. Everyone turns outward to act and inward to reflect. You must do both, but you are more comfortable doing one or the other, just as right-handers are more comfortable with the right hand, but do use the left one.

Circle the **E** or the **I** in the margin to show which pattern fits you better.

E stands for extroversion, which means outward turning.

I stands for introversion which means inward turning.

Which Pattern describes you better, S or N?

S		N	
S	pays most attention to experience as it is	N	pays most attention to the meaning of facts and how they fit together
S	likes to use eyes and ears and other senses to find out what's happening	N	likes to use imagination to come up with new ways to do things, new possibilities
S	dislikes new problems unless prior experience shows how to solve them	N	likes solving new problems, and dislikes doing the same thing over and over
S	enjoys testing skills already learned more than learning new ones	N	likes learning new skills more than practicing old ones
S	is patient with details but impatient when the details get complicated	N	is impatient with details but doesn't mind complicated situations

S pays most attention to the facts that come from personal experience. **S** can more easily see the details, while **N** can more easily see the big picture. **N** pays most attention to meanings behind the facts. **S** and **N** are two kinds of perception, that is, two ways of finding out, or giving attention to experiences. **S** stands for sensing and **N** stands for intuition. Everybody uses both sensing and intuition to find out things. You use both, but you use one more than the other.

Circle the **S** or the **N** in the margin to show which pattern fits you better.

Which pattern describes you better, T or F?

	T		F
T	likes to decide things using logic	F	likes to decide things using personal feelings and human values
T	wants to be treated with justice and fair play	F	likes praise, and likes to please people, even in small matters
T	may neglect and hurt other people's feelings without knowing it	F	is usually very aware of other people's feelings
T	gives more attention to ideas or things than to human relationships	F	can predict how others will feel
T	can get along with little harmony	F	values harmony; feels unsettled by arguments and conflicts

T makes decisions by examining data and staying impersonal and cool. **T** stands for thinking judgment. **F** makes decisions by paying attention to personal values and feelings. **F** stands for feeling judgment. You make **T** and **F** judgments every day, but you use one kind of judgment more than the other.

Circle the **T** or the **F** in the margin to show which pattern fits you better.

Which pattern describes you better, J or P?

	J		P
J	likes to make a plan, to have things settled and decided ahead	P	likes to stay flexible and avoid fixed plans
J	tries to make things come out the way they "ought to be"	P	deals easily with unplanned and unexpected happenings
J	likes to finish one project before starting another	P	likes to start many projects but may have trouble finishing them all
J	usually has mind made up	P	usually is looking for new information
J	may decide things too quickly	P	may decide things too slowly
J	wants to be right	P	wants to miss nothing
J	lives by standards and schedules that are not easily changed	P	lives by making changes to deal with problems as they come along

Circle the **J** or **P** in the margin to show which pattern fits you better. **J** stands for judgment and **P** stands for perception. **J** people run their outer life with settled judgments. **P** people run their outer life in an open, perceiving way.

Types Come From Patterns

Now you can put together the four letters of the patterns that describe you best. Draw a circle here around the same letters you circled in the margins above.

EI SN TF JP

Now write your four letters here: ___ ___ ___ ___

The four letters together make up a whole pattern called a type. It may be your type. There are 16 different "people types" as shown by the 16 combinations of the letters. Find yours.

ISTJ	ISFJ	INFJ	INTJ
ISTP	ISFP	INFP	INTP
ESTP	ESFP	ENFP	ENTP
ESTJ	ESFJ	ENFJ	ENTJ

Each type is different from the others in important ways. As you come to understand the type ideas better, you will see how type affects your life with your friends and family, at school, or in a job.

Source: Gordon D. Lawrence, *People Types & Tiger Stripes*, 3rd edition. Center for Applications of Psychological Type, Gainesville, Florida, 1993, pp. 2–4. Used with permission.

When Chakil and Desmond did this exercise, they found out that Chakil tested very heavily as an "N" person. This explains why Chakil is a great idea person. Both Chakil and Desmond tested as being "E"—people who like interacting with others—so that their intensive work with people was a real good choice for both of them.

This does not necessarily mean that you have one preference to the exclusion of another. We all have and use each of the type preferences, but we simply use them to differing degrees, depending on our background, interests, education, life experiences, and so on. Take Desmond as an example. He tested as borderline between "N" and "S," which helps explain why he is able to both brainstorm with Chakil and then implement Chakil's ideas systematically. Since we are always growing and changing as people, our description of ourselves may change and the outcome of our personality types may change as well. For example, if Desmond were to increase the idea-generating portion of his daily work—or if he joined a club where he generated ideas for projects—he may reach a point at a later date where he feels he is more of an "N" than an "S" simply because of how he is spending a lot of his time. But we do lean toward certain traits, and the personality tests will help you determine if there are career opportunities for you that you may not have considered.

By taking the personality quizzes suggested above, you have begun the road of obtaining objective information about your personality traits that can help you choose a career path. For instance, Jerelyn Burgess tested as an INTP—which means she is introverted, intuitive, thinking, and perceiving—and an ISR—investigative, social, realistic. The areas where she tested the strongest were in the introversion and thinking categories of the "Mental Habits" exercise and the investigative and social categories of the Holland test. This told her what she already had known subconsciously—that she loved helping people, but she didn't always have the energy to work with them one on one. She also recognized in herself the ability to be both a great idea person *and* good with detail, since she tested as an intuitive person with leanings toward being detail oriented. Armed with this information, Jerelyn started to investigate careers where she could help people in ways that were broader than giving day-to-day, individual assistance to others. She ultimately obtained a degree in political science and got a job with her state government analyzing the effectiveness of the state's welfare programs.

Use these kinds of tests and indicators as a guideline, not a prescription for what you should do. They are designed to give you ideas, but only you know which of them are most applicable to helping understand your unique personality. These tests are not intended to restrict you from being who you are, but can give you some idea of where you are coming from.

Don't rely *just* on these personality tests to help you discover who you are. Use the other techniques listed earlier—including reviewing your personal history, brainstorming with the people who know you best, and listing your strengths and weaknesses based on your own observations—to get a fuller (and ever-evolving) picture of yourself. Above all, keep questioning yourself. Our most vital answers come from within.

WHAT ARE YOUR VALUES?

Values are the things that we believe in, often unidentified but everpresent. Values give us a framework from which to make some of the most important decisions of our lives. The more strongly we hold a belief, the more we are motivated to make that belief a part of our lives. Defining what you value—what is most important to you—can help you a great deal in deciding your career goals and what paths to take in reaching those goals. Being clear on your values also provides the motivation and the *will* to help you make your dreams a reality.

The following is a list of "value" words. Put a checkmark by those qualities that are most important to you. Ask yourself in what order you would put the following values to complete this phrase: I am/want to be

_____.

____Honest/fair	____Educated	____Loyal	____Organized
____Wealthy	____Cooperative	____Powerful	____Peaceful
____Accepting	____Ambitious	____Joyful	____Athletic
____Adventurous	____Loving	____Needed	____Prompt
____Self-accepting	____Optimistic	____Prompt	____Funny
____Conscientious	____Mature	____Neat	____Intelligent
____Trustworthy	____Creative	____Secure	____Healthy
____Handsome/beautiful	____Independent	____Famous	____Efficient
____Full of integrity	____Serious	____Brave	____Kind
____Calm	____Decisive	____Strong	____Enthusiastic

How Does Your Career Fit into Your Value System?

In addition to personal values, you have things that you will want from your career, goals you will want to achieve. Remember, you will probably engage in three to six careers in the journey to reach a fulfilling career or position in your professional lifeline. Looking at that realistically, you could possibly hold two to three different levels of jobs in each of those career moves, which indicates a possibility of ten or more significant jobs during the course of your career.

First, determine your life values. If you are not clear on what you want from your whole life, then you may end up making incompatible career decisions. Your career choices should be a reflection of what you value in your life, not the other way around.

After you have thought through what is important in your life, then look again at your career values. Do they still fit? If not, rework them so that you will be able to accomplish your personal as well as professional goals. Examine your motives for setting your sights where they are. That way, you can decide what it is that you truly want from your career. It could be one of the following, or it could be a combination of two or more of them, or it could be different from the following motives:

Economic well being—riches, affluence, material prosperity

Position—a high rank or standing in a certain organization or community

Power—ability to do or act, strength, vigor, ruler or authority figure, ability to command or control others

Flexibility—adaptability or workable schedule

To make a difference—give something of yourself or of significance back to society or the world in order to make it better for everyone

Meaningful work—important, weighty work with significant consequential importance

Achievement—great professional accomplishment, changing the face of the workplace

Advanced technology—to further scientific, industrial, or business expertise

Place of work—outdoors/indoors? small company, large company?

Take a few minutes now to identify, examine, and evaluate your own motives by completing the sentences started in Table 1-1, Self-Examination:

TABLE 1-1 SELF-EXAMINATION

1. The kind of work I enjoy most is _____

2. The kind of work that makes me proud is_____

3. I can't see myself working as a _____

4. My starting salary goal is _____

5. My present-value, ultimate career salary is _____

6. The kind of work that I would get tired of after an extended period of time is _____

7. Self-fulfillment looks like _____

8. Being in charge makes me feel _____

9. Being responsible makes me feel _____

10. Directing the work of others makes me feel _____

11. If I could have any job in the world it would be _____

12. A successful person I know or have heard of is_____, and he (or she) is successful because _____

    _____

13. The special qualities that I have to offer an employer are _____

    _____

14. An employer would promote me after two years because I demonstrated these exemplary characteristics on the job _____

    _____

Remember to balance your personal and career values. Look for areas of conflict and make adjustments accordingly. Deborah Johnston, a biological engineer student, wants to earn a lot of money but also places great value on a clean environment. Given her values, she should probably avoid working for a corporation that is in constant trouble with the EPA and whose management does not seem interested in changing this situation. She would be better served making a lot of money in another way. That way, her value system does not have to conflict with itself, pulling her in two very different directions.

On the other hand, Deborah may see her involvement in such a corporation as an opportunity to improve the corporation's environmental policies. If she chooses to work for the corporation for this reason, she should stay aware of the conflicts that may arise between her work duties and her environmental beliefs and the perseverance that she may need to make the difference she wants to make. Perhaps making a difference in this way is part of her value system, making this rockier path the one that is most consistent with her values system.

Whatever her values, having an understanding of those values ahead of time will help Deborah make important career decisions. In the same way, you too can save yourself a lot of heartache and agony if you can ensure that your career harmonizes with your belief system. Stay true to yourself and the rewards will follow.

SUMMARY

Knowing yourself and your values, as well as what it will take to grow within yourself, encompass your first steps toward career success. Use the information in this chapter as tools for analyzing yourself and your potential as you start thinking about the career path you will travel.

ASKING QUESTIONS AND GETTING ANSWERS

1. **Identifying What Makes You Proud.** Make a list of three events in your life that you see as accomplishments. Try to include events that have occurred over the span of your lifetime, not just recently. Underneath the event, explain why this event was important to you. Use this list to help you understand a little more about who you are and what you value. Each event gives you confidence from which you can gather future strength to assert yourself and take new risks. For instance, Polly was especially proud when she won an award in elementary school from a drawing contest in the Sunday comics section of her newspaper. She had entered the contest in spite of the derisive comments made by her older brother and sister about how she would never win, so why bother trying. Why does that memory stand out for Polly? Three reasons: she loved the prize (a collection of toy farm animals), she was happy to show her siblings that they were wrong about her artistic abilities, and she was not thwarted by peer pressure.

   ➤ Event _studied in Guadalajara, Mexico_

   What You Learned _how to be away from home, how to_
   speak Spanish, how to appreciate another culture

   Why It Made You Feel Valuable _learned to deal with fear_
   of unknown

   ➤ Event _____

   What You Learned _____

   Why It Made You Feel Valuable _____

   ➤ Event _____

   What You Learned _____

   Why It Made You Feel Valuable _____

   ➤ Event _____

   What You Learned _____

   Why It Made You Feel Valuable _____

2. **Combining Your Values and Your Personality.** Who you are and what you believe in often are intertwined. Think about your personality traits that you have identified in this chapter. What values match those traits? For instance, Candace is an introvert (getting energy from within). She *values* her reading time, after she's put her children to bed and settled in for the night. Thus, her personality trait influences what she values.

➤ Personality Trait: _feels more calm after exercise/prone to_ _stress_

Corresponding Value: _makes running a priority each_ _week_

➤ Personality Trait: _____

Corresponding Value: _____

➤ Personality Trait: _____

Corresponding Value: _____

➤ Personality Trait: _____

Corresponding Value: _____

3. **Contemplating Careers.** Take some time to review what career options may be available to you based on the outcome of the personality tests that you have taken. Fill out the material developed by John Holland at your career center. Below, write down your resulting Holland code as well as your score from the "Mental Habits" exercise found in this chapter (which uses the same initials as the Myers-Briggs Type Indicator®). Then go to the library or your career counselor to determine careers that are recommended for these personality types.

➤ Your Holland Code: _____ _____ _____

➤ Your "Mental Habits" Type: _____ _____

_____ _____

➤ Possible Career Options: _____

_____

_____

COLLABORATIVE LEARNING AND TEAM-BUILDING SKILLS

1. **Getting to Know Yourself: Becoming Comfortable Discussing Your Strengths.** In groups of three or four, take turns describing yourself for three to four minutes to your small group. Imagine that your colleagues are part of a review committee and that you are trying to pass an initial screening process to get the job interview for your dream job. Leave your inhibitions and fears behind. Describe your strengths and tell your colleagues what is special about you and what would make you stand out in the work environment. For

example, talk about what you've learned in college, how you've developed your leadership skills, and what practical experience you may have from any part-time jobs you've held. After each person has taken his or her turn, give constructive comments on how your colleagues can improve upon their initial statements.

2. **Discussing Values that Are Important to You.** In groups of two to four, review your values lists from page 12. What are the differences in your value systems? Why do you value something differently from your classmate? Discuss why certain values are important to you. Listen to others and keep an open mind when listening to what matters most to others and why.

LONG-TERM PLANNING: KEY TO YOUR PERSONAL PORTFOLIO

1. **Knowing Where You've Been.** Sometimes in discovering who we are, we need to learn where we've been. Write a biography of one of your parents or grandparents. Be sure to include a discussion of the things that were important to them. What did they do every day? Where did they work? How many children did they have? What is their educational background? What did they value? Next, write a summary of what you have learned from them. What has their example taught you? What have their mistakes taught you? Finally, make a list of three qualities in this person that you would like to adopt. Make a commitment to try to incorporate these three qualities in your everyday life.

Biography of: _____

_____

_____

_____

_____

What I Have Learned from This Person: _____

_____

_____

_____

_____

_____

Three Qualities that I Will Try to Emulate:

a. _____

b. _____

c. _____

2. **Envisioning Your Future.** Take a moment to close your eyes and think about what you want in your future ten years from now. What job do you have? How much money are you earning? What kind of responsibilities do you have? What is your workweek like? How about your personal life? What kind of house do you have? How many children? Are you married? What kind of vacations are you taking? What hobbies do you have?

   Imagine that you are getting up on a typical workday. Describe that day in the space below. This may feel hard right now, before you've had a chance to investigate what you want to do for your career and in your life, but do your best. Let your imagination flow. Consider your personal and leisure life in connection to your career. Thinking about where you want to be can help give you great insight into who you are and what you like and value.

   _____

   _____

   _____

   _____

   _____

   _____

   _____

   _____

3. **What Will They Say When You're Gone?** One way to explore career paths is to think about where you want to end up. What do you hope your obituary would say about you after you've lived a full life? Write down what you want it to say. How do you want to be remembered? How do your career goals fit into your life goals?

   _____

   _____

   _____

   _____

   _____

   _____

   _____

STUDENT QUESTION

Glenda Rae, legal assistant in the Pacific Northwest

Glenda has been thinking a lot about changing jobs or going back to school so that she can really work on a career that's right for her. One of the hardest things for Glenda to do, however, is to leave "the comfort zone." She is having a real inner struggle in trying to decide what she wants to do, with whom, or where she wants to be. Now that she's made friends in one place and has a set network, "it seems very scary to go where you know nobody." Glenda would like help in learning how to adjust to something new. She thinks it would be helpful to get more information before making any changes, including information about herself, so that she can feel like she's making the right choices. It would help to make any changes make sense and give her some clarity. Her question:

How can I prepare myself ahead of time to help me feel that I'm making the right choices?

Leave the comfort zone! One of the best ways to grow personally and professionally is to venture forth from the safe and the familiar into new, uncharted waters. New challenges stretch the limits of your potential, teach you new things, and show you that you can adjust in a variety of situations, not just those in which you know. So the first step is to decide you want to really improve and maximize where you are currently so that you can prepare for your next move.

The second step is deciding that you want to do the hard work required to learn who you are and investigate fields which interest you. You have to dig deeply within yourself for those answers. The other part of the process involves spending time learning about fields and professions which intrigue you. As for "right" choices, there are many or few, depending on your determination to make them happen for yourself. You decide which path and which set of options best suits your interests. Even if the path you select is not ultimately your ideal, you will learn to take risks, you will take on new responsibilities and you will find that you can adjust and become "comfortable" in a wide variety of situations. Just don't let that "comfort" last too long. The comfort danger is complacency; strive to live up to your full potential.

CAREER PROFILE

PEOPLE WITH A CALLING

People accomplish tasks everyday that affect the world around us. Often we do not even know the names of those people whose pioneering efforts still impact our lives today. Just like anyone else, these people had to identify who they were so that they could get involved in fields that allowed them to emphasize their strengths. Below are condensed versions of three obituaries published in *The New York Times* in July 1996, paying tribute to three such individuals.

SAMUEL A. KIRK, 92; FOUNDED SPECIAL EDUCATION FIELD

Samuel A. Kirk, an immigrant homesteader's son who became so intrigued by his childhood experiences teaching illiterate farmhands to read that he went on to an acclaimed career as the father of special education—a term he coined in 1963—died on July 21 at his retirement home in Tucson, Arizona. Dr. Kirk wrote so widely and so authoritatively on many aspects of mental retardation learning disorders and was responsible for many innovations in diagnosis, training and social policy that it is not hard to understand why a former colleague, William C. Healey, once suggested he was "the last of the great generalists in his field." Dr. Kirk's most visionary contribution to public policy occurred in 1964, when he persuaded the Administration and Congress to begin providing financing to train teachers to provide the expert help such children needed.

(*New York Times*, Sunday, July 28, 1996)

RICHARD W. LONG, 46, BUILDER OF BICYCLES FOR OLYMPIC TEAM

Richard W. Long, a college drop-out who used a personal-injury settlement from a motorcycle accident to build a multimillion-dollar bicycle business that is supplying the most advanced equipment to the United States Olympic cycling team, died on July 12 when his motorcycle and a truck collided on a winding mountain road east of Los Angeles. Demonstrating a vision that would repeatedly characterize his business success, Mr. Long used the financial settlement to buy a bicycle store in Anaheim when cycling was becoming a passion in California. A marketing innovator from the beginning, Mr. Long spent his weekends at bicycle tracks to keep up with his customers' needs. Although sales grew steadily, continued expansion required so much capital that it was not until last year when the company went public with a 40 million offering, that Mr. Long was able to enjoy the full fruits of his success. "It's kind of ironic that he started his business from a motorcycle accident and died in a motorcycle accident," his son Jeff said. "But at least he lived to see what he had accomplished, and he knew that we got to see it, too."

(*New York Times*, Saturday, July 20, 1996)

ANNE HUMMERT, 91, DIES; CREATOR OF SOAP OPERAS Anne Hummert, the woman widely credited with creating the radio soap opera and spinning out many of the spell-binding classics of the 1930s and 40s, was a 91-year-old multimillionaire who had maintained a vigorous life almost to the end. At a time when commercial programming in the infant medium concentrated on working people who returned home to sit in front of their radios at night, advertisers were dimly aware that the housewives who stayed home all day were the nation's primary purchasing agents. But these women were considered too busy dashing here and there to pay more than cursory attention to the family radio. The Hummerts didn't argue with the theory of the distracted housewife. They simply seized her attention and changed the pattern of her life. Mrs. Hummert, who had a photographic memory, was renowned in the industry for her ability to remember each intricate twist of every one of her creations. It was a reflection of the grip the Hummerts had on their audience that their programs generated more than five million letters a year, and it was a measure of their commercial success that by 1939 Hummert programs accounted for more than half the advertising revenues generated by daytime radio. When television began to displace radio, the couple simply retired and enjoyed a life of travel and leisure.

(*New York Times*, Sunday, July 21, 1996)

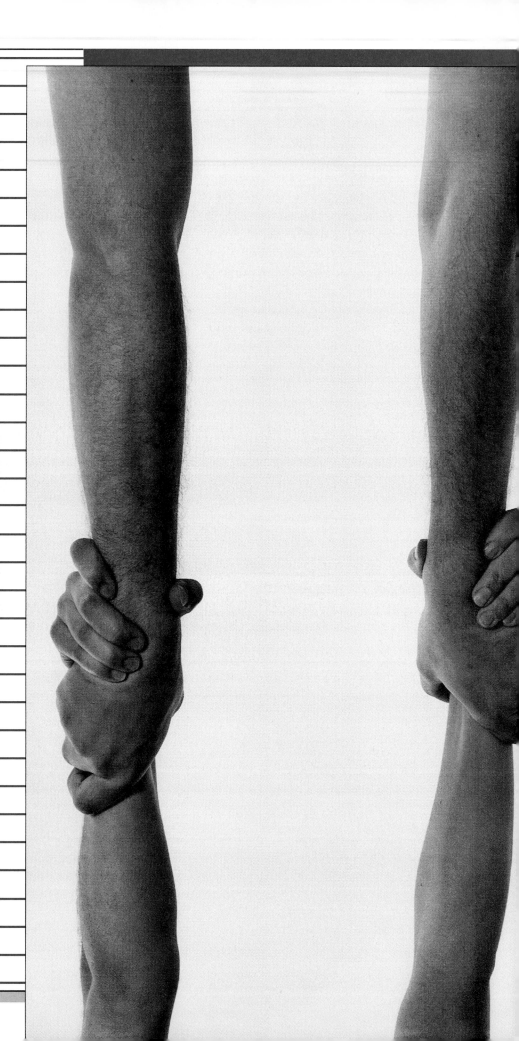

FIND

Assessing Your Interests and Abilities:

Defining Your Passions

Have you ever watched trapeze artists? They seem effortless. They swing back and forth on the trapeze, spinning and somersaulting from one trapeze to another, into each other's arms. They are synchronized, smooth, and invincible. They are undoubtedly very talented individuals who flawlessly accomplish a feat that virtually no one else knows how to do.

But how did they ever get there? Surely they began by falling into the net once or twice. How many other would-be trapeze artists started with them and then quit because they just couldn't do it? Successful trapeze artists are people who discovered an *interest*, learned that they had a *talent* in the area and, through hard work and perseverance, developed the *skills* necessary to make their interest and talent come alive. Their skills include physical strength and agility, the ability to communicate with each other, and the ability to work hard and develop an expertise, among many other qualities.

Each of us has interests, talents, and skills that we can develop to work for us as we pursue our career goals. Your abilities may not lead you to the ceiling of a circus tent, but identifying your strengths and preferences can help you figure out the career path that's best for you. This chapter is designed to help you think about where your talents, interests, and abilities lie so that you can choose career paths that will be most rewarding for your unique qualities and passions.

WHAT ARE MY INTERESTS?

Identifying your interests can help you take one big step toward finding a career that's right for you. It stands to reason that you will be more successful at something that you like, and you are more likely to be happy in a career that involves activities you enjoy. Therefore, consider your hobbies or interests—would any of them support you financially?

Realistically, there are very few professional athletes, cowboys, singers, or race car drivers (or trapeze artists, for that matter) who are actually able to support themselves with their hobby or interests. Even though you may not be able to support yourself in that manner, however, you may be able to find a career in a field that you like that keeps you close to your hobby or interests. For example, even though you may not be able to fulfill your lifelong dream of becoming a Hollywood movie star, there are many jobs in the movie or television business—like advertising, camera work, fashion design, or location management—that you could find rewarding and that would provide a decent income. And there are many, many jobs where the quality of being dramatic is a big plus. Becoming a teacher, lawyer, salesperson, or even a small business owner could take advantage of dramatic qualities.

Kathy Early is a good example of someone who has chosen career paths based on her interests. Kathy began her career with a fine arts degree. She loved photography, so she became a freelance photographer. Financially, the road was difficult, so she decided to go back to school and become an engineer like her father. She discovered that she had a love as well as talent for engineering, which should not have been a surprise, given the fact that both engineering and photography require analytical, logic, and mechanical skills. Nevertheless, she *was* surprised—in high school, she hadn't done well in math and science, and she hadn't realized her talent in this area. "There was such a gap between my art and engineering education, I thought the door was closed" to a new career. "But you can make changes and grow. I completed my electrical engineering degree when I was 35 years old."

Katherine Minges-Albrecht, the vice-president of a start-up computer company, encourages students to choose their careers based on things they enjoy doing. "What are you doing in your spare time? If you're spinning your wheels and waiting to get home to do what you enjoy, then you're in the wrong career." Katherine knows many people who "had a hobby on the side but didn't think it was 'career material.'" She recalls a friend of hers who was climbing the "corporate ladder," but what she really enjoyed was flower arranging. "She found *her* career success when she opened up a flower shop. Her life is *completely* turned around." Katherine anticipates her own career ultimately involving teaching, since she gets her "adrenaline rush" from tutoring. "Time just flies when I'm helping someone else understand something," she notes.

Jacob Stout agrees. Jacob has had numerous jobs in a variety of fields like publishing, sales, graphics, and advertising. Currently he is launching a new business venture with a computer company. According to Jacob, the greatest gift is being able to identify something that you can enjoy even if it takes you longer to get through college and/or choose your career. Jacob's son recently graduated from Southwest Texas State University with a degree in industrial construction. "It took my son seven years to get through school, but it is worth it because he took the time to find out what he really enjoys."

Therefore, the next step in gaining career success is to identify your interests. This may take some brainstorming or listing of all random ideas that come to mind associated with a topic. Use Table 2-1 to put down those ideas on paper. Remember, knowing what really interests you will help you to discover those fields that combine what you really like to do. So think broadly. Open up the parachute of your mind.

TABLE 2-1   WHAT ARE MY INTERESTS AND/OR HOBBIES?

NO.	INTERESTS/ HOBBIES	JOB POSSIBILITIES	PREPARATION REQUIRED	TIME REQUIRED	CHECK IT OUT/ YES/NO

Next, think through your favorite classes or organizations in school. Why did you like these programs? Was it simply the camaraderie? Or was there something unique about the program that drew your interest? Fill out Table 2-2 with a list of those things.

TABLE 2-2   FAVORITE SCHOOL CLASSES AND ORGANIZATIONS

CLASS/ORGANIZATION	WHY DID YOU ENJOY IT?
1.	
2.	
3.	
4.	
5.	

WHAT ARE MY ABILITIES?

What do you do well? *Aptitude* is an inclination, tendency, or natural ability to learn. Recognizing your natural talents will help you in the quest for career and life success. The more you know about yourself, the better equipped you will be to make meaningful career decisions, now and in the future.

As an example, Katherine remembers a marketing job that she didn't get. "I went to interview with all the businesses" that participated in the on-campus interviewing at her school "and I hated every one of them." There was one job as a marketing representative that all the students were coveting, and she was a final candidate. She could tell from the way her final interview was going that she would be offered the position. She panicked at the thought and started answering interview questions incorrectly just so she would not get the job offer. She felt depressed and spent a lot of time at home with her mother, crying. "I hated what I was trained to do. I was on the verge of graduating, and I was afraid I was locked into the future. I moped around the house with a 'woe is me, I'm pathetic' attitude."

To help her out, Katherine's mother hired a career counselor who worked intensely with Katherine. "That career counseling absolutely changed my life," Katherine says. The counselor "asked real detailed questions about who I was, my skills and strengths. We figured out that I'm not suited to a hard-lined, 8 to 5 working atmosphere," which was why she panicked at the marketing job interview. Ultimately, they decided that Katherine needed lots of flexibility "with the ability to change when something gets old and stale."

After the consultation, Katherine successfully began her own tutoring agency called the Learning Consultants. Within a year, the business grew into a big office with 12 employees. She eventually wanted to move on—as her career counselor had warned her—but that was okay because she simply graduated to another one of her careers (with a little c). "People tell me that opportunities come *my* way and not theirs," Katherine says, "but I think that often it's because they are not actively pursuing creative ways to have their career needs met."

Understanding Skills

One way to begin determining your aptitudes is to look at the skills that you have already developed. There are two ways to think about skills: first, skills are activities that you can do. Second, however, is the fact that skills can be the *style* or *method* by which you do activities. For instance, you may have word processing skills. That skill is something you do. But what are your skills as a word processor—what *style* or *method* do you use? Perhaps you are an accurate word processor. In that example, your "skill" is both your word processing knowledge *and* your ability to be accurate. Other word processors may be quick, while still others may be particularly adept at designing a document visually so that it gets attention. While all of you are word processors, each of you has a different strength in the same area. By identifying not only what you can do but also how you do it, you will be able to better identify your aptitudes—that is, where your natural talents lie.

Transferable Skills

In thinking about skills, recognize that many of them can be transferred from one job to the other. Word processing is a skill that can be used in a variety of jobs. What other kinds of skills are transferable? Chapter 10 (Becoming Employable and Promotable: Preparing for Change) lists in detail some of the business skills that are useful in virtually every job. The list is a reflection of "transferable skills." It includes communication, problem solving, decision making, teamwork, leadership, creativity or innovativeness, being tenacious or persevering, having drive or energy, having commonsense smarts, your ethics or honor code, independence, adaptability, and the ability to recognize your weaknesses. Are you developing these skills? Do you have them already? Where do your strengths lie?

Rama Moorthy, an engineer and products marketer, relies heavily on the transferable skill of communication—both orally and in writing. She can convey information to all levels of management and to a variety of personality types of all professional backgrounds. To focus her communication efforts, she plans all her communications from the point of view of the audience, whether the information is a formal presentation or a conversation with her boss. "I outline what I want as the end result and define my goal for the communication. I develop an outline and fill in the key information. I define the audience and then fine tune my presentation. I practice, practice, practice until it is clear, even if it's a conversation. I talk to myself a lot when I'm in my car. I always plan what to say for contingencies."

Kristen Shields, specializing in hotel/conference management, is another example. Kristen's key to success is to be "highly organized." She is organized with the details of meeting events such as booking speakers and entertainment engagements. Also, she is organized with her time. She sees procrastination as the root problem with work ethics. "When people put off what they're supposed to do, it creates problems for everyone, and it gives them so much stress. I learned a long time ago to keep focused and get my work done."

You too can develop transferable skills methodically as Rama and Kristen have. Above all, be creative in the way you think about what skills you have and how you can transfer them to new or different careers.

Assessing Your Skills

Take some time to think through what you do well—what your *aptitudes* are. Below, describe three things that you can do and explain how it is that you do them well.

SAMPLE CHECKLIST

#1 I can _conduct research_ . I do this activity well because _I am careful and thorough_ .

#2 I can _teach_ . I do this activity well because _I have a lot of positive energy_ .

#3 I can _write well_ . I do this activity well because _I'm a good thinker._

YOUR TURN

#1 I can _____ . I do this activity well

because _____ .

#2 I can _____ . I do this activity well

because _____ .

#3 I can _____ . I do this activity well

because _____ .

Review your list. Rather than just three skills listed (of something you can do), you have *many* skills listed (things you can do and the method or style you use in doing them).

Now think about what kind of skills you have that may fit well in the workplace. In 1993, the United States Department of Labor issued a report called SCANS (Secretary's Commission on Achieving Necessary Skills). This report identifies basic skills that you must have in the modern workplace as well as skills that will help you grow into a career path that's right for you. Look over the list provided in Table 2-3, which reflects the information found in the SCANS report. What skills do you already have? What skills do you want to develop?

Tables 2-4 and 2-5 give you a chance to rank the SCANS skills according to what you do best. The tables separate the SCANS competency skills from the SCANS basic skills. Rank which category in each chart you do best—and then rank *within* each category which subsections you do best. Thus, if out of the five categories you are best at using resources, then you should rank resources #1 (out of five). Then, if within the resources category you are best at allocating time, then staff, then space, then materials, then money, your ranking should reflect this. Under the above scenario, your "Resources" section would look as follows:

			allocating staff __2__
			allocating time __1__
__1__ Resources	(Rank 1–5)		allocating money __5__
			allocating materials __4__
			allocating space __3__

Table 2-6 (drawn in part from the SCANS report) expands on skills that are useful in the workplace as identified in SCANS. Think through your strengths. What skills do you already have? What skills would you like to develop? Put checkmarks next to the skills you already have and circle the skills you would like to develop.

TABLE 2-3 SCANS REPORT SKILLS

COMPETENCE

Effective workers can productively use

➤ *Resources*—allocating time, money, materials, space, and staff.

➤ *Interpersonal Skills*—working on teams, teaching others, serving customers, leading, negotiating, and working well with people from culturally diverse backgrounds.

➤ *Information*—acquiring and evaluating data, organizing and maintaining files, interpreting and communicating, and using computers to process information.

➤ *Systems*—understanding social, organizational, and technological systems; monitoring and correcting performance and designing and improving systems.

➤ *Technology*—selecting equipment and tools, applying technology to specific tasks, and maintaining/troubleshooting equipment.

THE FOUNDATION

Competence requires

➤ *Basic Skills*—reading, writing, arithmetic/mathematics, speaking, and listening.

➤ *Thinking Skills*—thinking creatively, making decisions, solving problems, seeing things in the mind's eye, knowing how to learn, reasoning.

➤ *Personal Qualities*—individual responsibility, self-esteem and self-management, sociability, and integrity.

As you go through each of these exercises, think about not only what you do well because of practice but also what you do well *naturally*. Some of us may have developed great typing skills through years of practice, but also would be unique public speakers as a natural aptitude. Where are you leaning? What would you *like* to do? Be creative and spontaneous as you go through these checklists.

TABLE 2-4   WHAT SCANS "COMPETENCY" SKILLS DO YOU HAVE?

RANK YOUR "COMPETENCY" SKILLS. WHERE ARE YOUR STRENGTHS?

Subject Area (Rank 1–5)	Subsections (Rankings per Section)
_____ Resources (Rank 1–5)	allocating staff _____ allocating time _____ allocating money _____ allocating materials _____ allocating space _____
_____ Interpersonal (Rank 1–6)	teaching others _____ working on teams _____ working well with people from culturally diverse backgrounds _____ serving customers _____ negotiating _____ leading _____
_____ Information (Rank 1–7)	acquiring data _____ evaluating data _____ organizing files _____ using computers/process information _____ maintaining files _____ communicating _____ interpreting _____
_____ Systems (Rank 1–7)	monitoring performance _____ correcting performance _____ understanding social systems _____ understanding organizational systems _____ understanding technological systems _____ designing systems _____ improving systems _____
_____ Technology (Rank 1–3)	selecting equipment and tools _____ applying technology to specific tasks _____ maintaining/troubleshooting equipment _____

TABLE 2-5 WHAT SCANS "FOUNDATION" SKILLS DO YOU HAVE?

RANK YOUR "FOUNDATION" SKILLS. WHERE ARE YOUR STRENGTHS?

Subject Area (Rank 1–3)		Subsections (Rankings per Section)
____ Basic skills	(Rank 1–5)	reading _____ writing _____ arithmetic/mathematics _____ speaking _____ listening _____
_____Thinking skills	(Rank 1–5)	thinking creatively _____ making decisions _____ seeing things in the mind's eye _____ knowing how to learn _____ reasoning _____
____ Personal qualities	(Rank 1–4)	self-esteem _____ self-management _____ individual responsibility _____ sociability _____

TABLE 2-6 LIST OF SKILLS

TYPING/COMPUTER SKILLS

Can you:

type accurately?

type quickly?

make graphs?

make spreadsheets?

use computer programs? which ones?

use macro commands?

make macro commands?

move text within a document?

spell check?

generate table of contents?

print envelopes?

print form letters for many recipients by just inserting addresses?

LEADERSHIP SKILLS

Can you:

make sure that work is getting done?

listen carefully to the opinions of others?

take less popular viewpoints into consideration?

justify your positions quickly and confidently?

stick by an unpopular decision?

establish credibility through competence and integrity?

provide feedback to other workers?

make good matches between workers and the work that needs to be done?

TIME MANAGEMENT SKILLS

Can you:

identify tasks to be completed?

rank tasks by their importance?

construct a timeline chart?

estimate key task priorities such as importance?

estimate time needed to finish task?

estimate time available to finish task?

develop and follow effective, workable schedules?

avoid wasting time?

evaluate and adjust a schedule?

PROBLEM-SOLVING SKILLS

Do you:

think creatively?

come up with new ideas?

like to brainstorm with others?

focus on detail?

listen to new ideas?

TABLE 2-6   LIST OF SKILLS (CONTINUED)

PROBLEM-SOLVING SKILLS (CONTINUED)

Can you:

research the opposition and the history of a conflict?

set realistic and attainable goals?

present facts and arguments objectively?

listen to, hear, and reflect on what has been said?

try to determine what each party's "bottom line" is?

clarify problems?

adjust quickly to new facts/ideas?

propose and examine possible options?

make reasonable compromises?

DECISION-MAKING SKILLS

Can you:

identify the various choices you have?

rank choices in order of importance?

make lists of positives and negatives for each of the choices available?

make a decision at the spur of the moment, if necessary?

make a decision methodically, over a long period of time?

put aside a big decision to give yourself time to think about options?

research questions you may have with regard to a decision you need to make?

COMMUNICATION SKILLS (WRITTEN)

Can you:

punctuate correctly?

write full sentences?

avoid run-on sentences?

use topic sentences in paragraphs?

write creatively?

write quickly?

draft a business letter?

outline a paper?

write a paper from an outline?

write memos?

COMMUNICATION SKILLS (ORAL)

Can you:

talk to your boss?

explain a problem?

exchange information?

speak to a small group?

speak to a large group?

give a formal speech?

TABLE 2-6 LIST OF SKILLS (CONTINUED)

COMMUNICATION SKILLS (ORAL) (CONTINUED)

decide what information should be communicated?

listen actively to identify needs and avoid misunderstandings?

stay calm, even when you're upset or angry?

explain your point of view in the middle of a debate?

MATHEMATICAL SKILLS

Can you:

add?

subtract?

multiply?

divide?

do fractions?

do story problems?

figure out sales tax?

split a check in a restaurant?

balance a check book?

find bargains?

pay bills on time?

use a budget?

prepare a budget?

project costs and revenues?

calculate future budget needs?

figure out whether actual costs and revenues differ from the estimated budget?

take action to adjust the budget?

Are you able to do math problems:

while talking it out with others?

in your head?

only on paper?

quickly? accurately?

with a lot of numbers?

TECHNOLOGICAL SKILLS

Can you:

use data and other information by entering it into the computer?
   by modifying it?
   by storing it?

put information in a chosen format?

read and follow instructions for repairing relevant equipment?

choose the best format for display?
   line graphs
   bar graphs
   tables
   pie charts
   written descriptions

TABLE 2-6 LIST OF SKILLS (CONTINUED)

RESEARCH SKILLS

Can you:

collect information from various sources?

analyze questions to determine what information is needed?

select information most helpful to answering your question?

evaluate that information?

use a card catalog?

use computerized programs to conduct word searches for your research topic?

find three different sources on the same subject?

speak to a reference librarian?

TEAMWORK SKILLS

Can you:

share tasks necessary to complete a project?

encourage each other by listening and responding to others' ideas?

recognize/build others' strengths?

resolve differences for the benefit of the group as a whole?

take responsibility to accomplish the goals set up by your team?

INITIATIVE/FOLLOW THROUGH

Can you:

develop a plan?

create a process for making the plan work?

involve others?

delegate responsibilities?

meet deadlines, regardless of obstacles?

encourage others to meet deadlines with that kind of dedication?

spontaneously develop solutions as problems arise?

make a commitment?

keep a commitment?

ADMINISTRATIVE SKILLS

Can you:

answer telephones politely?

manage more than one phone line at a time?

copy large volumes of paper?

collate and organize many copies of the same document?

use a filing system?

create a filing system for storing information?

develop a plan on how to staff a project?

make charts or spreadsheets?

organize information to place in charts or spreadsheets?

How Can I Package My Potential?

Now that you've thought about the skills that you have, you can use this information to start figuring out what type of career path may be right for you.

You may have noticed in Table 2-6 that *many* skills are used in many different ways and, consequently, many different professions. In today's workplace, the use of computers is commonplace. The need to use administrative skills is nearly universal. Certainly mathematical and scientific skills are more important for the science-oriented professions, but having the ability to figure out sales tax or a budget is useful in almost any field.

Take Amy Gargas as an example. Amy is an information services analyst with the Actuarial and Underwriting Department of Blue Cross. She believes that the most important skill that she uses is interpersonal communication. "You can be the best program designer or software manager and up to date on the latest applications, but if you can't express yourself, you can't help the people you're hired to assist." Amy frequently rescues other employees who are having systems problems; they call her with distressed pleas for help. In their confusion, they can't always articulate exactly what the problem or request is. It is Amy's job to determine what their true needs are. She calms them down, determines what their tasks are, and learns about their job responsibilities, so she can prescribe and build the best system for their needs. If she didn't sift through the information that her customers provided and instead gave them exactly what they asked for without any discernment, she would not be solving the real problems. Therefore, her ability to communicate is crucial in her job, especially since most employees depend so heavily on their computers to do their work.

In its SCANS report, the Department of Labor points out how many occupations use most of the generic skills listed in its report. The report explains how a travel agent must allocate material and facility resources when she or he obtains them and must store travel materials (i.e., brochures, catalogs, and forms) to distribute later to customers. Likewise, SCANS points out that a dental hygienist communicates information about a patient's condition to a variety of individuals—like the doctor, patient, family members and insurance companies. Thus, while a dental hygienist's job seems quite technical in nature, it actually requires many of the same skills that other professions require.

Table 2-7 gives you an opportunity to think through different kinds of careers using various skills. Portions of the chart are left blank for you to fill. What creative ideas do you have about what other kinds of skills these professions use—and how?

TABLE 2-7 CHART OF SAMPLE CAREERS AND CORRESPONDING SKILLS

BUSINESS MANAGER

Leadership Skills

giving directions and encouragement, having high expectations for yourself and others, complimenting work well done

Teamwork skills

_____

_____

What else?

_____

_____

ACCOUNTANT

Mathematical skills

_____

_____

Communication skills

_____

_____

What else?

_____

_____

TEACHER

Communication skills

_____

_____

TABLE 2-7 CHART OF SAMPLE CAREERS AND CORRESPONDING SKILLS (CONTINUED)

Leadership skills

_____

_____

What else?

_____

_____

NURSE

Communication skills

_____

_____

Scientific skills

_____

_____

What else?

_____

_____

COMPUTER PROGRAMMER

Technological skills

_____

_____

Decision-making skills

_____

_____

What else?

_____

_____

TABLE 2-7 CHART OF SAMPLE CAREERS AND CORRESPONDING SKILLS (CONTINUED)

JOURNALIST

Communication skills

_____

_____

Computer skills

_____

_____

What else?

_____

_____

ENGINEER

Mathematical skills

_____

_____

Analytical skills

_____

_____

What else?

_____

_____

MARKETING/SALES

Marketing skills

_____

_____

TABLE 2-7 CHART OF SAMPLE CAREERS AND CORRESPONDING SKILLS (CONTINUED)

Research skills

_____

_____

What else?

_____

_____

PARALEGAL

Administrative skills

_____

_____

Communication skills

_____

_____

What else?

_____

_____

OTHER JOB_____

_____ skills

_____

_____

_____ skills

_____

_____

What else?

_____

_____

IS MY ATTITUDE IMPORTANT?

Sometimes the world looks almost too large to tackle, and we think we don't have *any* skills to offer a prospective employer. But one of your most important gifts is looking back at you in the mirror—you. If you believe in yourself and respect yourself, you will be capable of doing anything that you decide to do. Chapter 4 goes into greater detail regarding the steps that you can take to keep up your energy and spirits as you prepare your career path. But having a positive self-image and believing that you really can do whatever you *want* to do is a basic premise to success in life—career or otherwise.

Have faith in your abilities, even if others don't. Don't be discouraged that you don't have experience or ability in a lot of *activities*; emphasize instead what you *can* do. Patty Smith enjoyed writing in high school but was repeatedly told that she was bad at it. Once, her high school English teacher "looked me straight in the eye and told me that I would fail college because I couldn't read and I couldn't write." Her first class in college was English 101, and Patty had to write a paper. She chose to write on Martin Luther King, Jr. The paper "was 10 pages long! I worked really hard on it, but when I went to turn it in I thought to myself, 'you're a total idiot.'" She gave her professor the paper and "told her she was going to have to get me a writing tutor. She took the paper, read it right there, and cried. She said I was a wonderful writer—I just couldn't *spell*. She explained that I thought I was a bad writer because I had been programmed to think I was a bad writer. She said that my problems with writing were workable and that whoever told me I was a bad writer was just wrong. It made me wonder—did Michelangelo always color in the lines?" Patty's experience is an excellent demonstration of someone whose *manner* of doing something (writing creatively) was camouflaged by her weakness in an activity (spelling). Once she could believe in herself, she could correct the weaknesses while relishing the strengths.

SUMMARY

Remember, these initial aptitudes and interests will grow, develop, and change throughout your life. We have different needs at different stages of professional and personal lives. These categories are a way to help you think about yourself and your goals today at this stage of your life.

ASKING QUESTIONS AND GETTING ANSWERS

1. Identifying Things You Like to Do. Sometimes we know our top one or two favorite activities but are not as aware of other things we like to do. By identifying a lot of different activities that you like, you can broaden your ideas about what types of jobs you may be able to do that involve your interests. Thus, spontaneously and quickly, write down five of your favorite things to do in the space below.

1. _____

2. _____

3. _____

4. _____

5. _____

2. Making Your Current Activities Work for Your Future. Think through your current activities to make sure you are getting the most out of them to help you prepare for your future. Make a list of the skills you have been developing through your current activities—be it sports, volunteer work, child-rearing, or a job. Next, make a list of the skills that you *could* be developing through these activities if you expanded your involvement in the activity—and plan to start working on those skills.

➤ Activity: __*photography*__

    Skills You Have: 1. *frame picture in camera*

                          2. *use soft filters*

                          3. *take good spontaneous photos*

    Skills to Develop: 1. *learn to use dark room*

                          2. *learn to take interesting nature shots*

                          3. *learn to use/understand shadows better*

➤ Activity: _____

    Skills You Have: 1.

                          2.

                          3.

    Skills to Develop: 1.

                          2.

                          3.

➤ Activity: _____

    Skills You Have: 1.

                           2.

                           3.

    Skills to Develop: 1.

                           2.

                           3.

3. **Reviewing the Material to Choose Careers.** Look back at the materials you gathered in Chapter 1—your Holland Code and your People Types and Tiger Stripes results—and review the skills and interests that you identified for yourself in this chapter. Make a list of five possible job categories which you think match your skills, interests, and abilities.

    Job #1: _____

    Job #2: _____

    Job #3: _____

    Job #4: _____

    Job #5: _____

COLLABORATIVE LEARNING AND TEAM-BUILDING SKILLS

1. **Describing Your Best Skill.** In groups of two or four, take turns describing the skill that you believe is your best. Describe *why* you think this is your best skill. Give some detail to your classmates. On a piece of paper or on the chalkboard, write down the skills that everyone shares to get an idea of how diverse your skills and abilities are. Which skills do you think are universally required in the world of work?

2. **Brainstorming Universal Skills and Talents.** In your same group above, pretend that you are managers making hiring decisions. What kind of skills and talents are you looking for in prospective employees? Brainstorm two separate lists: one that has skills on it and another that has talents on it. Rank the relative importance of each of the skills and talents on your list. Assume that you only have one position open to hire and you are interviewing 100 applicants. Be picky! You have to make the best decision.

LONG-TERM PLANNING: KEY TO YOUR PERSONAL PORTFOLIO

Developing Skills. Think through the career paths that interest you. Is there a skill that is common amongst those careers that you would like to develop? For instance, Janice Holmes has thought about becoming a sales manager for a large company. She has also contemplated opening her own travel agency some day. Since both of these occupations require a lot of presentational skills, Janice decided to buy a book on artistic advertising. Her friend Bill (who may become her business partner) decided that *his* career choices would require a lot of public speaking, so he joined Toastmasters to improve on that skill. In the following spaces, list a skill that you would like to develop, explain why you think you need to develop it, and list two ways that you could work on developing that skill. Give yourself a time frame within which to develop this skill more (Janice gave herself a month, Bill gave himself three months). After that period of time, come back to this chapter and explain what you have done to improve the skill.

Skill: _____

Why I Need to Develop This Skill: _____

_____

First Activity That Will Help Develop This Skill: _____

_____

Time Frame: _____

What I Have Done to Develop This Skill: _____

_____

_____

_____

STUDENT QUESTION

Q **Pam Rud, marketer and researcher in San Diego, California:**

Pam has done a lot of different things in her career and is proud about how diverse her experience is. She has a bachelor's degree in advertising. Her first job was with a full-service advertising agency. She moved through numerous departments, each time increasing her responsibilities and giving her a well-rounded agency background. When she began her second job with a nonbank division of Security Pacific, she was able to transfer her agency skills to the client side and work in the marketing department. In her seven years of employment there, she continued to advance through the ranks and take on more responsibilities. Her advancement was not only vertical but horizontal, in that she added operations, systems, training, policy and procedure, and audit to her list of skills. Her broad range of knowledge seems to work as a disadvantage rather than as an advantage, however. When she has interviewed for positions, she has the sense that her experience is too broad, and the skill sets do not seem to pigeonhole into a nice, neat package. Her question:

How do I use the diversity of my skills as an advantage when looking for a job? Also, since my most recent work experience was with a financial institution, how do I demonstrate my ability to work in other industries? The financial name of the company sometimes brings a negative connotation of "banker's hours" and that my skills are only financial related. How do I promote my skill set as versatile to various industries?

A First, choose the industry that interests you most. Trying to look at too many options at once will cause you to lack focus and not clearly see what a given industry requires and what you have to offer. If you have two to three industries which interest you, fine. Second, focus more on the jobs you held—what you learned, what you contributed and what real progress you made—so that a prospective employer realizes that you have learned and mastered a number of capabilities and can do the same in the future. Emphasize the functional areas of your resume—review the example of a functional resume in Chapter 8 for ideas. Keep in mind that your needs may be changing because you may not be as satisfied or as happy in a cookie cutter type of job. Think out of the box for jobs that really interest you and keep looking for the best fit for you. It may take time to find the match.

Third, anticipate any negative perceptions that a prospective employer may have about your past. There are many ways you can gently and directly make your point: "You may have some perceptions about the financial industry. I know I did before I began working in this industry. While some people worked the stereotypical banker's hours, I worked long and hard to learn and contribute on my job so that I could exceed what people expected of me when I was hired. Those same characteristics of hard work, love of learning, passion for my work, and pride in making a contribution are a part of who I am. That is why I am confident that I can make a difference in your company."

CAREER PROFILE

LISA ALDISERT a bank executive turned motivational speaker, encourages people to be flexible with their career plans. "I do a lot of talks to baby-boomer types in career distress because of downsizing or other changes. I help them see the possibilities in starting over." Lisa uses herself as an example. She spent 16 years as a banker, she owned and operated her own apparel business for a while, and now she has her own consulting and seminar business. Lisa left the banking field because she felt she was not growing or developing as well in the structured corporate environment as she would with her own business. She encourages other people to go through the same self-evaluation, especially if they find themselves repeatedly feeling unhappy or disenchanted. She believes it is possible to achieve whatever you set your mind to do. "If you get the broadest education possible and get a good background, you can truly do anything you want," Lisa says. "Just because you start one type of career, you can still change."

Lisa decided to begin her seminar business when she realized that she was "more in love with the message than the manufacturing" of clothing. "The decision to make *that* change was incredibly difficult. It could have been perceived that I had 'failed.' The message again to students is it's okay to have questions. It's okay to think gee, maybe this isn't the right thing. As long as you're growing from the experience, I think there's nothing to worry about. As long as you truly feel that you learn from" whatever endeavor you try, "then you can't even consider it a failure as long as you learn from it. You have to be true to what you are and what your passions are—it *all* will come into play in whatever you do next."

Lisa stresses the importance of looking at the whole picture when looking for work. "Break it down. Skill is knowing what to do on the job. Behavior is how you do what you're doing. Values and attitude are *why* you do it. When employers hire people, skills are the easiest" to identify with regard to the job being advertised, but "behavior and values are most important. An employee has to be on the same value basis as I am. They could have all the skills in the world, but you need matched values."

Lisa knows that one of her strengths is appreciating diversity in cultures. "There's no question that that's a huge part of who I am," she explains. "I was raised in an Italian-American home where we were exposed to lots of cultures. It's just a more interesting way to live. I think I learned a lot about tolerance and inclusiveness from my family." In fact, learning about other cultures is one way that Lisa grows. When she travels, she's always open to learning from the new and different people who she meets along the way. "When I meet people, it's always fun to figure out what their history is, and how their background and culture will help me improve."

Lisa gives workshops to companies on how to interact together and appreciate each other's values. In her workshops, she draws on her personal experiences. Emphasizing the way personalities work together is "something I've been doing all along anyway." Now she's taking "all that experience and giving back to people in a way that makes them feel better all day long."

DISCOVER

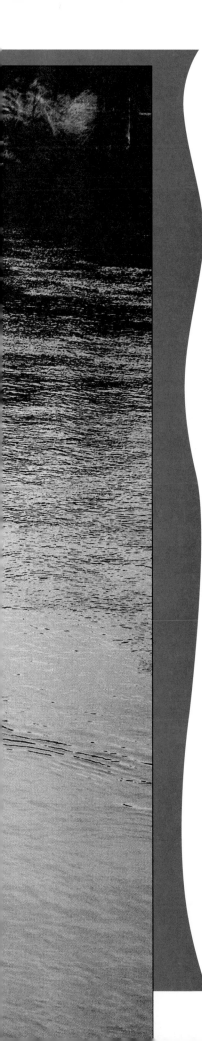

Career Explorations:
What Does and Does Not Interest You?

Christopher Columbus traveled across the seas from Spain to discover America. But how did it all come about? How did Christopher Columbus reach the conclusion that he should spend part of his life traveling across the Atlantic Ocean to see what he could find? Columbus, the third of three sons, did not know what his future had in store for him. In his country, the eldest son inherited the family land and the next eldest usually dedicated his life to the church. The leftover sons had to fend for themselves. Columbus could have chosen to play it safe and do nothing more with his life than what was immediately available to him. In fact, had he been the eldest (rather than third) son, he very well may have settled for his birthright to inherit his father's lands rather than take any risk. Instead of "settling in" at any level, however, Columbus chose a path that changed the world forever. He promoted his sailing skills and used his charm to convince the queen of Spain to appoint him Admiral of the Ocean Seas and sponsor a voyage into the unknown. Columbus had no crystal ball to tell him that he would succeed. In fact, a few people told him that he was just going to fall off the edge of the world. Think of how nervous Columbus must have been, standing at the helm of the *Santa Maria* as it got ready to sail off into uncharted waters. But he gathered up his courage and chose to set sail anyway. He took the risk. And what a wonderful risk it was!

You, too, are at the brink of choosing to take a journey into the unknown. Sure, you can choose the safe route instead and limit your exploration to one or two careers that you already know, even if those career ideas may not satisfy you. Or you can choose to take a risk and challenge yourself to find a career path that will fulfill you as much as Columbus' career path fulfilled him. Your exploratory journey may lead you to a career path that is just right for you. Even if you return from your journey convinced that your current path is the right one, the journey of exploring careers will have helped you solidify that decision.

HOW DO I BECOME AN EXPLORER?

Before you delve too deeply into this journey of resources, take a deep breath and remember for a moment who you are and where your interests lie. It would be easy to lose sight of the point of this book—that is, to find a career path that is right for *you*, not to spend a lot of time looking at careers that hold no interest for you. Also, as discussed more fully in the next chapter, don't be discouraged if your career path doesn't develop exactly how you plan. Frequently, the marketplace takes unexpected turns and changes, which you may have to consider and incorporate into your career plans. In addition, your goals may change from time to time, and your ideal career may take on a new shape and look different at the end of the climb than it did when you started. In fact, an "ideal" career is a fallacy for most of us, in that there are probably a number of careers that we would both enjoy and do well.

Remember that your career path will affect your personal life choices. For example, if you choose to specialize in an area where there are very few jobs, you may be limiting yourself to live in the areas of the country where there is a market for that specialty. As another example, if you choose a career that tends to demand a lot of hours of work a week, you are also choosing to spend less time at home. You may be more willing to do this earlier in your career rather than later. Or, if you spend beyond your means, you may have to work hours on end your whole life to compensate for your habits. Thus, keep in mind your personal life goals when deciding your career choices. They *will* overlap.

HOW DO I RESEARCH CAREERS?

The amount of information available today is almost overwhelming. You can find written sources of information in local libraries and a plethora of knowledge in cyberspace. If you can think of a source, career information is probably available there.

Computers

If you have access to computers, use them. The Career Information Service (CIS) has perhaps the largest amount of information available in any one spot. CIS provides information specific to the state where it is located, including information about occupations, job descriptions, locations for training, and financial aid information. QUEST, a part of CIS, can help you identify work characteristics that are common to certain occupations. SIGI (System of Interactive Guidance and Information), also a part of CIS, can help you match your values to possible occupations. GIS (Guidance Information System) has national information on it. DISCOVER identifies career sources. CIS should be available through your career counselor. In addition to CIS, however, assistance in selecting majors and obtaining employment information should be available on the computer. For instance, "Moody's Corporate Profiles" on Dialog (1-800-955-8080) lists thousands of companies with information on annual earnings, financial data, and the like. Of course, on-line services such as Prodigy, America OnLine, and CompuServe will have bulletin boards with company or job information and even job openings under an incredible array of areas. (Further discussion on searching for jobs on the Internet can be found in Chapter 5.) A new computer program called "Career Choices" may be useful as well and may be in your career center.

Access to computers also can help you focus on whether you are choosing a career that is limited to certain areas of the country. For instance, Dun & Bradstreet's review of top companies on CD-ROM will allow you to conduct a search for certain kinds of companies in the region of the country where you want to live. If your search turns up empty, you need to take a closer look at whether this career choice is right for you (or, conversely, if you really must live in the area of the country that you have chosen).

Figure 3-1 provides a list of places on the Web (originally compiled by the University of Texas at Arlington) where you can find career and job search information.

The "DOT" System

There are over 35,000 job titles and over 20,000 occupations listed in the *Dictionary of Occupational Titles* (DOT), a publication of the United States Department of Labor. The descriptions are broken down into nine different types of occupations as follows: (1) Professional, Technical, and Managerial; (2) Clerical and Sales; (3) Service; (4) Agricultural, Fishery, Forestry, and Related Occupations; (5) Processing; (6) Machine Trades; (7) Bench work; (8) Structural Work; and (9) Miscellaneous. Thus, if you know the general area of your career interests, you can simply skim through the career titles in that area to figure out career titles that might interest you. An added benefit

FIGURE 3-1 PLACES TO START ON THE WORLD WIDE WEB

Career Information "Clearinghouses"

1) http://www.jobtrak.com/jobguide (The Riley Guide)
2) http://www.clearinghouse.net/tree/busemp.html (Univ. of Michigan Career Center)
3) http://rescomp.stanford.edu/jobs (Stanford Univ. Career Center)
4) http://www.100hot.com/jobs (HotBot)

General Career and Job Search Information

1) http://www.tripod.com/work (Tripod)
2) http://www.careermag.com (Career Magazine)
3) http://www.newwork.com (New World of Work)

Employer Research Sites

1) http://www.yahoo.com/business (Yahoo)
2) http://www.hoovers.com (Hoover's On-Line)
3) http://www.jobweb.org/careers.htm (JobWeb)

Newsgroup And Networking Information

1) http://www.altavista.digital.com (Newsgroup archives)
2) http://www.dejanews.com (Newsgroup archives)
3) http://www.lliszt.com (Directory of discussion lists)

Job Posting Sites

1) http://www.monster.com (Monster Board)
2) http://www.ajb.dni.us (America's Job Bank)

Source: University of Texas at Arlington.

to the DOT system is that the jobs are categorized numerically by the types of basic skills necessary for that job. If you already think you want to be a copy writer, for instance, but aren't sure of what that job entails and what skills are necessary, the DOT publication will give you some ideas. The DOT is a good tool, especially for those people who truly are exploring a lot of different career ideas with the hope of reviewing a broad array of choices. There are thousands of occupations for you to explore. This reference will open your mind to many ideas to get you started.

The Princeton Review of Occupations

This is a helpful guide, matching personality types to job titles. This review also includes salary ranges for various occupations, percentage of males and females within that occupation, what organizations people in various careers join, what periodicals they read, occupation growth trends, and what a typical day is like for a professional.

Other Publications

There are a number of publications, both government and private, that could be useful to a career search:

A. Government publications
  - Encyclopedia of Careers and Vocational Guidance
  - What Can I Be? A Guide to 525 Liberal Arts and Business Careers
  - A Guide to Careers Through College Majors
  - The Encyclopedia of Second Careers
  - The Occupational Outlook Handbook (published every two years in terms of nature of the work, places of employment, training, other qualifications, advancement and employment outlook) (http://stats.bls.gov/ocohome.htm)
  - The Occupational Outlook Quarterly (http://stats.bls.gov/empooq0.htm)
  - Bureau of Labor Statistics (this has a wide range of information!) (http://stats.bls.gov)

B. Publications listing organizations
  - Encyclopedia of Associations
  - Encyclopedia of Business Information Services
  - Guide to American Directories
  - Standard Periodical Directory
  - Standard Rate and Data Business Publications Directory (listing trade publications)
  - State directories (each state has a directory of trade and industry that should be in your library or can be obtained through the state's chamber of commerce)

C. Publications identifying companies or executives
  - Dun & Bradstreet Million Dollar Directory (companies earning more than $1 million annually)
  - Dun & Bradstreet Middle Market Directory (companies with assets between $500,000 and $1 million)
  - Thomas's Register of American Manufacturers
  - Standard Directory of Advertisers
  - Poor's Register of Corporations, Directors, and Executives
  - Who's Who in Commerce and Industry
  - Geographical Index (lists companies by cities and towns)

D. Publications on using the Internet for job hunts (a resource list compiled by the University of Texas at Arlington)

➤ Be Your Own Headhunter Online: Get the Job You Want Using the Information Superhighway, by Pam Dixon and Sylvia Tiersten

➤ The Guide to Internet Job Searching, by Margaret Riley

➤ Electronic Job Search Revolution: Win with the New Technology That's Reshaping Today's Job Market, by Joyce Lain Kennedy and Thomas J. Morrow

➤ Finding a Job on the Internet, by Alfred and Emily Glossbrenner

➤ Hook Up, Get Hired! The Internet Job Search Revolution, by Joyce Lain Kennedy

➤ NetJobs: Use the Internet to Land Your Dream Job, by Michael Wolff

➤ The On-Line Job Search Companion: A Complete Guide to Hundreds of Career Planning Resources Available via Your Computer, by James C. Gonyea

➤ Using the Internet in Your Job Search, by Fred E. Jandt and Mary B. Nemnich

WHAT IF I DON'T DO EVERYTHING RIGHT?

There are no right or wrong answers to exploring careers. Whatever feels right to you probably is right *for* you, as long as you are committed to the process. Certainly there is advice that we can give—for instance, we know that the more creative you are in your explorations, the more likely you are to come up with ideas that meet your individual career and life goals. Be

creative with the sources you use, too. Don't limit yourself to reviewing government publications, periodicals, and trade journals to cast a broad net in learning about various occupations. Review other sources like newspaper want ads; you're sure to see the description of occupations that you haven't thought of before. Review business magazines for ideas about innovative projects in the business world. Look for magazines that are geared toward college students, such as *Business World, College Placement Annual,* or *Business Week's Guide to Careers.* Check in-house publications of corporations, especially large, nationwide corporations that may have monthly newsletters, to find postings of recent job openings and descriptions so that you can learn about the types of jobs that exist in your fields of interest. Your career explorations are limited only by your imagination and time.

SHOULD I CHOOSE MY CAREER BASED ON FIELDS WITH A FUTURE?

It is virtually impossible to predict what will be a growing career field ten years from now, or even five years from now. You can make some educated guesses, and your hunches may turn out to your benefit. Most important, however, is to choose a field that matches your skills and interests as closely as possible.

One way of choosing career paths that have growth potential is by entering fields that will allow you to expand your transferable skills (described in Chapters 2 and 10). That way, you don't get locked into a situation where your ultimate career goal becomes obsolete.

Ned Smith's experience is a good example. Ned chose to major in political science with an emphasis on nuclear strategy and national security and weapons analysis. "It was great in 1989," when he began the major but, with the end of the Cold War, "it was no longer a required field of study," Ned recalls. Ned's interviews in his senior year were necessarily limited to the government (given his emphasis), and the government was no longer hiring in his chosen field.

Luckily for Ned, he had more than just his major to support him in his search for a career. He had developed leadership and management skills when he was the drum major of his college band, and he had participated in other extracurricular activities along the way. Also, he had approached his political science major from the perspective that he was learning to learn (not just studying to get a job in the nuclear weapons industry), which means that he used his classes to challenge himself, think critically, and increase his knowledge. He ultimately has succeeded in becoming a manager in a leadership development program in the fast-growing business of telecommunications. His work as a drum major had taught him how to get a large group of people to work together as a team. His interest in learning allowed him to appear as a well-rounded, industrious person at his interview. By being aware of growth occupations and fields, as well as by focusing on developing transferable skills along the way, Ned has landed on his feet.

One consideration in selecting a career is how the field/industry is now and what the growth prospects look like for the future. As a career seeker, you must match your individual capabilities and interests with an occupation or field that at least has potential for growth—both in the number of jobs in the future and in the potential salaries you could earn. For instance, if you want a career in computer programming, you must be aware of what the future in computers appears to be and which languages have longevity. Also, the argument between personal computers or workstations versus mainframe computers will make a huge difference in which languages you learn.

All fields and occupations are not on the rise, but many, such as farming and some systems analyst positions, are on the decline. Also, because of downsizing and budget cuts in most industries, middle management jobs have been eliminated as corporations are "flattening" their organization charts and cutting out many management positions in the middle of the chart. Therefore, some members of middle management (no longer on the leading technological edge and not high enough in the organization to guarantee job security) have found themselves unexpectedly changing careers. Of course, some fields—such as agriculture—may be welcoming new participants even though the general field is on the decline just because the individuals currently in that area are leaving for different occupations. Others, such as law, may be predicted to increase the actual number of positions to be filled over the next decade but already have more than enough qualified candidates to fill the new positions. These examples show that exploring the ramifications of trends—looking below the surface—is important to understanding the future.

In addition to being aware of trends in the world of work and having a good game plan, Ned's experience shows that you should always have a backup plan in the face of unexpected events. You may be required to take a temporary detour from your career path and reevaluate your goal timetable. Having an alternative plan may help you get back on target.

Here is an example: Joe Jordan has an ultimate goal of being the CEO of a computer company. Companies usually do not hire job seekers directly into management positions. New hires must prove themselves before being considered for upper management or even a management training program. In most cases, people begin at the entry level, prove themselves by doing well in their first few jobs, and then get promoted. Given these circumstances, Joe must be constantly cognizant of the business environment and his industry's growth potential as he makes changes in his career path.

Tables 3-1, 3-2, 3-3, 3-4, and 3-5 are published in the U.S. Department of Labor's *Occupational Outlook Handbook, 1996–97 Edition* and show (1) projected job openings due to growth and replacement needs; (2) occupations with the largest projected numerical decreases in total employment, 1994–2005; (3) occupations having the largest numerical increase in employment, 1994-2005; (4) occupations projected to grow the fastest, 1994–2005; and (5) jobs growing the fastest and having the largest numerical increase in employment from 1994-2005, by level of education and training.

HOW ABOUT RESEARCHING INDUSTRIES?

If you're trying to learn about whether a particular industry is open for new players, you can research that industry in much the same way that you've been researching possible careers. Begin your research with a broad net, as you identify the industries that most interest you. Your first resource can be the *Readers' Guide to Periodicals*. This publication indexes by subject the various articles that periodicals report. Choose a library that offers an extensive selection of business magazines such as *Fortune, Forbes, Harvard*

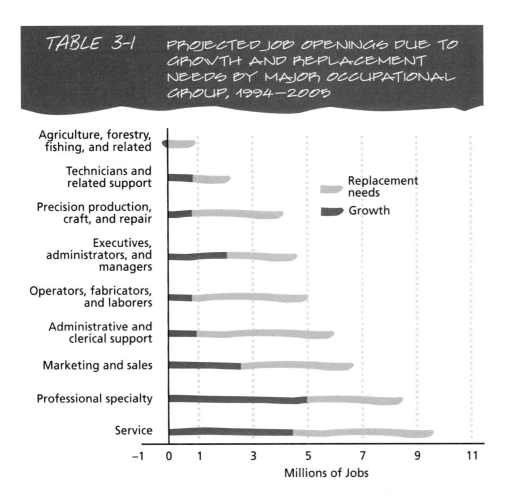

TABLE 3-1   PROJECTED JOB OPENINGS DUE TO GROWTH AND REPLACEMENT NEEDS BY MAJOR OCCUPATIONAL GROUP, 1994–2005

Source: U.S. Department of Labor, Bureau of Labor Statistics, *Occupational Outlook Handbook, 1996–97 Edition* (Washington, D.C.: U.S. Department of Labor, 1996), p. 2.

Business Review, Business Week, Industry Week, Barron's, Money, Nation's Business, U.S. News & World Report, Time, Newsweek, and specific industry trade journals. Major metropolitan newspapers publish industry trend articles as well. Local business journals many times produce an annual directory of companies organized by industry.

What are you looking for in all of this industry information? When perusing your resources you want to determine current trends, vocabulary, company rankings/competition, government regulations and issues, customers, distribution channels, new products and the health of the industry. This information will give you the framework–the background–in the fields which interest you.

TABLE 3-2 OCCUPATIONS WITH THE LARGEST PROJECTED NUMERICAL DECREASES IN TOTAL EMPLOYMENT, 1994–2005

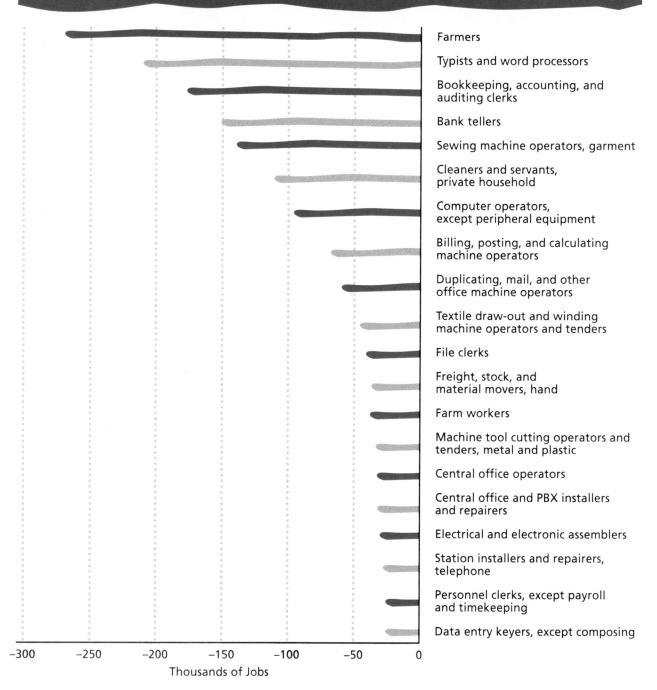

Source: U.S. Department of Labor, Bureau of Labor Statistics, *Occupational Outlook Handbook, 1996–97 Edition* (Washington, D.C.: U.S. Department of Labor, 1996), p. 4.

TABLE 3-3 OCCUPATIONS PROJECTED TO GROW THE FASTEST, 1994–2005

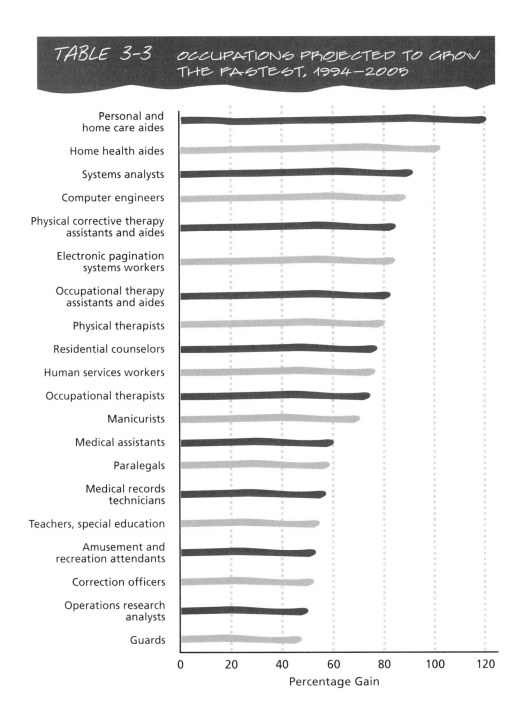

Source: U.S. Department of Labor, Bureau of Labor Statistics, *Occupational Outlook Handbook, 1996–97 Edition* (Washington, D.C.: U.S. Department of Labor, 1996), p. 3.

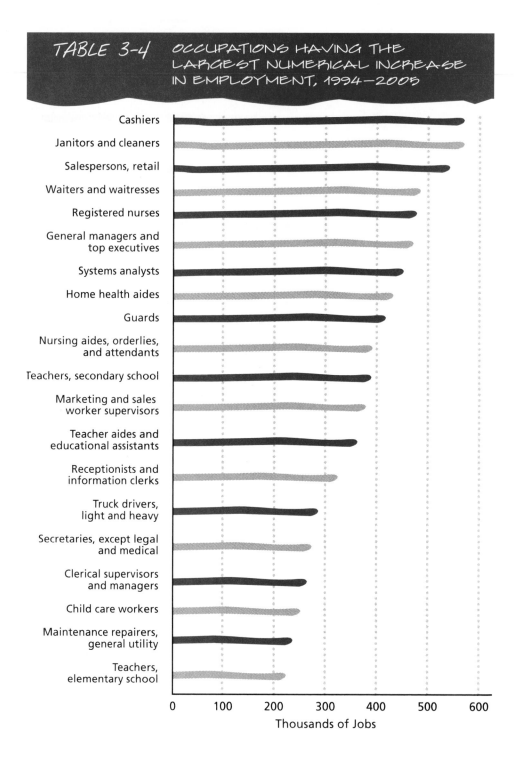

TABLE 3-4 OCCUPATIONS HAVING THE LARGEST NUMERICAL INCREASE IN EMPLOYMENT, 1994–2005

Source: U.S. Department of Labor, Bureau of Labor Statistics, *Occupational Outlook Handbook, 1996–97 Edition* (Washington, D.C.: U.S. Department of Labor, 1996), p. 3.

TABLE 3-5 JOBS GROWING THE FASTEST AND HAVING THE LARGEST NUMERICAL INCREASE IN EMPLOYMENT, 1994–2005, BY LEVEL OF EDUCATION AND TRAINING

FASTEST GROWING OCCUPATIONS	OCCUPATIONS HAVING THE LARGEST NUMERICAL INCREASE IN EMPLOYMENT

First Professional Degree

Chiropractors	Lawyers
Lawyers	Physicians
Physicians	Clergy
Clergy	Chiropractors
Podiatrists	Dentists

Doctoral Degree

Medical scientists	College and university faculty
Biological scientists	Biological scientists
College and university faculty	Medical scientists
Mathematicians and all other mathematical scientists	Mathematicians and all other mathematical scientists

Master's Degree

Operations research analysts	Management analysts
Speech-language pathologists and audiologists	Counselors
Management analysts	Speech-language pathologists and audiologists
Counselors	Psychologists
Urban and regional planners	Operations research analysts

Work Experience Plus Bachelor's Degree

Engineering, mathematics, and natural science managers	General managers and top executives
Marketing, advertising, and public relations managers	Financial managers
Artists and commercial artists	Marketing, advertising, and public relations managers
Financial managers	Engineering, mathematics, and natural science managers
Education administrators	Education administrators

TABLE 3-5 JOBS GROWING THE FASTEST AND HAVING THE LARGEST NUMERICAL INCREASE IN EMPLOYMENT, 1994–2005, BY LEVEL OF EDUCATION AND TRAINING (CONTINUED)

FASTEST GROWING OCCUPATIONS	OCCUPATIONS HAVING THE LARGEST NUMERICAL INCREASE IN EMPLOYMENT
Bachelor's Degree	
Systems analysts	Systems analysts
Computer engineers	Teachers, secondary school
Occupational therapists	Teachers, elementary school
Physical therapists	Teachers, special education
Special education teachers	Social workers
Associate Degree	
Paralegals	Registered nurses
Medical records technicians	Paralegals
Dental hygienists	Radiologic technologists and technicians
Respiratory therapists	Dental hygienists
Radiologic technologists and technicians	Medical records technicians
Postsecondary Vocational Training	
Manicurists	Secretaries, except legal and medical
Surgical technologists	Licensed practical nurses
Data processing equipment repairers	Hairdressers, hairstylists, and cosmetologists
Dancers and choreographers	Legal secretaries
Emergency medical technicians	Medical secretaries
Work Experience	
Nursery and greenhouse managers	Marketing and sales worker supervisors
Lawn service managers	Clerical supervisors and managers
Food service and lodging managers	Food service and lodging managers
Clerical supervisors and managers	Instructors, adult education
Teachers and instructors, vocational and nonvocational training	Teachers and instructors, vocational education and training

TABLE 3-5 JOBS GROWING THE FASTEST AND HAVING THE LARGEST NUMERICAL INCREASE IN EMPLOYMENT, 1994–2005, BY LEVEL OF EDUCATION AND TRAINING (CONTINUED)

FASTEST GROWING OCCUPATIONS	OCCUPATIONS HAVING THE LARGEST NUMERICAL INCREASE IN EMPLOYMENT

Long-Term Training and Experience (More than 12 Months of On-the-Job Training)

FASTEST GROWING OCCUPATIONS	OCCUPATIONS HAVING THE LARGEST NUMERICAL INCREASE IN EMPLOYMENT
Electronic pagination systems workers	Maintenance repairers, general utility
Correction officers	Correction officers
Securities and financial services sales workers	Automotive mechanics
Patternmakers and layout workers, fabric and apparel	Cooks, restaurant
Producers, directors, actors, and entertainers	Police patrol officers

Moderate-length Training and Experience (1 to 12 Months of Combined On-the-Job Experience and Informal Training)

FASTEST GROWING OCCUPATIONS	OCCUPATIONS HAVING THE LARGEST NUMERICAL INCREASE IN EMPLOYMENT
Physical and corrective therapy assistants and aides	Human services workers
Occupational therapy assistants and aides	Medical assistants
Human services workers	Instructors and coaches, sports and physical training
Medical assistants	Dental assistants
Detectives, except public	Painters and paper hangers, construction and maintenance

Short-Term Training and Experience (Up to 1 Month of On-the-Job Experience)

FASTEST GROWING OCCUPATIONS	OCCUPATIONS HAVING THE LARGEST NUMERICAL INCREASE IN EMPLOYMENT
Personal and home care aides	Cashiers
Home health aides	Janitors and cleaners, including maids and house keepers
Amusement and recreation attendants	
Guards	Salespersons, retail
Adjustment clerks	Waiters and waitresses
	Home health aides

Source: U.S. Department of Labor, Bureau of Labor Statistics, *Occupational Outlook Handbook, 1996–97 Edition* (Washington, D.C.: U.S. Department of Labor, 1996), p. 7.

Some of the reference materials that will help you analyze your particular industry include:

> **Directory of Industry Data Sources.** Lists publishers of data information; provides more sources to review.

> **Moody's Industry Review.** Organized by industry; ranks companies on the basis of financial information; lists industry leaders and provides a quick view of industry's health.

> **Directory of Corporate Affiliations.** Lists the parent/owner of companies; provides insight into corporate culture, financial health, management structure.

> **National Trade and Professional Associations of the United States.** Lists general information about industry organizations which can be further researched for information.

> **Corporate Technology Directory.** Gives the names, addresses, and telephone numbers of companies that are within an industry, including information on competitors and geography.

> **Dun and Bradstreet's Billion Dollar Directory.** Provides parent company, financial, and SEC information, important for industry leader information and financial status.

WHAT ABOUT SELF-EMPLOYMENT?

Many people leave the employment of others after acquiring business experience to start their own company because they value more freedom and/or flexibility. What they may overlook is that, despite the glamour of self-employment, being self-employed is a never-ending job with long, hard hours. Another aspect of self-employment is that more than half of all new businesses do not see their sixth anniversary—and it is the consensus that new businesses are not considered stable until their fifth anniversary. People often don't post a profit until the third year of being in business. So, if you want this for yourself, you have to really be committed to making it happen.

A few self-employment opportunities are listed in Figure 3-2.

WHAT IF I WANT TO CHANGE CAREERS?

Some people may decide that the career they have had for many years is not the right one for them, and they start to explore what they really want to do. Over and over, you'll hear stories of people who left one field to "follow their passions" in another field.

FIGURE 3-2 SELF-EMPLOYMENT OPPORTUNITIES

Service-Oriented Business

1) Computer Instruction
2) Catering
3) Seminars/Workshops
4) Consulting
5) Exercise Programs and Facilities

Retail Business

1) Home Video Rental
2) Bookstore
3) Children's Educational Games
4) Home Health-Care Aides

Food Business

1) Gourmet Coffee Shop
2) Drive-Through Coffee Vendor
3) Ethnic Restaurant (Ethiopian)
4) How to Cook Seminars

Tourism or Recreational Business

1) Travel and Learning Vacations
2) Backpacking Outings
3) City Sight-seeing Tours
4) Child-Related Entertainment

Technology

1) Web Master
2) Web Designer
3) Technical Repair
4) Technical Service

Unusual

1) Artisan
2) Weight/Body Trainer
3) Communication Auditor
4) Motivational Speaker

As individuals change from one career to another, they often make a gradual (instead of abrupt) change so that they are not without work while they are making their transition. Often people try to prepare themselves for the transition by choosing careers that are compatible with or related to the areas or fields in which they are interested. Taking responsibility for your own future in this way will position you to make the change as smoothly as possible with the least amount of personal upheaval. As an example, a computer programmer who wishes to teach at the university level during the last phase of his or her career life will prepare for this change by completing the necessary college courses (to ensure marketability in the new profession as well as acquire the essential professional experience). Also, retired professionals or executives are being hired after retirement as consultants in the field they left. Many professionals approaching retirement will enter new careers on a part-time basis before making a change.

If you are contemplating a career change, think about how your current career has taught you skills that you will need in your new career path. Make a list of what you still need to be successful at your newly chosen field. If your current career can't get you those skills and allow you to transfer easily into the new field, then look through the various resources outlined in this chapter and see if there is an occupation or occupations that would help you create a bridge between what you are doing now and what you would like to be doing. This way, you can help yourself make the more gradual change and keep on a specific career path too.

SUMMARY

Career exploration is a process of discovering which career you are going to follow and creating a strategy for that career. Once you realize your motives, values, aptitudes, and personality traits, you are ready to start making your career journey. You now have resources to help you identify the jobs that will lead to your career interest and help you get started toward the career that will be the most rewarding and fulfilling for your personal set of criteria.

ASKING QUESTIONS AND GETTING ANSWERS

1. Exploring DOT. Go to the library and locate the *Dictionary of Occupational Titles.* Look through the directory and choose three occupations you think you might enjoy. List them below, along with a list of the primary skills they require.

➢ Occupation:_____

Required Skills:_____

_____

➢ Occupation:_____

Required Skills:_____

_____

➢ Occupation:_____

Required Skills:_____

_____

2. Getting to Know What You Are Seeking in a Career. To better know yourself and your career motives and be able to set future goals, write a paragraph on each of the following career topics:

➢ How do I see myself professionally? How will I appear to other people?

_____

_____

➢ How would I describe the kind of career that would be satisfying for me?

_____

_____

➢ What are my salary goals (both presently and for the future)?

_____

_____

➢ What kind of family do I want? Do I plan to stay at home to raise my kids?

_____

_____

➤ How would I describe my dream home?

_____

_____

➤ What kind of education will it take to satisfy my needs?

_____

_____

➤ What kind of education will it take to satisfy my wants?

_____

_____

➤ What does career success mean to me?

_____

_____

➤ What kind of work environment would be ideal (number of hours, size of company, etc.)?

_____

_____

COLLABORATIVE LEARNING AND TEAM-BUILDING SKILLS

1. **Helping Each Other Choose a Career.** Get in groups of two and take turns interviewing each other about values, hobbies, likes and dislikes, strengths and weaknesses, challenges and fears, previous employment, extracurricular activities, and so on. Use sections in the preceding chapter in developing your questions. Don't ask what the interviewee's current career goals are. After the interview, write down five career choices that you think would suit the interviewee—and be ready to explain why. Share your ideas, and find out how close you've come to the interviewee's career goals.

A.1. Interviewer's Career Ideas

a._____

b._____

c._____

d._____

e._____

A.2. Interviewee's Career Goals

a._____

b._____

c._____

d._____

e._____

B.1. Interviewer's Career Ideas

a._____

b._____

c._____

d._____

e._____

B.2. Interviewee's Career Goals

a._____

b._____

c._____

d._____

e._____

2. **Making Career Choices.** Mark D'Avila is a computer analyst with 15 years of experience. He loves his computer profession but feels it is time for him to make his move to his second chosen career—management. You have been hired to be his career counselor. In groups of two, discuss among yourselves what Mark should do to prepare himself for this new career. What steps should he take? How should he figure out what new skills he needs to acquire? Does he need additional education? If so, how would you counsel him? If his ideal job is CEO of a computer company, what should his interim career look like? What do you need to know about his current skills and personal life to counsel him in the best manner possible? Make a list of the five questions you think are the most important to ask him in helping him develop towards his next career move.

➤ _____

➤ _____

➤ _____

➤ _____

➤ _____

LONG-TERM PLANNING: KEY TO YOUR PERSONAL PORTFOLIO

1. **Researching Industries.** In this chapter, we reviewed methods to use in researching industries. Now is time to put those methods to use. Select one industry and research the following information at your local library:

    Industry_____

    a. List three current trends or challenges in the industry

    #1_____

    #2_____

    #3_____

b. Who are the top five market leaders?

#1_____

#2_____

#3_____

#4_____

#5_____

c. Describe the industry's primary products, customers, vendors, and distribution channels.

_____

_____

_____

_____

d. List the types of positions that the industry has to offer that would interest you.

_____

_____

_____

_____

e. List three questions that you would ask if you had an opportunity to speak with an expert of this industry.

#1_____

#2_____

#3_____

f. What skills or experience do you have that could assist a company with the current trends or challenges facing this industry?

_____

_____

_____

_____

2. Making Sure Your Path Is Working for You. Sometimes we get starry-eyed about what we believe will be our perfect career without exploring whether the day-to-day work involved in that career will be interesting to us. It may be that our strengths do not match the requirements of that career. Investigate a career that you might like by doing a task that gives you information about that field—read a book, watch a talk show, read a news article, interview someone in the field. After your investigation, make a list of six activities that someone in that profession must accomplish in their job—three that you think you would enjoy and three that you think you would not enjoy.

    a. Things I Would Enjoy

        #1_____

        #2_____

        #3_____

    b. Things I Might Dislike

        #1_____

        #2_____

        #3_____

3. Knowing the Facts. With regard to the occupation that you have chosen, find out more details. What kind of education is required? What is the average salary? How many hours a week would you be working? What are related fields? Does it still interest you? Fill in the blanks below. Then choose a second occupation and repeat the exercise.

    a.

        1. Title:

        2. Educational Requirements:

        3. Salary:

        4. Hours:

        5. Current Job Market:

        6. Projected Job Market:

        7. Your Personality Traits Likely to Help:

    8. Your Personality Traits Likely to Impede:

    9. Opportunities for Advancement:

   10. Related Occupations that May Interest You Down the Road:

   11. How Does This Occupation Fit in with Your Life Goals?

b.

    1. Title:

    2. Educational Requirements:

    3. Salary:

    4. Hours:

    5. Current Job Market:

    6. Projected Job Market:

    7. Your Personality Traits Likely to Help:

    8. Your Personality Traits Likely to Impede:

    9. Opportunities for Advancement:

   10. Related Occupations that May Interest You Down the Road:

   11. How Does This Occupation Fit in with Your Life Goals?

STUDENT QUESTION

Q **John Weaver, junior at Middlebury College in Middlebury, Vermont**

John has a double major in psychology and economics. Right now he is looking in two directions for a career—human relations and the business track, something like Wall Street. He has always been interested in the business side of things (his uncle is a stockbroker and seems to enjoy it), which is why he has thought about Wall Street. To John, jobs on Wall Street seem to be a route that lots of people take for two years or so. On the opposite side of the coin, John doesn't know if he wants to work with numbers all the time, which is one reason why he has kept psychology as one of his majors. John feels that doing work in psychology is more personal. John has even thought about doing something like teaching "rather than spending 12 hours a day crunching numbers." John says, "I'm kind of like a lot of kids these days—I have no idea what I want to do. About five times I've known what I *definitely* wanted to do and then I changed my mind and thought 'huh—what am I doing?' Basically, my 'gut' is split." John doubts whether he could pick a career even if someone told him that he would be given all the tools, everything he needed—that he just had to choose. John doesn't want to do what his older brothers have done, which is graduate from college without a lot of direction or goals for the future. John's question:

How do you find out what you're interested in? How do you know? How do you discover your interests? What leads do you go off of?

A You need to do two things. One, learn more about the fields you think you want to pursue. Talk to some stockbrokers who work on Wall Street. What do they like about the job? What do they hate? How did they get there? Are they salespeople, traders, analysts? What qualities do they think got them where they are now? How much do they really work with numbers? What questions did they wish they had asked before they got into this field? What do they know now that they wish they had known when they were in your shoes? Ask the same questions of teachers so that you can determine if that field suits you better. Through this process, it is quite possible that you will learn new, undiscovered avenues which will lead to jobs of interest. Investigate as much as you can to find out which fields really resonate with you—which areas really spark your passions.

The second thing you need to do is try some of these areas, through internships or part time jobs, before you make up your mind. These are the "leads" which you yourself create. Even if you get into a career and decide to switch gears later, that's okay. You can make as much of an informed decision as possible and then reevaluate once you're there. People often take circuitous routes to their "ideal" job. Just don't let fear of making the "wrong" decision keep you from getting going.

CAREER PROFILE

MARK KIRSCHNER

Choosing a career that's exciting, fun, *and* profitable seems a near impossibility to many of us. It seems like only a few people have the serendipity to land the perfect employment situation. Mark Kirschner, vice president of marketing MTV consumer products, seems to be one of those "chosen" few. At age 32, he is working at a job that many would love, and he has a lot of fun doing it. But as Mark's career path shows, his employment at MTV has little to do with serendipity and much more to do with planning, determination, and simple hard work.

Mark started college as a pre-med major but, rather than just taking classes in his major, Mark used his summers to explore careers. He worked in a medical lab running assays and gels one summer—he found the work interesting but he learned that medicine was not his passion. He thought about law and worked in a law firm one summer but decided against it. "I thought law was really interesting, but at the end of the day it was not something I wanted to build my career around." Then one summer Mark worked for a graphic design firm and then the next summer for an advertising agency. "It kind of clicked," he remembers. "I thought it was a fun, creative business." He decided that this should be his career.

Once Mark decided to enter the field of advertising, he worked hard to get a job. "I made New York my target city," he says. "I went to *every* on-cam-

pus interview and targeted *every* agency." In the fall of his senior year, he organized his class schedule so that he had Mondays and Tuesdays free, "commuted every weekend to New York, and set up interviews every Monday and Tuesday morning. I did that almost every weekend. I was a maniac—because I was scared to death I wouldn't get a job!" Although he didn't get the precise job he was looking for, he ended up working for an agency where he learned all steps of advertising from the ground up. He attributes his success at this job hunting to his energy, among other things. "I was on them and all over them until they gave me an interview," he says. He also researched the companies extensively. "I was able to look at a client list, see the accounts" of the company he was going to be visiting, "and then tell them how I could help them on particular accounts."

Key to Mark's career development is his belief that, in choosing a career, you first and foremost must "follow your passion. If you're not passionate, if you're not having fun, then you're not in the right place." According to Mark, "At the end of the day, whether you're in accounting or marketing" or any other field, "if you're excited and passionate about what you're doing— about your product—that makes your work more interesting and makes you more productive." As examples, he uses his colleagues from the various industries where he has worked. "Most of the people at MTV love music. Most people in videogames love them or love technology. A lot of them always took things apart as kids but just didn't become engineers. Which is not to say that someone doing ads for Preparation H has a passion about hemorrhoids, but they probably do have a passion about helping other people. Following your passion doesn't have to be as blatant as working at MTV. It can be more subtle than that." Mark's ability to be flexible while at the same time staying focused on his goals and following his passion has allowed him to develop an exciting and fun career path.

Preparing To Realize Your Goals:

How to Get from "Here" to "There"

GENIUS IS ONE PERCENT INSPIRATION, NINETY-NINE PERCENT PERSPIRATION.

—THOMAS ALVA EDISON

Picture a local park where you live, or the downtown area of your town, or a building that recently was constructed. Everything there didn't just appear overnight. It took many people and many years to care for the trees, flowers, and grass planted in your local park. Someone built the benches and designed the bike path that runs along its edge. In the same way, the appearance of your downtown is not random. It may have begun with a random design many years ago, when its first settlers arrived. But someone had to decide when to pave the roads, where to put up traffic lights, whether to allow free or paid parking. And the recently constructed building required many steps to be taken along the way *before* construction ever began. An architect had to design the building plans; the city council had to approve the building's design; the property owners had to figure out whether water and sewage would be available; the building materials had to be chosen and purchased. Whether it is the park, the downtown area, or the building, nothing appeared by magic. It took a lot of hard work and a lot of steps along the way to create the finished product. In fact, without proper planning and preparation, the project can fail or become too expensive to maintain. For instance, construction of that building could be stopped midstream if the owners forget to ensure water and sewage access. Therefore, preparation is key to a successful outcome.

The same is true of most projects—including a career path. In the last three chapters, you've gathered a lot of information about who you are and how to explore career choices. But what should you do with this information? Now that you know more about what you have to work with, it's time to plan your own "park." Through this chapter, you will discover some of the tools that are available to make your career what you want it to be. These tools include learning how to make decisions to set you on your career path; how to set career goals and timelines, and how to plan for resources such as money, education, and a support system. You should take these tools and make a plan to carry out what you want for your career. It's up to you to decide how to use those tools to design your ultimate career game plan and outcome.

HOW DO I MAKE DECISIONS FOR MY FUTURE?

You gathered a lot of information in the first three chapters. How do you use this information to decide on a career path? Everyone handles decision making in his or her own way. Some people make impromptu decisions; others agonize over their choices. Some people make lists to visualize the positives and negatives to the decision they might want to make; others go with their gut instinct. In fact, you may use all these methods at various times when you make your decisions.

Preparing for your future includes reaching some conclusions about the career path you want to take. Look back over the information you have gathered so far—what have you learned about yourself? your abilities? the career paths that best fit you? Discard those career options that you know are wrong for you, and you will be left with a set of choices from which to choose your career path. Now make some decision in the way most comfortable to you about which career path you will concentrate on.

Keep in mind that you can *change* your decision if you're not satisfied. Don't fall into the trap of believing there is a "right" choice and a "wrong" choice—a "perfect" choice that you must find or ruin your future forever. Kathy Shannon learned this lesson. She initially chose a career in politics, and then realized that this career was not right for her. Campaigns made her feel uncomfortable. She changed careers and became a journalist instead. "It is important to know when you're absolutely miserable and what you're miserable about and avoid it again in the future," Kathy says. It was difficult for Kathy to admit she was unhappy because she was afraid she was admitting that she had lost direction. Looking back, though, she knows she made the right decisions—both to at least try politics and then to leave it when she was unhappy.

Life is an ever-evolving process, not one set in stone. Making a choice that you change later at least helps you get started on your path. Making no decisions at all will just leave you stagnant.

HOW DO I SET CAREER GOALS?

Some people have always known their ultimate career goal. For instance, Becky Parker has known she wanted to be a doctor ever since she was nine. Others discover the perfect career through a life-changing event. Roger Quick had no idea what he wanted to do until he watched a friend's life fall apart because of actions taken by law enforcement officers. From that point on, Roger knew he wanted to become a police officer because he wanted to help make the system work for its citizens rather than work against them. Still others may be unsure of where they want to wind up, although they know the general category of their career ideas. Terry Bhola knows he likes marketing and is pretty sure he likes fashion, so he'll study marketing as his college major and get as many jobs and internships in the fashion industry as he can to build his career in that area.

Regardless of whether or not you have a specific or general idea of your career interests, you need to begin to set some goals and make a plan to carry them out. The path toward your ultimate career goal can be just as important as the ultimate goal itself. Career success means you must be serious about securing a series of relative job successes and eliminating an "I just need a job right now and will worry about my career later" attitude. For instance, even though Becky knew she wanted to be a doctor, she had to plan her steps along the way to get into medical school and to choose a specialty. She participated in internships, worked part time at the student health center during college, and tried out many different areas of medicine before settling on emergency care. She tried to make each of her employment opportunities work toward her ultimate career goal. Even when she worked as a baker in her college cafeteria, she focused on the positive skills she was learning and worked her way to a supervisor's position (which would ultimately help her in managing a staff at a hospital).

If you are to have career success, you must treat every job you get as a necessary piece of a career jigsaw puzzle. If one piece is missing, it could jeopardize the finished product. Treat every job as the most important piece of the puzzle of your well-organized career success plan.

Since we will probably have more than one career in our lifetime, we must go further than just planning the first career, but use those first, second, or third careers as stepping stones toward those fourth, fifth, or ultimate steps. Use these first careers as catapults to rocket you from one situation to another that's better—wherever that is for you. For example, suppose your ultimate goal is to teach computer science at the university level. You need to identify (1) what skills are needed for such a job and (2) how to go about developing those skills. Perhaps you identify teaching, computer literacy, and administrative tasks as three major skills needed. What jobs or activities will help develop these skills? Volunteering as a teaching assistant? Working at a job that requires a lot of computer work? Joining a club that will have opportunities to strengthen administrative skills? Whatever the steps, you should try as much as possible to have each of your jobs help develop skills that will be needed for your career.

Now how should you go about tackling the awesome task of taking your steps toward your ultimate career goals? *Set goals and develop a plan.* Successful people set goals, develop plans, establish deadlines, and list priorities. It's no surprise that these are some of the same tactics you need to do well once you enter the work force. Employers want to hire employees who know how to set goals. The most common reason that people don't achieve their goals is that they never set them in the first place. Think of a marathon runner—if he or she doesn't train gradually for the race, he or she will not finish it and/or may experience a great deal of pain in trying to finish it. The best way to start "training" for your career is to set small, manageable goals that can be achieved. As you gain confidence through those small victories, increase the size and importance of the goals. On the lighter side, there is a lot of truth to the old saying that, "you can only eat an elephant a single bite at a time." If your end goal looks impossible at first, break it into small pieces and then attack. Another very important trait that you need to develop is *tenacity*—holding fast or firmly, retentive, and unyielding. In other words, don't give up.

Following are some of the steps for successful goal setting and achievement:

1. Set written goals and determine the benefits of accomplishing each goal.

2. Before you start, make a plan of action. Outline your goals and take it to the lowest level you can to be able to make each "bite" edible.

3. List priorities and stick to them. If your goals change so will your priorities, so set new goals and establish new priorities.

4. Deadlines will keep you going. If a goal slips, reset the deadline and take steps to meet it. You may need to pick up the pace to get your schedule back on target.

5. Make a commitment in writing and make a mind set that you can and will succeed. Commit to success. If you don't know what that looks like, find a role model and observe your role model to get a mental picture of what success looks like.

6. Tell someone. By telling someone else, you put pressure on yourself to get started and not look back. It also gives you outside support. Sometimes a little pep talk from an outsider is all it takes to get back on target.

7. Set realistic goals and benchmarks in order to have continuous victories. Setting unrealistic goals not only can dampen your enthusiasm, it can put unnecessary pressure on yourself.

8. Make a list of affirmations, like the following, to keep reminding yourself that you are a "winner" and you do "finish" what you start.

   a. I am well organized.

   b. I finish what I start.

   c. I meet my goals every day.

   d. I am successful.

   An affirmation list should be short (not more than ten entries) and said aloud four or five times a day until you are living proof that the affirmation is real. When you have one of your affirmations comfortably handled permanently, you may replace it with a new one. Repeat your affirmations day after day. They should be spoken automatically, just like brushing your teeth.

9. To support your affirmations, visualize yourself in your mind's eye doing your difficult task. If you can see yourself doing something, the actual doing may even seem anticlimactic. It may be as though you have always done it. For example, go to bed at night picturing yourself accomplishing the task. This will give you subliminal messages while you sleep. Carol Pendley had not been skiing for eight years when she made the reservations. Every night for the next month she went to sleep practicing her parallel turns. When she reached the slopes, she was a better skier than she had been eight years earlier. *It works!*

10. Be tenacious! Never give up. You will never know how close you are to success if you give up your dreams.

11. If you feel yourself burning out, step back and give yourself a break. Go to a movie, mow the yard, or give yourself a treat. Take a weekend off and allow yourself to forget the goal for a short period of time. When you start to feel reenergized, you will know it is time to hit it hard again!

12. Reward yourself at milestones. Give yourself a present you've always wanted, eat a banana split, read a book. You know what makes you happy. Also, give credit where credit is due: remember to thank those who have helped you—they deserve credit for supporting you.

13. Keep score. How are you doing? Did you accomplish what you set out to do?

Now that you know the reasons and the "how to's" of goal setting, let's do it. Following is a goal-setting exercise that will help you get accustomed to making written goals for everything you intend to accomplish. The most difficult part of any task is getting started, so *just do it*! Goal setting is one of the few exercises that you start at the end and work backward. Start by putting down the time frame you will follow, what the end product looks like to you, and the steps you anticipate it will take to accomplish that goal. Now go through the time line and set milestones next to the appropriate date needed for accomplishment in a timely manner. To practice goal setting, complete Table 4-1, Getting Started Setting Goals.

TABLE 4-1 GETTING STARTED SETTING GOALS

TIME FRAME	CAREER-BUILDING GOAL	STEPS YOU'LL TAKE
Retirement		
Twenty years from now		
Ten years from now		
Five years from now		
One year from now		
Six months from now		
One month from now		
One week from now		
Tomorrow		
Today		

How Long Will It Take Me to Reach My Goals?

When you set those goals and attach that top priority label to them, you must then assess the amount of time it will take to achieve them. Of course, you must make a decision to complete your series of goals and commitments. You must also take responsibility for the final outcome, keeping in mind that goals are not meant to be inflexible but will change from time to time. By setting up a career map, you can help keep yourself on track. Study the career map in Figure 4-1 to develop ideas about your own map.

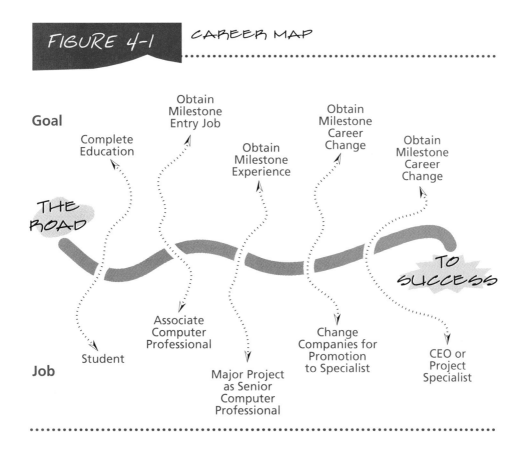

FIGURE 4-1   CAREER MAP

Goal

Complete Education

Obtain Milestone Entry Job

Obtain Milestone Experience

Obtain Milestone Career Change

Obtain Milestone Career Change

THE ROAD

TO SUCCESS

Student

Associate Computer Professional

Major Project as Senior Computer Professional

Change Companies for Promotion to Specialist

CEO or Project Specialist

Job

In the midst of setting up your career map, you should add an anticipated completion time in weeks, months, and years for each goal. When you create this career map, you must remember that it can be changed from time to time, that your circumstances and priorities most likely will change, and that you may make other possible choices for your optimal career outcome. These changes may create detours along the way, but you can use those detours to your advantage, if only as learning experiences. For instance, an expanded career map may appear as shown in Figure 4-2:

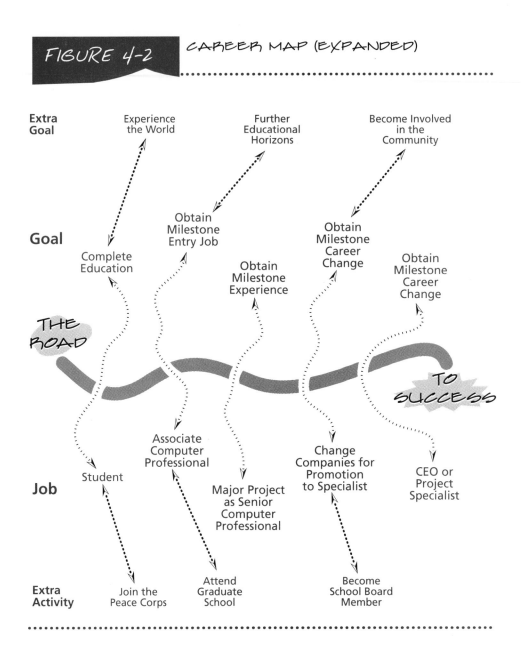

FIGURE 4-2 CAREER MAP (EXPANDED)

Keep your goals and your time line in mind, and allow yourself the strength to recover from any setbacks and get back on track. If you miss a milestone, restructure your career map and reschedule your completion. For example, Kevin had to drop out of school because of an emergency appendectomy. Instead of letting the detour devastate him, he made an appointment with his counselor as soon as he was out of the hospital and revised his degree plan. This action gave Kevin a target to aim at and he never let the word "quit" enter into his vocabulary or his mind. Kevin was constantly looking forward. But he didn't stop there. Kevin took out his career success goals and corrected his timeline. Therefore, Kevin had a temporary setback but never slipped into a negative mind set about his completion.

In addition, you can design a career map for shorter periods of time. For instance, Brad is on the ski team at his university and plans to try out for the 2002 Olympics. Brad's physical training has taught him a lot about setting goals. Right now, he has set daily, monthly, and yearly goals. His current long-term goal is to be in the top ten in his field in a year and in the top five soon thereafter, so that he ultimately will be eligible for the 2002 Olympic team. His short-term goals are the steps that he believes he has to take to reach his long-term goals (i.e., he has a set regime for a certain number of hours a day when he is committed to working out). Brad's constant discipline in skiing will help him not only as he tries to reach his dream of being an Olympian but also as he tries to get the most out of his college education. "No matter where my maturity was in other things, I was always mature in sports, and it's helped to develop other parts of me," Brad says.

WHAT IS THE RECIPE FOR SUCCESSFUL CAREER PREPARATION?

Once you have set yourself career goals and a career map, you need to create a recipe for career success that works for you. There are a number of ingredients in such a recipe: you may need further education; you may have financial concerns; you will need to think about how you budget your time; and you will need to develop a support system among your family and friends. Only *you* know what needs to go into your recipe for success, and in what amounts.

Education

Some degree of education will be necessary for most jobs in the twenty-first century, whether it be a high school diploma for the unskilled jobs, associate degree for semiprofessional jobs, or the graduate degrees or special certificates for the professional, managerial, and executive positions. It is imperative that you be aware what the minimum requirements are for each job you seek and prepare yourself accordingly. Keep in mind that jobs in the United States require more education than ever before, and with the inclusion of the computer in every field of work, your education could be the difference in getting that desired position or coming in second to someone who completed his or her educational requirements.

Also, in the event that your experience and that of the competition are the same, the tie-breaker could be education. Don't let your career goals slip away because you didn't complete your educational goal. Be sure to pin down what the educational requirements are for your career goal. What is absolutely necessary? What is optional but preferred (and more likely to give you a variety of choices)? Be sure to place your educational goals on your career map.

Money

Money is a major concern in every phase of reaching your career success as reflected in the cost of education or special training, the opportunity cost of not having a full-time job while going to school, and the salary goal that you set for yourself.

> ➤ The cost of an education has a wide range. For instance, it costs $20 per credit hour at Tarrant County Junior College in Tarrant County, Texas, while it costs as much as $420 to $480

TABLE 4-2 YOUR MONTHLY BUDGET

INCOME AND EXPENSES	(+)	(-)
Part-time job		
Car payment or public transportation		
Rent		
Phone		
Food		
Car insurance		
Medical insurance		
Entertainment		
Gasoline (if you drive your car)		
Other		
Total		

per credit hour at Harvard. Budgeting one's money is very important to both students attending college full time and employees working full time and attending college in the evening. Table 4-2 is a sample budget of a college student. Fill out this budget based on your own financial circumstances.

➤ Opportunity costs means the amount of money you could be making if you were working full-time instead of going to school or training for a certification. Table 4-3, Opportunity Costs, adapted from the U.S. Department of Labor's *Occupational Outlook Handbook*, presents a scenario that a high school student might face. This scenario shows the various salary possibilities over a limited period of time.

TABLE 4-3 OPPORTUNITY COSTS OF ATTENDING COLLEGE

JOBS FOR WHICH HIGH SCHOOL GRADUATE QUALIFIES	POTENTIAL MONTHLY SALARY
Sales clerk	$1,212
Auto mechanic	2,000
Secretary (if you have computer skills)	2,000
Nanny or day care worker	1,000
Lawn work	866
Construction worker	1,500
Social worker (experienced)	2,500
Truck driver (must have commercial driver's license with good driving record)	2,000
Receptionist	1,000

JOBS FOR WHICH COLLEGE ASSOCIATE DEGREED APPLICANT QUALIFIES	POTENTIAL MONTHLY SALARY
Computer operator	$ 2,500
LVN nurse	1,500
Technician	2,700

Source: U.S. Department of Labor Bureau of Labor Statistics, Occupational Outlook Handbook, 1996–97 Edition (Washington, D.C.: U.S. Department of Labor, 1996), pp. 7, 134, 209, 224, 243, 261, 280, 289, 329, 341, 345, 457, & 462.

➤ Expected salary is a consideration that one must address when choosing a career and making educational decisions. Table 4-4, also taken from the *Occupational Outlook Handbook*, is a list of potential jobs for the twenty-first century and the expected salaries.

➤ People with good budgeting skills carry those skills with them into the business world. No matter what you decide to pursue, having a strong sense of money management—which begins with personal financial planning—will strengthen your overall contribution as an employee.

Support System

As important as the foregoing requirements for career success is the emotional aspect of setting a goal and seeing it to its successful conclusion. This is perseverance, and it is a hallmark of an accomplished individual. A good positive support system is a valuable asset in goal achievement. After you have named, developed, and written your career goals, share the goals with someone or a system of people who have a keen interest in your successful conclusion and are willing to support you in accomplishing that goal.

When you start doubting your ability to complete your goal, you develop concerns about the time limitations, you worry about the money sacri-

TABLE 4-4 EXPECTED JOB OPPORTUNITIES IN THE TWENTY-FIRST CENTURY

POSITIONS REQUIRING FOUR-YEAR DEGREE	AVERAGE MONTHLY SALARY (PRESENT VALUE)
Administrators and officials, public administration	$ 2,000
Managers—marketing, advertising, public relations	3,685
Managers—personnel, human resources, labor relations	3,131
Buyers—wholesale and retail trade	2,143
Engineers (experienced)	3,945
Mathematical and computer scientists (experienced)	3,533
Natural scientists (experienced)	3,226
Physicians	4,412

Source: U.S. Department of Labor Bureau of Labor Statistics, Occupational Outlook Handbook, 1996–97 Edition (Washington, D.C.: U.S. Department of Labor, 1996), pp. 3, 7, 25, 40, 41, 48, 65, 66, 71, 78, 96, 162.

fice, or you just need a pep talk by someone who has your success at heart and is willing to help you, pick up the phone and give a friend the opportunity to help. Or see the friend in person so that you can regain a positive perspective.

We all need help from time to time! Asking for help is not a sign of weakness; on the contrary, it is a sign of a confident person with specific goals doing what it takes to get energized. Developing a support system can help you stay on or get back on track. It can help you achieve the success you want and keep up your spirits when the road becomes hard. You may just need to vent to your supporters. They, in turn, may help or give you just the right "golden word" of advice that turns out to be all you need to keep you in the hunt for your career success. Regardless of your needs, give your supporters the opportunity to help; it may help them feel they had a part in your success, and they may need to help you just as much as you need their help.

The first step is to make a support system list. Use Table 4-5, My Support System, to make your list. This support can come from many areas of your life, from family members, friends, teachers, or counselors. Once you have made your list, call all the people on the list and ask their permission to add them to your support group. Let them know that you will call them whenever you think they can help or you need support or advice. If they say no, they just don't want the responsibility, say "thank you" and take them off your list. It is probably not a reflection of you but of their comfort level in helping others, and it does you a favor to know in advance not to waste your time. If they say "yes," thank them

TABLE 4-5   MY SUPPORT SYSTEM

NAME	HOME ADDRESS	HOME #	WORK ADDRESS	WORK #

sincerely and when you hang up the phone, send them a note to affirm your appreciation. When you have completed your support system list, put it in your time management system (discussed next), so it is always with you.

Time Management System

A time management system is one of your most valuable career success work aids or tools, so make sure you keep it with you at all times. What? You don't have a time management system? Remember, the majority of successful executives make written goals. To help you realize those goals, you should break them down into small, manageable pieces and work through them one at a time. You break your pieces into a time system—years, months, weeks, and days. In this manner, your goals can be met one at a time in little, manageable portions. Table 4-6 is an example of a week's planner, and Table 4-7 is a monthly planner. Where do you get these? There are many commercial brands at the office supply stores or stationery stores, or you could copy these pages and make your own system. The important thing to remember though is just *do it!*

TABLE 4-6 WEEKLY PLANNER

	ACTIVITY	ACTIVITY	ACTIVITY
Monday			
Tuesday			
Wednesday			
Thursday			
Friday			
Saturday			
Sunday			

TABLE 4-7 TIME MANAGEMENT

MONTH OF _____

SUNDAY	MONDAY	TUESDAY	WEDNESDAY	THURSDAY	FRIDAY	SATURDAY

SUMMARY

Preparing to meet your career goals does not happen overnight. To be able to realize career success in a timely manner, you must stay focused on where you are going and reflect on how far you have come. Think through all the tools you have at your disposal in working toward your ultimate career goal. Each step along the way is a challenge. Be proud of yourself for accepting the challenge!

 ASKING QUESTIONS AND GETTING ANSWERS

1. **Designing Affirmation Cards.** Through the power of positive thinking, you can help yourself focus on believing in yourself and your goals. Write down three short-term goals that you would like to achieve (a good grade point average this semester, a work-study job at the school newspaper, etc.) Below, write those three goals in the positive (e.g., "I will get a 3.0 GPA this semester," "I will get a job as a reporter at the newspaper").

   a. _____

   b. _____

   c. _____

   Now transfer these goals to separate pieces of paper or cards. Read them (both silently and aloud) in the morning, during the day, at night. The more times you read them, the stronger the idea will be in your mind. For reinforcement, rewrite the phrases over and over on a separate sheet of paper.

2. **Setting Financial Goals.** Think through what your financial needs and wants are. For example, you can set a goal to save a certain amount of money over the next five years. Perhaps your goal is that you want to be debt free over a certain period of time. Or you could set a goal to pack your lunch every day to save money during the week. List three financial goals that you have or want to make.

   Financial goal #1:_____

   Financial goal #2:_____

   Financial goal#3:_____

3. **Designing Your Own Career Map.** As discussed in this chapter, you can design a Career Map to cover a short period of time. Think of where you would like to be this time next year. What educational goals do you want to reach in the next six months? What personal goals? What job do you want to get in that period of time? Fill out three goals that you have for the next year. Then design your own career map to meet those goals, and identify the activity that you will do to meet the goal. Expand that map to include more goals if you desire.

   Goal #1 for the next year:_____

   Activity to Meet Goal #1:_____

   Goal #2 for the next year:_____

   Activity to Meet Goal #2:_____

Goal #3 for the next year:_____

Activity to Meet Goal #3:_____

CAREER MAP FOR NEXT SIX MONTHS

Goal _____   _____   _____

By: _____   By: _____   By: _____
    Date   Date   Date

THE ROAD

TO SUCCESS

Activity _____   _____   _____

COLLABORATIVE LEARNING AND TEAM-BUILDING SKILLS

1. **Helping Each Other Design a Support System.** In groups of three or four, review each other's support system list that you filled out in Table 4-5. Brainstorm with each other for more people to put on that list. Did some of you think of *types* of people (like a professor or a service provider) that others forgot to explore? Through this brainstorming, come up with at least three new people to put on that list. Identify qualities in those who you list. What makes them good people for a support system?

NAME	ADDRESS/PHONE	MENTORING QUALITIES
1.		
2.		
3.		

Next, take turns "being" one of the people on someone else's list and practicing what would be said during a conversation that you might have when that person is in a crisis. What should you say? What was the other person's response? The person in "crisis" should discuss an issue that is currently a problem for him or her (such as the loss of an internship or the lack of time to do homework). Discuss how the conversation went. Was the person in crisis clear enough? Was the supportive person empathetic enough? Discuss what types of topics would be the most productive to discuss with people in your support system.

2. **Supporting Each Other.** Pair up with someone in your class. Agree to be each other's support system. Share the goals that you wrote down in this chapter. Share your affirmation cards, your timelines, and so on. Over the next few months, check with each other at least once a week about the progress being made toward your goals. Give each other the support that each of you needs.

LONG-TERM PLANNING: KEY TO YOUR PERSONAL PORTFOLIO

1. **Designing Your Long-Term Career Map.** Set up your own career map for the two career paths that you investigated at the end of Chapter 2 or any other two careers that you think you may like to begin. Try to anticipate possible unexpected events such as getting married, having children, moving to a new city or state, and so on as you draw up your own personal timeline. Be sure to draw in optional choices. Follow the structure designed in Figure 4-1.

2. **Designing Long-Term Affirmation Cards.** As noted in the first section of these exercises, there is much power in thinking positively. As with the first section, write down goals that you would like to achieve, only this time make them long-term goals rather than short-term goals. Again, state them in the positive (e.g., "I will become a regional sales manager for my company," "I will graduate from college with honors").

a. _____

b. _____

c. _____

As with the previous exercise, write down these goals on separate pieces of paper or cards and read them whenever you can, or rewrite them over and over for reinforcement. Certainly succeeding in your career requires more than reciting a few lines off of a card every day. But by reading your affirmations, you can help yourself keep a positive, optimistic attitude. They're *your* goals; it's up to you to figure out the best way to reach them. Believing that you *can* reach them is one very important step toward succeeding.

CAREER MAP 1

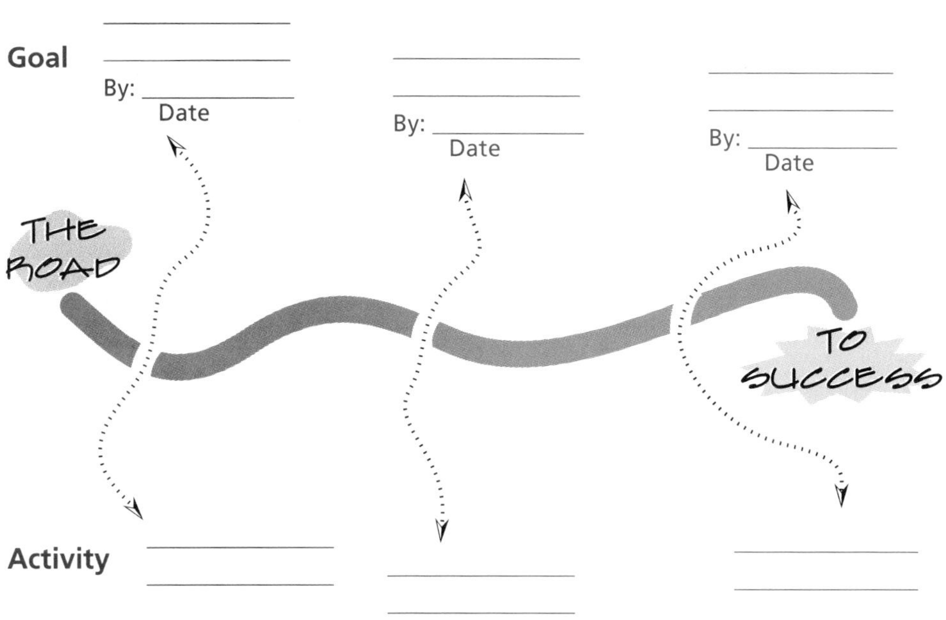

Goal _____

By: _____
    Date

_____

By: _____
    Date

_____

By: _____
    Date

THE ROAD

TO SUCCESS

Activity _____

_____

_____

CAREER MAP 2

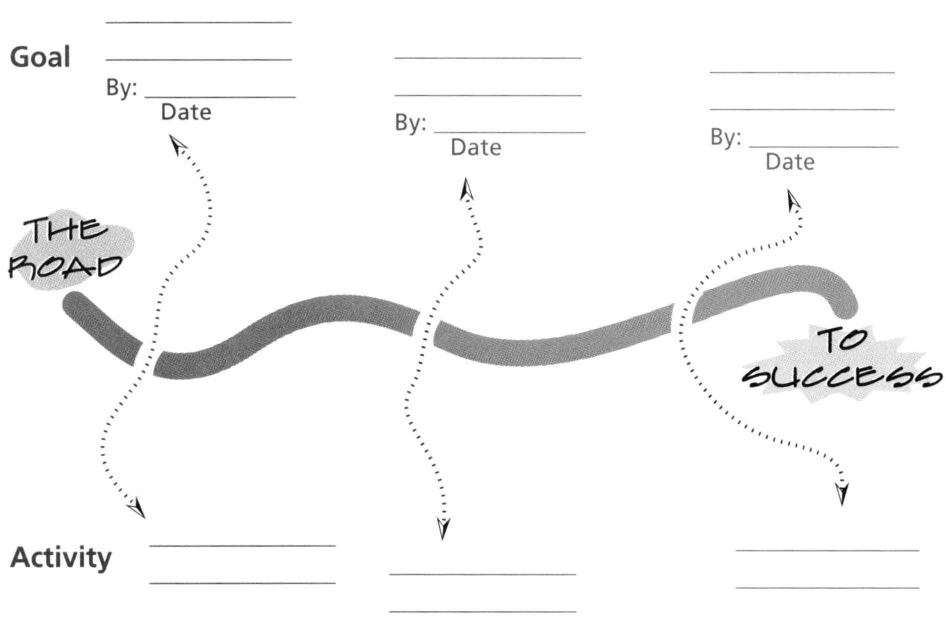

Goal _____

By: _____
    Date

_____

By: _____
    Date

_____

By: _____
    Date

THE ROAD

TO SUCCESS

Activity _____

_____

_____

STUDENT QUESTION

Q **Hiipoi Kauahi, student at Kapi'olani Community College in Honolulu, Hawaii**

Hiipoi is in his fourth year of college, technically, because of many stops and starts. He graduated in 1988 after two years at a community college. He had a drama scholarship, but his first two years were terrible—and really affected his GPA. He views those first two years as being "dumb and young." He went to work for a Hawaiian airline, and it definitely helped him to take time off. Now his GPA is 3.8, and he knows that he wants to be in film. Right now, he's studying liberal arts. He wanted to get into the film school at USC and went there to take a tour of the campus, but he has just found out that he's been turned down. The school told him that it wants to see more progress, more high-level courses taken. He expected the rejection because of his first two years of grades. It just stalls his plans for now. But he really wants to figure out how to set up career goals. He would like to know who he would contact to set up those goals. Also, he has a lot of family responsibility right now, because he and his wife have a new baby. His question:

I know I would like to do documentaries on Hawaiian life and life-style, but I would like someone to help me direct my energies and learn how to choose a career that would complement my goals (since there's not a lot of demand for filmmaking). I'm juggling a lot while trying to hold onto my dream of filmmaking. Any suggestions?

A There are many people, like campus career counselors and advisors, who can help you to set up a career plan. You can also pay career advisors to help you think through these issues. However, you can set up a career game plan on your own as well. If your goal is to ultimately do documentaries on Hawaiian culture and life-style, then focus on the process of learning to make documentaries. Find out who in Hawaii currently does this type of work and ask to apprentice with them. Sometimes you can learn as much if not more from "masters" in the field who are willing to take you under their wing and expose you firsthand to the secrets of the trade. Once you have experience like this, you may have a better chance of getting into a formal program like the one at USC. Or you may learn so much from your apprenticeship that you get your foot in the door working on a documentary with someone else or on your own.

Once you get some more exposure to the field you want to pursue, you can make sure it is what you really want to do. For instance, maybe you will learn the art of producing documentaries, but you find that the market is risky for the type of documentaries you want to create. So maybe you hedge your bets initially by working on something safe, like programming for kids, until you can build a market for documentaries on Hawaiian life.

CAREER PROFILE

MIKE PATTERSON At age 29, Michael Patterson is the youngest city administrator in the state of Washington, and one of the youngest nationwide. Finding this career path was not automatic for Mike, however. It took many turns and bumps along the way to wind up where he is now.

Mike has wanted to be a politician since he was 9 years old. "I had always wanted to have a life that mattered—to make a difference for people," Mike remembers. Then, during the 1976 election campaign, "I started listening to what candidates said, and how much impact these guys had on the world. The Jimmy Carters, the Ronald Reagans—Bob Dole was running for president even back then!" To Mike, politics seemed the best way to achieve his goal of making a difference. Mike decided that he should become a lawyer to reach that ultimate goal. "I started looking at what politicians were, and they were all lawyers," Mike says. "So I thought, that's the way I've got to do it." Thus, at age 18, Mike had his life all mapped out as he started college.

But Mike's life took unexpected turns. At age 19, he got married and he and his young wife Aggie quickly became parents. Aggie nearly died in delivery, and for that first year after the baby was born Aggie was housebound, recovering. Mike worked three jobs and went to school fulltime. He remembers many classes where he fell asleep or just didn't show up because

he was stretched too thin.

Then, as a sophomore in college, Mike found out he had dyslexia. He was taking English 101 and doing well in the course. When he went to take the exit exam, however, he failed. He was forced to take English 101 a second time, and was one of the best students in the class, but he failed the exit exam again. "My professor said something wasn't right," Mike recalls. "He told me I should be able to pass this thing." Mike was sent to the learning disability lab, where he was diagnosed with a mild case of dyslexia. "They told me to concentrate harder, that my mind was playing tricks on me," Mike says. "I got out of English 101. I didn't have to worry about exit exams. And I always concentrated more."

In spite of his dyslexia, Mike started law school. He was determined to achieve his ultimate career goal, and law was the way he saw to achieve it. However, Mike's dyslexia really hurt him in law school because the entire grade for any one class was based on a test given at the end of a semester—a test that did not make accommodations for people with dyslexia. Mike remembers "bombing" on his contracts final the first semester. He went to speak with his professor, who knew that Mike was well versed on the subject. "He said this would be tough for me" to continue with law school with the dyslexia problem. "He told me I'd be fine as an attorney, but there was nothing he could do about my testing. He knew I understood the material but it wasn't coming through on paper." That's when Mike told him he was in law school because he wanted to be involved in politics. His professor suggested that Mike seek a master's degree in public administration instead, where the testing methods are different. Mike followed through with this suggestion, which is how he has gotten where he is now.

Mike's flexibility and tenacity have helped him along his career path. Rather than allow potential obstacles to deter him, Mike molded his career path around them. Becoming a politician is still in Mike's future—if he wants it. "There's an awful big cost to being a politician, I'm starting to learn," Mike admits. "Before I only saw the positives. Now I see you also have to give up a big part of yourself, your privacy." As Mike has shown, he is open to changing the path he has chosen if the change is a good one for him. Whatever he chooses, he seems to understand the tools that he needs to help him prepare for the future.

Part 2

THE JOB SEARCH

AND

GAME PLAN

EVALUATE

Researching and Ranking Companies:

How to Evaluate Companies that Interest You

> WHEN THE GOING GETS TOUGH, THE TOUGH GET GOING.
> —KNUTE ROCKNE

An investigative reporter has just learned that all the medical malpractice insurance carriers in her state are refusing to renew doctors' malpractice insurance unless her state's legislature does something to reduce the amount of money awarded to plaintiffs in medical malpractice lawsuits. The reporter knows that she could just report what she's learned and leave it at that. But she also knows that this is an important issue to her readers—without malpractice insurance, doctors won't practice medicine! So she starts researching. She reviews all the public documents at the state insurance commission and learns that the losses for the insurance companies have not been as bad as the insurers have implied; she interviews local lawyers who say that the insurance companies are just trying to put pressure on the legislature and that the companies won't actually leave the state since they threatened to leave ten years ago for the same reason and are still around; and she verifies this information by gathering newspaper clippings about what happened ten years ago. She hears rumors that a company in a neighboring state may be willing to insure her state's doctors. She calls this company, confirms its intention to become a presence in the state, and suddenly she has a copyrighted story on the solution to the state's medical malpractice insurance woes. In the process, she has become one of the foremost authorities on medical malpractice insurance in her state.

What the reporter sought was full information about a crisis. What she found was a solution. In the same way, your investigation and research of where you want to work can be both informative and solution oriented. You can choose to know no more than what you're given on the surface (like the reporter could have done), or you can investigate further to find a work environment that suits you well. The more you research and investigate the available choices, the better you will understand both what you're looking for and what options are available to you. And perhaps you will come across the *solution* in a way that you didn't quite expect.

WHERE DO I START?

Start your research by knowing what you want to find out. Develop a goal and get to work finding the companies that may be suitable prospective employers. You have already reached some conclusions in Chapter 3 about the career field you want to enter, and you have spent some time setting career goals in Chapter 4. Now you must fit your goals to the various organizations in your chosen field of interest. You may want to look at the size of the companies, whether they are domestic or international, commercial or government oriented, family owned or open market, located close to home or in another state or country. The choice is yours. Don't fall victim to only interviewing with the companies that have interest in you. By researching and ranking your top choices ahead of time, you are taking control of the search for prospective employers and aggressively seeking the best organizations for your talents.

Your goal in researching is twofold: first, it's important to know as much about different corporations as possible so that you can decide which ones would suit you best. In addition, however, having knowledge about the details of a corporation is sure to impress recruiters and managers of the corporation. Remember Mark Kirschner (profiled in Chapter 3), who interviewed with company after company in New York? He got his first job because of his intricate knowledge of the company where he was interviewing. And he knows that he made his own job hunt easier by highlighting those companies whose products and work interested him the most. He interviewed in New York every weekend for a semester, and that was *after* narrowing the companies to his top choices!

Here are some things that you might want to learn about when researching companies (also outlined in the U.S. Department of Labor's *Occupational Outlook Handbook, 1996–97 Edition):*

> ➤ **Type of Business.** What is the purpose of the organization? Does it provide services or products? Does it have a different function? Who are its customers? Is it large or small? What are its plans for the future? Does it have a unique product, or does it promote itself in a unique manner? What are the other businesses in this field—do they do a better job? Is the organization's business or activity in keeping with your own interests and beliefs?

➤ Job Descriptions. You may like the type of business of a certain company, but you also should inquire about whether they have the type of work that you want to do. Even if everything else is perfect, you won't be happy if you don't like the work. What types of positions are available? What are the duties of the person or people in the position that you are seeking? What kinds of projects are those people working on? You should also make sure that you meet the requirements of the job you are seeking. For instance, your dream job may be to become the regional sales manager for a particular company. But what if that company requires all their sales managers to have advanced degrees in engineering—something you don't have? You have to analyze whether the company is really a good fit for you, or whether you are going to have to improve your skills to keep up with the company's expectations—especially in the technological world of today and in the future.

➤ Work Environment. Is the job outdoors? indoors? with a big company or small company? with regular or irregular hours? 40 hours a week or 60? What types of people work there (especially in a smaller company where everyone gets to know everyone else)? Do you feel comfortable with them? Does the work require travel? What matters to you?

It's easy to say that you don't really care—you're just as happy being in the spotlight as you are being a small cog in a very big wheel. But some people flourish in certain environments, while others wilt. Beth recalls her summer associateship with a huge law firm in Baltimore. Beth thought she wouldn't mind the anonymity, but found that it was uncomfortable for her to walk down the hall and not know a lot of the people she was passing, even after three months. Her officemate Linda, on the other hand, loved the huge firm. She felt secure because of its size, and she enjoyed the ever-changing faces. Two different people, two very different reactions to the same work environment.

➤ Benefits. Of course, one of the first questions will be about the salary range. But there are more benefits than just salary. What about health benefits? Is dental included? What is your monthly fee for medical insurance? Is there a pension or profit-sharing plan? paid vacation? What other services do they offer you or your family? Is there child care? Are there physical fitness programs or health club memberships? Make the inquiry about these things, but also decide how much they matter to you. Which ones matter the most?

Another kind of benefit that can be important to your career growth is educational opportunities. Does the employer offer participation in certification programs and seminars? Who pays for them? Does the employer encourage employees getting higher education? only tolerate it? discourage it (because it appears to be a distraction from a 60-plus-hour work week)? How important are these educational opportunities to your career growth? Are you learning enough on the job so that you can forego the formalized education?

➤ Location. Where is the job located? in your town? in a neighboring city? far away? close to family? If it is in another city, can you afford the cost of the commute? Would you plan to move? Will your bottom-line salary be enough in the new place? What are you looking for? If you're thinking of moving to another city at a later time but not now, you may want to plan ahead by exploring companies in your area that have offices in the area where you want to move.

As noted in Chapter 3, location may not appear important now but may become crucial at a later date. Thus, you may want to think through location issues with an eye toward your long-term future. Certainly you may not have the flexibility to be choosy about where the job is located because of a difficult job market overall (or in the place where you want to end up). Nevertheless, *where* you live may be quite important to your happiness overall, and thinking about location now can give you some reassurance and/or ideas later.

➤ Potential for Growth. What are the long-term prospects? Has the company been doing well so far? Are they looking to expand? Is the organization in an industry with favorable long-term prospects? What are *you* looking for?

➤ Other Factors. Other job factors are not so neatly defined and the answers can only be found within yourself. It is important to capture these intangible pieces of your job description that are unique to what is important for your life and values. Consider what type of company culture would best suit you. Do you want a company with an established reputation or do you want one with an entrepreneurial setting where you can contribute to its growth? Do you like a structured work environment or one that is more relaxed? Do you want a company that solicits participation from all members of staff and management? What type of boss would you like to have? Does the company have a mentoring philosophy?

Once you have identified the things in a company that are most important to you, you will have a better sense of what type of company you seek. For instance, Julie Rhodes will graduate in May with a degree in business. She wants to find a company with a lot of growth potential where she can get a lot of experience. Her ultimate career goal is to become an office manager, but she's a little afraid to start out in that position without having more work experience. Realistically, she won't get hired right out of college for that level of job. She'll have to work her way up. She lives in Aurora,

Colorado, just outside Denver. Although she's not thrilled about commuting to Denver, she is willing to do so if she finds the right company. She believes that there will be more options for her in Denver, so she's resigned to the fact that she'll probably end up working there. She feels she needs a starting salary of at least $18,000 with basic health benefits to help support her family. Using the sample budget outlined in Chapter 4, she has budgeted her monthly costs and has decided that she can manage on that sum. (See Table 5-1.) She also wants to find a company that is flexible about child care issues because she is a single mother with two young children. She's a small-town person, so working with a small company would feel most comfortable. She is also a little shy and feels that a smaller company will be more like a family where she can get to know a few people well (rather than a lot of people more superficially).

Julie's priority goal list looks something like this:

1. Need salary of $18,000 or more, with health benefits.

2. Need a place big enough for both an office manager and an assistant; need opening for assistant, and an office manager who likes teaching. Need a lot of responsibility, so I can learn.

TABLE 5-1 JULIE'S MONTHLY BUDGET (AFTER TAXES)

INCOME AND EXPENSES	(+)	(-)
Job	$1,000	
Child support	600	
Rent		$505
Utilities		60
Phone		40
Food		300
Car insurance		100
Medical insurance (with expected employer's plan)		125
Entertainment		70
Gasoline (if I have to commute)		120
Child care		250
Other		
Total	$1,600	$1,570

3. Need some flexibility, in case kids get sick. Maybe find a place that will let me work out of the house in times of emergency. They're pretty healthy kids, so I just need a *little* flexibility.

4. Prefer smaller, family-atmosphere company.

5. Look to Aurora companies first, then Denver and surrounding suburbs.

6. Other things that would be nice: paid vacation, higher salary, pension plan (not as important because I'm only 25), shorter workweek (like 35 hours instead of 40 hours, so I can be home with my kids).

Notice that, although Julie would like a shorter workweek, she didn't put it high on her priority list. That's because she decided it was more important to get a job with a lot of good experience. Also, Julie believes that most companies willing to train new employees are going to have high expectations that the new employees are willing to go the extra mile and work really hard. Julie thinks that, if she can find a company where she can learn a lot and get a lot of responsibility, she can grow into a situation where the employer will ultimately trust her with working out of the home sometimes or reducing her hours as long as she gets her work done.

These are Julie's priorities. What are yours? Fill out the end-of-chapter exercise asking you to make a list of your goals in seeking companies that are best for you.

How Can I Find Out Which Company Is Best for Me?

Research—systematic inquiry, investigation, or exhaustively studying in a particular subject or field —should be approached as you would any other problem or inquiry. Remember, you have a choice too. Don't let your choices of prospective companies default to only the companies that put an ad in the paper, are in your hometown, are referred to you by your college placement office, are in the recruiter's database, or who are interested in you.

You already spent some time researching industries that interested you, back in Chapter 3. If you didn't complete that investigation, you may want to revisit that section of Chapter 3 before you start researching specific companies within the industry that interest you the most.

In trying to determine how best to find out what companies are out there, turn back to Chapter 3 again. Many of the resources used to explore careers can also be used to identify companies in your field of choice. Thus, the Internet, for instance, has bulletin boards of prospective private and public employers with job announcements. The publications listed on pages 51-54 will give you an idea of companies to research. Every year, Fortune Magazine publishes the top 500 and top 1,000 companies in terms of atmosphere, benefits, opportunity, etc.

Other publications are:

➤ *The Industrial Directory* (listing companies and products of the manufacturing sector)

➤ *Encyclopedia of Career and Vocational Guidance*

➤ *Occupational Outlook Handbook* (explains the various industries that hire your occupation)

➤ *American Almanac of Jobs and Salaries* (lists job and salary information)

➤ *Dun & Bradstreet Career Guide* (categorizes occupations and industries)

➤ *The Bureau of Labor Statistics* (has a variety of publications regarding occupations, salary ranges, employment rate, etc.)

These resources would certainly be a good beginning for compiling a list of companies for you to consider.

Libraries are a logical starting place also because they have such a large variety of resources under one roof in which to research. In the reference section, you can get almost any kind of information on companies. There are resources that show companies' financial stability, their officers (complete with a biography of their business experience), and so on. A reference librarian can help you explore companies that you select as your top interests. Most of the resources listed in this chapter can be found in your local library.

Use the following resources for your company search:

➤ The Internet. Although already discussed in Chapter 3 and mentioned earlier, this resource deserves a second plug. On-line computer resources are relatively inexpensive and offer an expansive array of information. You can be "on-line" 24 hours a day, 7 days a week. Many libraries offer free access to the Internet, and many companies, professional societies, colleges, and government agencies have "home pages" where you can find announcements about job opportunities, upcoming events, useful documents to obtain, and so on. The more you learn about the Internet, the more useful it is to you. You may want to study resources such as the *Internet Yellow Pages* to figure out what is available for you in researching your specific field of choice.

The Internet can create a new way to search for a job with usenet news groups, mailing lists, letnet sites, gopher servers, and the World Wide Web. On the Internet, you can find job postings that are not listed anywhere else. According to the National Association of Colleges and Employers, there are over two million job-related sites on the Internet. Their own home page (www.jobweb.org) offers a directory of career and internship opportunities and job postings that can be searched by key words.

An example of an Internet search is as follows: Net Search gives a menu of career topics. Three of the topics of interest are Find a Job, Job Fairs, and Career Placement. Clicking on Career Placement gives at least ten new options. Five intriguing ones are Skill Search, Career Web, America's Employer, Career Mapper, and Career & Job Searching. And so on and so on.

Be careful, though: the Internet can be addictive. Also, look out for claims and promises from companies who match you up with jobs for a fee. Their promises may not be reliable, and there are many areas where the services are free.

➤ Company Annual Reports. These provide information on a company's finances, products, subsidiaries, locations, company culture, and senior management names. If your library doesn't have a public company's annual report, you can contact the company directly and request one. Also, review the reports that are in the same industry for trends, structure, government regulations, industry health, and so on. For privately held corporations, the information is much more difficult to obtain. Since many companies have home pages on the Internet these days, this is another area to find these reports.

Annual reports can be dry reading between a glossy cover. To digest the information, read the chairperson's letter and the company synopsis at the beginning of the report. These usually give some insight into the management style and the company's personality. Next, read the overview sections of the major business divisions or subsidiaries for specific trends, products, and recent successes. Make an outline of each section of information—it can help you view the company's organizational structure and explains which portion of the company is doing well, has the most employees, most potential for growth, and so on.

Dig through the financial information, too. The annual report will show a comparison to previous years' figures. To do a quick assessment of the company's financial health, determine the current ratio (total assets divided by total liabilities). The larger the ratio, the healthier the company. A stable ratio is 2 to 1 (assets to liabilities). In addition, make sure the net worth is growing. Also, read the auditors' statement, which summarizes the company's accounting practices. If the audit team is satisfied with the compilation of numbers, you can feel comfortable with the information and are ready to interpret it for your own use.

➤ Periodicals. Although periodicals result in only a small percentage of all job hires, they are a good source to identify corporations that may interest you. Local newspapers, national newspapers like *The Wall Street Journal*, magazines, and trade journals will have articles and advertisements regarding corporations and possible job openings. If a company that you have already placed on your potential list appears in the newspaper, you will have information about the company prior to applying for the position. (It may also save you a fee if you are working with a recruiter because you can make the application on your own.)

➤ Yellow Pages. One less obvious way to locate companies in your field is to check the Yellow Pages. Along with the well-known companies will be the start-up companies and companies that are on the local job market only. A great place to acquire experience is with small companies (with historically less pay but typically more flexibility and opportunity than the more structured nationally and internationally known companies). Where better to find the smaller company but in the Yellow Pages?

➤ Word of Mouth. You have a natural resource in the people you know. For instance, your college professors have probably worked outside academia or are presently doing so in a consultant capacity, so they will have an idea about which companies are the strongest and which ones specialize in the field you're pursuing. They may have first-hand information about one or more of the companies on your "most desirable" list. Your friends may also be a great source of information. When your fellow students graduate, they could possibly go to work for one of your top 25 companies and can give you inside information on how the company is run. This could be a valuable resource either in the near or distant future. Doesn't it stand to reason that if a particular company is at the top of your prospect list, it may also be at the top of your friends' list? Another resource could be the friends of your parents or other family members. Remember, the older members of one's family usually hold the best positions. If that is the case, a friend of the family or one of your own family members could give you not only firsthand knowledge of the company, but also could possibly help get that first important interview or even give you a personal reference.

➤ Job Fairs and Career Expos. One type of job fair is the type that colleges sponsor. These fairs are arranged by the college to give graduating students an opportunity to talk to representatives from the corporate world, and you will find that the corporations hand out a lot of information about their companies at these fairs. Another source of vital information and maybe referrals is your college placement office. Many companies make contact with the placement office and even give them a listing of their available positions. Your placement office may not only have information about available openings, they may also have information from former students that would confirm your opinion of the company and could help get information about the company for you. Another type of career fair is the one that is produced by the company that is seeking new employees within its own facility or at a rented site. Again, information will be supplied at these fairs. In addition, company representatives at the fair accept resumes and interview prospects, so you can both conduct your research and make use of an excellent opportunity to get your "foot in the door." Therefore, when you attend these affairs, be sure to dress formally as if you were on an interview. (In-depth advice on how to dress and conduct yourself during the interview process is in Chapter 9.)

➤ **Chamber of Commerce.** You can probably find a great deal of information about a corporation at the local Chamber of Commerce of the city where it is located. It is the Chamber of Commerce's business to know about companies in its city— and to *promote* their existence in the city in order to keep them there. Therefore, if positive information is what you are seeking, call or go see the Chamber of Commerce. It will sell you on the company. Also, the information should be free.

➤ **The Company Itself.** Most companies will have public documents that can give you a lot of information about them. In addition to annual reports, you can find promotional materials, advertising, or an employee's handbook.

You have your goals. You know your resources. What now? Think back to that investigative reporter. She also knew her basic goal and knew her resources. From that point, she just worked. She followed leads. She was patient and methodical. She kept her mind open to adjusting her goals when new information changed her focus. She gathered her energies and made difficult telephone calls in her search for information. You can use that same patience and energy in your own research. Even though you're researching a different subject, the idea is the same—work hard, be creative, and relentlessly pursue the information you're seeking.

Keeping the investigative reporter in mind, make a list of 20 companies that interest you the most. Go through your checklist of things you want to learn about the companies and seek out that information. Use the skills you've developed in other kinds of research projects, where you had to have different sources for writing a paper. Even though this is researching a different kind of topic than a history paper for example, it's still research and a lot of the same steps apply. Be as methodical as you can, and have fun! It's exciting to start narrowing down where you want to work and learning about those places. And a prospective employer will be *very* impressed with your knowledge about the company. Think of how flattering it is when someone you meet for the first time knows about a project you did or an accomplishment you've had. Your prospective employer will feel the same way.

Also, keep your eyes open for the unexpected. For example, Julie—our friend from Colorado looking for an assistant office manager position—started her research but found that most of the smaller companies didn't have much room for growth. She also realized that some of the larger corporations had smaller departments that ran somewhat independently of each other and often were run by close-knit groups. By adding these kinds of companies to her list, Julie was able to get both the growth potential and the family-like atmosphere that she was seeking. In addition, to her surprise, Julie's research showed that some of these larger corporations actually had day care in the building, which meant she could see her children during the lunch hour and other breaks. She added "day care" to her list of preferences and ranked it pretty high on her list.

In another example, Sean was reading *The New York Times* on a Sunday morning when he saw a feature article on the owner of Chic-Fil-A, a fast-food chain that serves chicken in a variety of forms. According to the article, the owner was a good person who was very fair to his franchise owners and employees. He required only $5,000 as a start-up cost to buy a franchise; guaranteed a certain annual income for the franchise owner with a generous share in profits, and sponsored educational grants for employees who also wanted to attend college. Sean cut out the article and keeps it for future reference—either for himself, once he gets some funds together, or for friends or family members looking for a business venture.

WHAT SHOULD I DO WITH THE INFORMATION I COLLECT?

It's great to have a lot of information. Now comes the time for applications. Where do you really want to work? What would be your first choice, your second, and so on? Put your decision-making abilities into action. Set priorities. Rank the companies according to your preferences and where you think you have the best chance. Think back to your list of priorities. Which corporations meet your most important priorities? How many of your goals can be achieved by which companies? For example, you will probably have one goal that is your highest priority, so you should give the highest priority to companies that will help you meet that goal. After her smaller experience with a large law firm, Beth decided she wanted to work at a firm that would give her a lot of responsibility and a lot of contact with clients. She got her wish! What she didn't have at her new job (working in a ten-person firm in Washington, DC) was a lot of the efficiency of a larger firm. But that wasn't a priority for her, so it didn't seem to matter as much. Sure, there were negatives about not having immediate access to certain things and not having some of the "perks" available at larger firms, but those were things that Beth was willing to give up in exchange for the responsibility she was given on every case.

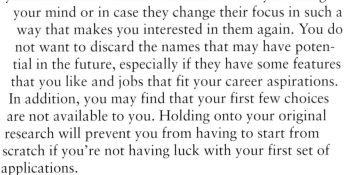

As you eliminate companies from your list during your research, switch them to an alternative list for future reference so that your research on them is available in case you change your mind or in case they change their focus in such a way that makes you interested in them again. You do not want to discard the names that may have potential in the future, especially if they have some features that you like and jobs that fit your career aspirations. In addition, you may find that your first few choices are not available to you. Holding onto your original research will prevent you from having to start from scratch if you're not having luck with your first set of applications.

For instance, none of the companies on Julie's first list worked out. However, during her search, she had told her career counselor about her priority list. The counselor suggested she contact a very large Denver corporation where the main office manager is known for being a good mentor. Julie found out the corporation also had an on-site day care center. She made the contact and got a job as one of the office manager's assistants. Although the job isn't as immediately challenging as she wanted and although she spends a lot of time on simple tasks, she is learning a lot and making a good salary.

Also, keep your goals realistic. Not every job will fulfill everything you want for your career. Mark Kirschner, the marketer for MTV profiled in Chapter 3, recognized that as he developed his career. Mark believes that you may find that you need to work a certain job you don't particularly like because it will teach you a skill that you need to know for your later career goal. "It's like taking vitamins," he says. "If you know you need a certain kind of experience, you have to go out and get it." In fact, Mark found that when his current employer understood he was seeking another job so that he could get a particular kind of experience, that employer helped him in his search. "To this day, we're friends," Mark notes.

SUMMARY

All the information you've collected will be invaluable as you attempt to locate internships, information interviews, or job interviews. Your in-depth knowledge of the company will be impressive. Don't let all your research go to waste. Incorporate it into the work you do to prepare for interviews, send out applications, obtain internships, and so on.

You may be like the investigative reporter and not be exactly sure about where each step is taking you. If you trust your instincts and follow the flow, however, you'll most likely do a good job leading yourself down your career path. At the very least, you will be learning a lot about the field that you have chosen to pursue.

ASKING QUESTIONS AND GETTING ANSWERS

1. **Setting Goals for Research.** Before you begin researching companies, you should decide what matters most to you in the working world: work experience? salary? other benefits? environment? Only you can know what is best for you. Below, outline your goals for employment. This list will be your guide as you conduct the research to find the corporations where you want to work. Review Julie's list on page 105-106 for ideas of how to structure what you're looking for. Write down as many or as few goals as you feel will help get you started on your search for the right company. After the goal, write down a source or sources where you think that you can get the information that you're seeking.

   Goal #1:_____

   Source:_____

   Goal #2:_____

   Source:_____

   Goal #3:_____

   Source:_____

   Goal #4:_____

   Source:_____

   Goal #5:_____

   Source:_____

   Alternative Goals:_____

   Sources:_____

2. **Selecting Companies to Research.** Look over the list of goals that you've outlined. What companies do you think may match those goals? List five companies where you think you might be happy and that you would like to begin investigating.

   Company #1:_____

   Company #2_____

   Company #3:_____

   Company #4:_____

   Company #5:_____

COLLABORATIVE LEARNING AND TEAM-BUILDING SKILLS

1. Helping Each Other Select Goals. Sometimes we are not quite as in touch with what is important to us as we think. Through this exercise, you can help each other decide whether the goals you outlined above really reflect your priorities. Without looking back at your priority list and without telling each other what your priorities are, sit down in groups of two and interview each other about your lives, your likes and dislikes, the things that matter to you, what kind of work you're seeking, and so on. After the interview, write down what you believe are some of the other person's priorities in a job search and in what order you think that those priorities lie. Compare the list that follows with the lists you've filled out in the earlier section. Are there any differences? Are there any new goals that you want to add to your previous list? For instance, Sally was able to identify that Jess not only was looking for a job with a lot of responsibility but that he also would prefer a job with weekend work hours, given the circumstances of his family life. Thus, because of this exercise, Jess was able to add to his list of priorities that he wants to work weekend hours.

INTERVIEWER'S IDEAS OF INTERVIEWEE'S GOALS

Goal #1:_____

Goal #2:_____

Goal #3:_____

Goal #4:_____

Goal #5:_____

Alternative Goals:_____

2. Critiquing and Adding to Sources of Information. In groups of three or four, evaluate each other's decisions regarding what sources to use in finding out which companies meet particular goals that we have. Have you each selected the best source to research? For instance, George planned to determine the starting salaries at his chosen companies by calling office managers at those companies. The people in his group suggested that a better starting place would be with the career counseling office at his school. What advice can you give each other about sources of information?

Alternative Source for Goal #1:_____

Alternative Source for Goal #2:_____

Alternative Source for Goal #3:_____

Alternative Source for Goal #4:_____

Alternative Source for Alternative Goals:_____

LONG-TERM PLANNING: KEY TO YOUR PERSONAL PORTFOLIO

Researching Companies. You will need to begin researching the companies that you want to rely on. Either in the space provided or in an easy-to-carry notebook of your own, begin to make notes about what you learn about the companies. Jot down the information you can find and keep track of the corporations that don't quite meet your needs (so that you can go back to them at a later date if you need to).

	#1	#2	#3
Company			
Address			
Contact People			
Top Officers			
Senior Management			
Competitors			
Profitability			
Type of Business			
Purpose			
Product			
Type of Positions			
Duties			
Projects			
Specific Skills			
Number of Employees			

	#1	#2	#3
Work Environment			
Outdoors/Indoors			
Types of People			
Management Style			
Level of Professionalism			
Team Atmosphere?			
Work Independently?			
Travel?			
Supervisor			
Strengths			
Weaknesses			
Growth Potential			
Long-Term Prospects			
Expansion?			
Competitors?			
Publicly or Privately Owned?			
Customers			
Benefits			
Salary			
Medical			
Dental			
Pension			
Vacation			
Location			
Require Move?			
Close to Family?			
Commute?			
Does It Fit with Next			
Career Step?			
Culture/People			

STUDENT QUESTION

Naomi Shidake, college student in Honolulu, Hawaii

Naomi is majoring in medical assistance. She took a year to choose this career and is really happy with her choice. It combines both administrative and clinical work—the best of both of her interests. She feels that she will not just be taking temperatures or blood pressures, but will also be more diverse than just doing front office and accounting work. In choosing this major, Naomi did a lot of career shadowing. She spoke to career counselors and researched the financial side of this career. By the time she got to college, she knew exactly what she wanted to be. Now, though, she is getting ready to choose a company or doctor's office to work in, and she's not sure how to conduct the research. She can't get a job during school because few offices will hire medical assistants before they're certified. She doesn't know where to go to do this research, other than her library, the consumer protection agency, or the Better Business Bureau. Her question:

I know I would probably like to work for a family doctor in a small or midsize company, but how do you research a small company? How can you go up to this strange office and ask the employees, how do you like this doctor? I'm sure they won't be so open until you start working there. Also, it's important for me to figure out how I will fit in with the people where I work—I think that's very important. What should I do?

Both your librarian and the World Wide Web are great sources of information. You might also want to call a few of the local hospitals and ask if there is a register of new doctors who are trying to build their practices. Often, these people will be more likely to work with you, even if you take a volunteer position initially, because they are trying to build their business. You might also check with the local medical school, if there is one, to see how many of last year's graduates started their own practice. It takes a fair amount of investigative work to get the answers to these questions. You might have to make these phone calls on your lunch hour each day to get this information.

In terms of finding someone you would "like" to work with, be patient. Often in your first job, it is not possible to be that picky because you lack experience. If you take a job with someone who is demanding or whom you don't especially like, think about the larger lessons you will learn from dealing with someone who is not like you. None of us can choose our bosses. It is rare to find someone you both like and respect, although it does happen. It is more important to have respect for your bosses—or their ethics, their judgment, and their sense of mission. While you may not be able to gauge ahead of time whether or not you will "like" your first doctor as a manager, go with the best opportunity. Learn to adjust to different people and styles. When you have more experience under your belt, and a better sense of the industry as a whole and who is good to work for, you may be able to be more selective about where you work and for whom.

CAREER PROFILE

JUDE ZEMPER Jude Zemper has tailored his career around his life's priorities. In doing so, he has been selective about the companies that he has worked for so that they will provide the necessary balance to his life. He has managed to develop a successful career around the geographic requirements of his field, a downturn in the defense industry, military responsibilities, an interest in personal travel, and the responsibilities of marriage and a family.

Jude earned a bachelor's degree in industrial technology from Ohio University in 1983. When he graduated, he found that his degree was not quite as well known as some other engineering degrees. It focused on the various aspects of manufacturing and manufacturing engineering. Jude determined which type of companies recruited engineers that specialized in manufacturing. His first career move was to San Diego, California, where he worked for a defense contractor that produced a variety of electronic products. When the defense industry declined, however, Jude needed to make a career transition to an emerging market. He considered telecommunications because it had growth potential and the possibility to transfer his experience in electronics. And so his search began.

He started his search by identifying all of the telecommunications companies in San Diego. He prioritized the list to a few companies and tackled them one at a time. "I researched as much published industry information that I could find at the library or through the Internet. I wanted a company that was of a particular size and was in a growth mode." Jude received financial information for public companies by requesting the information directly. He worked with recruiters; reviewed trade journals and magazines; and networked with family, friends, and past coworkers. "After I finished with all of the general information about a company, I tried to contact as many people as I knew that might have more information or could provide me with another contact that could provide additional insight."

Jude made the transition to the telecommunications industry and has been satisfied with the career change. Due to family priorities, his next job change may be to another geographic location. "When you're looking for a position out of state, it's so much more difficult; you have to make the most out of on-line and paper information. I've checked all the on-line job boards on the Internet to determine which companies have job opportunities. Once you identify these opportunities, the trick is to determine the best way to get your foot in the door."

Jude recommends that a person identify companies that will offer career enhancements, as well as match skills and abilities. "You need to do a self-assessment and define which areas you would like to enhance and which areas will be necessary for marketability in the next five years." Jude thinks that to identify the areas of growth, we sometimes need the assistance of others. "This doesn't always have to come from your boss at performance appraisal time. In order to gain some perspective, I discuss my plans and goals with my wife, friends, coworkers, and mentors."

Networking:
How to Connect with People

> LUCK IS A MATTER OF PREPARATION MEETING OPPORTUNITY.
>
> —OPRAH WINFREY

"Mr. Meyer here."

"Hello. This is Gabe Caballero. I'd like to speak with Howard Kim. I got his name from Maria DeAngelis who said that he would be a good source of information on careers in management. I'm a college student interested in obtaining an entry-level management position, and I would very much like to interview him about any advice he may have for me."

"Well, he's a very busy man and keeps a tight schedule. I'm his assistant. Can I help you?"

"I realize that he's busy, which is why I mailed my resume and a cover letter to him in advance. I wanted him to know a little bit more about me before he agreed to speak with me briefly for 10 to 15 minutes."

"Well, I do remember seeing your resume. And Mr. Kim admires persistence...I'll speak to him and see if there is a time when he can speak with you by phone."

"Thank you very much. I know Mr. Kim's busy, and I want to assure you that I won't take up a lot of his time. I will be pointed and direct in my questions. I truly appreciate the opportunity to ask him his advice."

"I'll call you back and let you know if there's a time and day that he can speak with you."

"Thanks, again. Have a great day."

Networking is about talking to people—just like Gabe spoke to Mr. Meyer above. In truth, you probably "network" all the time through basic human interaction—you just may not realize what you're doing. Networking is really just about people talking and sharing ideas. When you meet someone new at a party who has similar interests, don't you file away his name and information in your memory? Of course you do. In fact, if the opportunity exists, you both probably share information about your similar interests to help broaden each other's knowledge in the area—or you may even offer to help on an upcoming project related to your interest. That's "networking," plain and simple.

The mystery of networking is not so much that we exchange information or services—that we try to *help* each other—but that we are not quite sure how to use this kind of exchange as a tool for career development. For instance, that person you met at the party with whom you had similar interests—if you decide six months later that you are interested in pursuing a career similar to his, you should contact him to ask him questions about the career. That also is "networking."

This chapter will help prepare you not only to take advantage of the contacts you make but also to preserve them. For instance, you may be hard pressed six months later to remember the name of the person you met at that party—or the company he works for, how to get in touch with him, and so on. You may not even remember what he looks like. On the other hand, if you had gotten his business card during the initial meeting and written some notes on the back of his card to remember specific details while they were still fresh in your mind, you would not be so lost when you wanted to recontact him. Through this chapter, you will get some ideas on how to set up your own networking strategy so that, among other things, you'll be better able to recontact people like your acquaintance at the party.

WHAT IS THE NETWORKING PROCESS?

Networking comes in all shapes and sizes. It can involve two people finding out that they share common interests, one person acting as a go-between for two people at different companies, or a group of people across the country working toward a common goal through the Internet. It can be deliberate or coincidental, proactively helpful or simply informational.

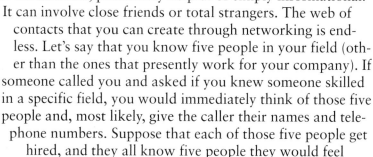

It can involve close friends or total strangers. The web of contacts that you can create through networking is endless. Let's say that you know five people in your field (other than the ones that presently work for your company). If someone called you and asked if you knew someone skilled in a specific field, you would immediately think of those five people and, most likely, give the caller their names and telephone numbers. Suppose that each of those five people get hired, and they all know five people they would feel comfortable recommending, and they all get hired, and they all know five people, and so on. Ultimately, you will have a web of contacts like that outlined in Figure 6-1.

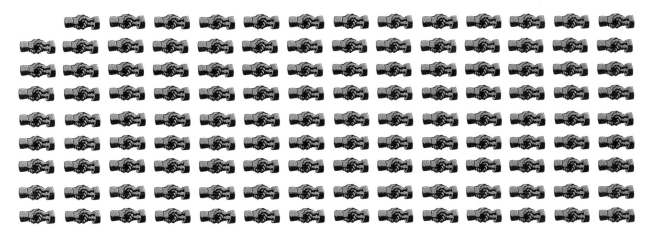

At the Base: The Exchange

As discussed, we have the opportunity to network virtually every time we come into contact with another person. That doesn't mean that every contact with another human being must turn into networking. The difference between a simple contact and networking is that networking, by definition, involves an exchange of information, ideas, or services. Many contacts will not result in an exchange—at least not right away. We might meet someone we like a lot, or have a lot in common with, but there won't be any immediate issues to address with that person. Developing a positive interaction with that person from the beginning, however, may lead to a positive interchange down the road.

Dan Hoyt, an insurance salesman, sends "support" notes to his friends and acquaintances—just because. He writes one every day. The note is usually simple but affirming to the reader. He firmly believes that everyone he meets is worth the time and effort to get to know and support. He believes that he will miss something if he doesn't take the opportunity to visit with them. These interactions are done from the goodness of his heart. At the same time, though, Dan is building a group of wonderful friends and a reliable network.

Recognize the emphasis on the concept of "exchange" in networking. You may feel uncomfortable with the idea of calling someone to "network," especially if you're on the side of asking rather than receiving. But the idea of networking is that both sides can have something to offer. Try to be creative in thinking of ways to help out someone who is working with you to solve a problem or make a connection. By actively thinking of ways to help the people who help you, you can be participating in the networking process rather than just asking for help without giving anything in return. As a bonus, a considerate attitude can help to make your contact a lifelong connection. Even if you have nothing to offer right now, a simple thank-you letter for someone's help can mean a lot.

Also recognize that "networking" rarely means that we call up our acquaintance to make him get us a job. That would be great, but unusual. Instead, there are several types of benefits we can both give and receive through the networking process. In fact, some networking is purely informational. For instance, you may tell a friend that you're looking for a certain type of job. Your friend says she knows someone in the field that you're investigating and suggests that you call that person to learn more about the field. She offers to let you use her name, which you do. You have a wonderful conversation with this individual and leave feeling committed to your newly chosen field. But there was no hint of this person actually being able to assist you in finding a job. That's okay—you benefited just from spending some time with him. And who knows? Maybe he'll hear of something later that will change your networking relationship from purely informational to proactively helpful.

Think of networking as building bridges rather than asking for favors. What a treasure it is to find a person who shares our same interests! Whether the person is 6 years old or 60, it's fun to meet people with common interests and goals. Indeed, the "networking"—exchange of information—may have nothing to do with your career goals and everything to do with building a new friendship around one of your favorite hobbies. And maybe a newfound friend will also be able—and willing—to help in your career goals, too.

Coincidental versus Deliberate Networking

Much of our networking occurs by accident. When you meet someone in class, at a social event, or at a seminar who has just the kind of information you're seeking in a career field that interests you, don't pass up the opportunity to get to know that person and share your thoughts! Rodney Ahart was at a multilevel sales meeting. During the introductory ice breakers, everyone was asked to stand up and give his or her name and one wish. Rodney's wish was that he would find a better paying job that was more fulfilling for him and gave his wife and him more opportunity to settle into a home of their own. After the meeting, Judy—a stranger to Rodney—approached him and asked him what kind of job he wanted. He told her he was a laboratory technician with a two-year degree. Judy told him that she was in human resources for a larger manufacturing plant, that they were searching for laboratory technicians, and that she just happened to have an application in her briefcase. The next week Rodney went on an interview, was offered and accepted a job, and he and his wife started looking for their dream home.

As Rodney's experience shows, speaking up can make the difference in your career path. Stay alert to the possibility that there may be networking opportunities anywhere you go.

Other networking occurs over time without a lot of concentrated effort on your part to network. This is especially true when you make sure that your personal network is aware of your ultimate career goals, as Carol did. Carol's ultimate career goal was to become a college instructor and/or author. To be an instructor, Carol knew she must first have a college degree in a subject that she would want to teach. Since she didn't have the funds to go to college, she took a secretarial position with a company that offered tuition assistance to its employees. As a college student, she made sure that many of her new acquaintances and colleagues became aware of her ultimate career goals. One of those connections helped her change careers from secretary to editor in another company and helped her develop toward one of her career goals of being an author. Carol then sought a master's degree, continuing to keep others informed of her goals. She received a telephone call from one of these individuals, asking her if she still wanted to teach at the college level. Carol immediately replied "absolutely" without even asking what courses, hours, pay scale, or when. Even though Carol did not have the exact experience the college was seeking, she ended up with the job—in large part because she had been personally referred.

In each of these career opportunities, Carol had had an edge because she had taken steps to be prepared when an opportunity appeared, and she had consistently kept her contacts informed of her ultimate career goals. Just like with accidental networking, however, you need to make a conscious effort to speak up. As Carol's experience shows, keeping your colleagues, friends, and family informed of your goals can ultimately help them think of you when they hear of an opportunity in your chosen career.

One of this chapter's goals is to help you think of ways to network deliberately, too, with people or in places where you think you might get results. Although deliberate networking can absorb a lot of energy, it has a good chance of giving you quick results. For instance, in putting together this book, the authors thought of people they had met who would have interesting questions or opinions about careers. They then asked the people they had contacted if *they* knew of anyone who would have interesting comments to make about careers. Everyone was helpful and thought of great people to contact. Most likely, they would not have thought to suggest the other contact without prompting from the people interviewing them, though. This is deliberate networking.

Ned Smith is a great example of how deliberate networking can reap benefits. As you may recall from Chapter 3, Ned was unable to use his college degree in political science with an emphasis on nuclear strategy and national security because this career area became virtually obsolete with the end of the Cold War. Ned spent the year after he graduated from college selling sweaters and renting cars while he contemplated his next move. Ned geared up and started to explore career options, focusing on the business world. He used every connection he could think of, from his own friends to his parents' friends. He had a lot of interviews that didn't turn into jobs just because of his own newness to the interview process. Ultimately, though, he got an interview through a friend of his with Southwestern Bell and is now in a leadership development program that has given him invaluable experience at every level of managing a business.

Ned encourages students to use all the contacts they have. "I don't understand it" when people refuse to use their parents' contacts, for instance. "I do have a sense of independence because I got my job through my own contacts, but there is no dishonor in calling a friend of your parents." At the very least, making lots of contacts can generate a lot of interviews, as it did for Ned. This is a learning process in and of itself.

Networking by Reputation

One way to ensure some of the best networking opportunities is to develop a reputation for yourself as a hard-working, dedicated individual. Think of your own experiences: aren't you more likely to make a connection for a reliable, easygoing friend over an unreliable, cantankerous friend? You personally may be willing to do anything for your more difficult friend but may be equally *un*willing to subject a total stranger to her mood swings. Reputations can take you a long way, as Carol's own experiences show.

Virginia Cone, a real estate agent with Coldwell Banker, does what she likes to do the most—help people. Virginia's goal is to be known for her "super services" and not as a "super salesperson." She builds her client base almost strictly through referrals and succeeds because of her ethical belief in helping her clients first and worrying about her commission second. "It doesn't matter to me what type of property someone is looking for," Virginia says. Whether it is a first home or a multimillion-dollar property, she is energized by the process of getting to know the person, determining needs, researching options, counseling on the commitment, negotiating the buy, and finding that perfect match. "It is important to treat everyone with dignity and respect. It only takes one person to be dissatisfied with your service to create a major obstacle."

So far, Virginia has had the success that her kind of enthusiasm virtually guarantees.

Another way to help increase your networking opportunities is to develop a skill that others will rely upon. We can all think of the computer genius in computer lab who helped out less knowledgeable students at the drop of a hat. Certainly that computer whiz got tired of helping out so many people all the time, but he did develop a reputation for knowing all the answers in a particular area. Chances are that, sooner or later, his skills will be recognized by someone hiring computer programmers. At the very least, he is developing references for the future.

What are People Thinking when I Try to Network with Them?

Sometimes we can get so wrapped up in worrying about whether we're making the right impression in our networking efforts that we forget that networking is really about communication. Part of the networking process is understanding that people are just people and networking is simply communicating with people with whom you have a connection—in this case, in an effort to gather information or assistance that helps you develop your career goals.

What are the Other Person's Goals?

To understand the human dynamics taking place in a networking situation, you should ask yourself what you think is the goal of the person or people you're contacting. Sometimes their goal is purely magnanimous: they just want to help. This is especially true in mentoring situations, where the purpose of the relationship is to teach someone younger or newer to the profession. In fact, a lot of your networking may be tied directly to mentoring, especially if you are still a student and just learning about your career goals.

Other times, you may be networking with people whose primary interest is looking good. For instance, you may be known as an expert in the photography field. An acquaintance contacts you for a one-time photography session not just because she knows you're looking for work but because the photographs will be of her boss's daughter. Although she doesn't tell you this, common sense dictates that at least a part of her goal in contacting you is to look knowledgeable and reliable to her boss. Don't let her down! Her additional purpose is getting you the work you want.

Any time you begin the networking process, you could learn a lot just by taking a moment to think about where the other people are "coming from." Are they just trying to help without any thought to any other benefit? Are they trying to set up a contact for themselves in the future? Would they like to get another good softball player at the office for the summer softball league? There is nothing wrong with having many purposes behind networking—it just helps you to evaluate what those purposes might be so that you can better address them specifically.

What are Your Responsibilities?

One of your primary responsibilities in networking is to handle the networking opportunity efficiently. A lot of times, the people you're contacting are very busy. They may want to help, but haven't focused on what you're looking for. This is especially true with deliberate networking, when your goal is to collect information and/or assistance. Thus, be specific about the kind of help you're seeking.

In addition, be riskworthy. As discussed, a good worker with good credentials will be easier to promote than a lazy, crabby person with no credentials at all. Part of being riskworthy is being conscientious about the contacts that you're making. If someone puts you in touch with a prospective employer, be extra careful about writing thank-you letters, returning phone calls, and so on. In these circumstances, it's not just your reputation that's on the line.

Also, be patient. Your contact may want to help you but may not know of anything right now. Listen to what your contact tells you. If she says you should call back in a month, then do as she asks. Certainly being persistent can help emphasize how interested you are in accomplishing certain tasks. Be sensitive, though, that your persistence doesn't become nagging or irritating.

Above all, be yourself. Relax, be sincere. Let the other person know that you appreciate the help, but don't overdo it. Networking is just like any other human interaction. Sometimes we can get so caught up in our networking "goal," however, that we forget this basic premise.

One way to meet each of these goals is to think ahead of time about what you'd like to say. Some people write out word-for-word what they will say; others may just map out an outline. Nonetheless, having your thoughts in order will help immensely as you try to network, especially if you don't know the other person well.

Dan Hoyt has found himself over time sharing his own formula for success with people from all walks of life and experience levels. He mentors many young people all at the same time. His experience is that people don't know themselves and their abilities well enough to determine how to communicate them during networking opportunities. "If a student comes to me and wants the name of my friends and their telephone numbers, they at least should be able to tell why I should give it to them," he says. "What do they have to offer?" He has a series of exercises for people to follow:

> ➤ Write down 30 characteristics that describe your ideal job or career.

> ➤ Make a list of mission statements for yourself, family, business, and community. Make a list of positive and negative qualities about yourself.

> ➤ Write down at least ten accomplishments from the last year and state three things you are looking forward to each month for the next year.

He encourages his student mentees to use this list to give them courage and self-esteem when they network with others.

How Do I Develop My Own Networking Strategy?

Now that you've started to dissect the mystery of "networking" into workable, manageable concepts, you can begin using what you've learned in a systematic way. Networking is a valuable resource that can be used for many different needs, especially achieving your career success. Like most valuable resources, however, you must be aware of its value and organize a process for using it. Effective networking requires a strategy—some thought and planning—just like anything else. We can't all be as lucky as Rodney (from page 125) when he obtained his long-desired goal by accident through a one-time event. The more methodical and prepared we are in our networking efforts, the more likely it is that we will achieve what we are seeking, especially with regard to career goals. Having a method along the way will save you time and effort in the future.

As you design your personal strategy for networking, guard against trying to develop contacts that are *too* attenuated. Making contacts can be a lot of fun, but it also can be time consuming and exhausting if you stretch yourself too thin. The very term "strategy" suggests a plan of action rather than a shotgun approach. You need to decide what's best for you given your personality and your current goals. Who knows? Maybe your strategy with regard to a particular subject will *be* a "shotgun approach" (making calls to a lot of people, even if you don't know them well or have a strong connection to them through friends or family) because you've evaluated your options and have concluded that reaching out to as many people as possible as quickly as possible is the best way to achieve what you're seeking in that particular case. Whatever you conclude, creating a plan—a strategy—will help organize your thoughts as you figure out how to use your resources.

Identify Your Networking Goals

When we meet other people and exchange ideas, we should be ready for anything. Many precious gems can be found at unexpected times. But as you develop a *strategy* for networking and actively try to implement it, you will help keep focused if you identify what it is you would like to achieve through your networking. Think through your current career goals. Are you looking to learn more about a particular field? Are you interested in getting a job with a particular company? Are you still trying to decide what your ultimate career goal is? Identify a few general and specific networking goals that you have. Don't worry if these goals change over time—that's natural, especially if you're still deciding what your career goals are. Developing goals does not mean that you should ignore other contacts that you're making that don't match your goal. It's just a way to help you focus on the networking opportunities that appear the most important to you at this time.

Don't get *too* caught up in your career goals. Remember—networking really is about people communicating. As you're trying to network, keep in mind that you're a person with a variety of interests. Your love for cooking, for instance, might be just the icebreaker needed to get the attention of that vice president of a company you've targeted.

WHAT I WANT TO ACHIEVE FOR MY CAREER THROUGH NETWORKING

_____

_____

_____

Identify the People in Your Network

Identifying the people in your network can be crucial, since networking is accomplished through people. For instance, did you know many new hires are made through a current employee's referral? In fact, an extremely high percentage of job openings are never even advertised. Very few people, in comparison, get jobs through newspaper ads, agencies, executive search firms, or cold calls. Also, approximately half of the agency-placed applicants were referred to the agency by one of the search company's personnel. The new company, if it is still hiring, will invariably ask new employees if they know anyone else that would be qualified and interested in a position with the new company. In fact, Kent Kirch (National Manager of Recruiting for Deloitte and Touche) says that one of D&T's tools for hiring experienced employees is through its employee referral program. According to Kent, getting a great job often is a function of "who you know," and getting your foot in the door through a friend or a friend of a friend is a good option.

Thus, once you focus on how to make and cultivate personal contacts, your road toward both defining and achieving your career goals just may become a lot easier.

Networking bases have ready-made resources as well as resources that are not as accessible. Whether it is a ready-made resource or one you need to develop, however, your networking system necessarily is personal to *you*. You may think that you don't know anyone that would be of value to start or add to your networking database, but you'll be surprised as you start figuring out your resources. Table 6-1 lists a number of suggestions of the types of people you could contact. Add names next to the list. If you are too shy about placing your doctor, dentist, or other professional on a networking list, remember that they probably would not hesitate to use your name. *Ask* them if you can rely on them. All they can do is tell you "yes" or "no." If it is yes, you will really feel good that they think that much of you. If it is "no," you haven't lost anything.

TABLE 6-1   NETWORKING LIST

INSTRUCTIONS: Fill in the names of people who might be able and willing to help you (use list below), and tell what it is that you would like for them to do for you.

Former employers:

Fellow workers:

Current employer:

Family members:

Friends:

Organizations in which you belong:

Church members:

Minister:

Teachers:

Professional organizations:

Clients:

Doctors:

Attorneys:

Neighbors:

Former neighbors:

Bankers:

Insurance agents:

Real estate agents:

Classmates:

Former classmates:

Accountants/CPAs:

Counselors:

Financial planners:

Other:

Don't forget to branch out by using the resources of your parents, other family members, or friends. Perhaps they have someone (like a former boss, a friend, a minister, an organization, a neighbor, etc.) that they can contact on your behalf. Use the list in Table 6-1 when you start to network with people who you know well. Having a list at their disposal might help them think of people that could help you. As mentioned earlier, be careful—the networking possibilities can seem endless and time consuming without being productive. The further you personally are from the contact, the more like a "cold call" the contact will feel to both you and the person you're calling. Be energetic but realistic about what you personally can achieve through the networking process.

Identify Where to Network

Anywhere! The beauty of networking is that we can and do have access to it all the time. You can make networking an integral part of your life. Do it everywhere you go—church, parties, meetings, school, work, or any other place where there are people you don't know.

There are ready-made networks that are easily accessible. Think of the places where you spend a lot of time—school, work, home, an organization where you volunteer. At least some of the people that you see at those places (professors, other students, colleagues, family members, other volunteers) will know you well and should not hesitate to help you out in your networking efforts.

In addition, today's technology gives us a great resource of networking through the Internet or e-mail. Through the computer, you very likely will find a bulletin board that deals with topics you've targeted. If nothing else, you can "meet" a lot of people who share your interests.

Beth used to work as a federal public defender and was appointed by the federal court to represent indigent people accused of committing federal crimes. As a federal defender, Beth could send requests for information to other federal public defender offices all over the country through an e-mail system. In the summer of 1995, Beth was trying to obtain a continuance for a client's sentencing because a proposed change in the law (effective in November) would potentially cut her client's sentence from four years down to two. The judge hesitated to grant the continuance, since 17 other defendants in that district were in the same circumstance and continuing one sentencing would require continuing all of them. "I knew that the judges would feel more comfortable granting the continuance request if I could show them that other federal courts in the country had continued other sentences under similar circumstances," Beth says. She sent out an e-mail to all the federal defender offices, explaining her dilemma. "Within 24 hours, I had heard from federal defenders from all over the country telling me that they'd gotten similar sentencings continued. The attorneys wrote and faxed letters about their experiences. I placed the information in a packet for the judges in my court, and they decided to grant the continuance!"

You can identify new places for networking as part of your strategy for "deliberate networking." Such deliberate networking could include joining a club or volunteering at an organization that focuses on your area of interest, attending professional organization and society meetings where you may run into people in your chosen field, subscribing to local newspapers or trade journals and checking them periodically for business meetings and activities that may interest you, or attending trade shows and career fairs. Check with convention centers near you to see what conventions are coming to town in the next few months. Sometimes these conventions have reduced fees for students. Along those lines, check with the professional organizations in the field that interests you for student groups or sections. If you do not know whether your targeted organizations have chapters near you, write or call them to ask.

Create a Networking Database

Now that you are starting to identify *where* to network, *who* to network with, and *what* to network about, you should begin thinking about how to organize the information that you'll be collecting. Figure out a system for keeping track of the people you meet, how to contact them, how you know them, and what your mutual interests are. You can file this information in a tin box, a business card holder, a Rolodex file, your computer file, or whatever filing system that works for you. Don't file the information in alphabetical order by the name of the person, since it's easy to forget people's names (especially if you have no need to contact them again for several months). Also record the information under the person's company or school (if the person is a student) or by your mutual interest. (You can make photocopies of the information—or the business card, if you have it—rather than tediously writing down the information three or four different times.) Then when a need arises, you simply pull out your networking file, find the person you're looking for, call him or her, and say, "Remember me, I met you at Joe's retirement party. During our visit you mentioned that you repaired computers as a hobby. Do you still do that or do you know someone who does?" In addition, if you have listed people according to interest, you will be able to identify all of your resources in that area simply by looking at that part of your filing system.

Now is the time to get started building your networking database. Use Table 6-2 to identify your file. You can begin your list with the people you identified in Table 6-1. When you have all the information in place, transfer it to your computer or a card (like a Rolodex card or 3 x 5 card) to start your networking database.

Keep up with your database regularly. Before you know it, you will have a huge file.

TABLE 6-2   NETWORKING DATABASE

NAME	OTHER INTEREST	WHERE MET	ADDRESS/PHONE

Pursue Networking Opportunities

Now comes the scary part: putting your networking strategy into action. Gathering ideas, names, and places for networking is of little use to you unless you take steps to activate the information you've identified. This probably will take not only work but also courage on your part. It's not easy to contact someone and try to "network" for information or a job. Take consistent, methodical steps to make the contacts and begin the networking and, it is hoped, you'll find it easier and easier to do.

Be Methodical. You're ready to begin making your contacts. Start with the people who would be the most receptive to your calling them to ask for help. In fact, start with a close friend or relative (someone who is likely to forgive any initial awkwardness). Also choose which places you would like to go first in trying out these networking techniques. In the exercises at the end of the chapter, there is a chart where you can plan out a strategy of whom to contact and where to go month by month. Use it!

Practice How to Make Contacts. Using your resources is important. Whether your contacts are made through letter writing, e-mail, or telephone calling, the more practice you get at making contacts, the more polished you will appear to the people in your network.

Your first decision in making a contact is whether to write or call. Use your best judgment as to how this contact should be handled. If you decide to write first, be sure to include a short letter and a copy of your resume. Use a letter format similar to that shown in Chapter 8 but give it a personal touch as well. Explain how you came in contact with this person (e.g., through the recommendation of a friend or family member), and spell out what you are looking for—a mentor, some information about a company, a job, and so on. Be both enthusiastic and sincere.

If you decide to call first, plan ahead for contingencies. Making a telephone call sometimes can be harder than writing a letter because everything happens very fast. Make yourself a checklist before every call:

➤ How can I make sure that I will get through to the right person?

➤ Is there someone I can trust to take a message and make sure I make contact with the right person later?

➤ What will I say when I get through to the receptionist? Do I want to leave a voice mail? How many times can I call without leaving a message before this receptionist will get annoyed?

➤ How can I explain the reason for my phone call in a clear, quick way so that my listener understands me?

Let People Know about Your Networking Goals. Speak up! Try to bring up subjects related to your networking goals with new people or in new situations—or even with old friends or places that you frequently visit. Like Rodney, you never know when someone may share one of your interests or may have information or ideas for you that you haven't considered. If you say nothing, you'll never find out if the person sitting next to you loves fly fishing as much as you do.

Exchange Business Cards. One of the most important things you can do for yourself is to trade business cards with *everybody* you meet, *everywhere* you go. Turn the card over and write the common ground you share with this new person, her occupation, and where you met her. This immediate collection of information will help immensely in recording thorough information for your database. If you don't have business cards, make them! Most discount office suppliers will print 100 cards for around $10. The business card does not have to have a company name on it. You could use the following as an example:

JOHN SMITH, STUDENT
(Name of College, University)

Phone: Address
Fax: City, State, Zip
E-mail address:

If you don't want to make a generic business card, you could keep 3 x 5 cards with you at all times and when the occasion arises, pull out the card and have the other person put vital information on one card, and you complete one on yourself to exchange. You should still turn the card over and enter the same information on the back that you would if it were a business card.

Attend Information Interviews. One way to learn a lot of information about a career and build a contact at the same time is to ask for an information interview—that is, an interview at a place of employment where the employer is simply telling you about the work that is done at the company rather than interviewing you for a specific job. In fact, the interview is really being conducted by *you* about the company. This is "deliberate networking" at its finest. Don't expect to get a job when you attend an information interview—don't even ask! And be careful to be prepared with informed questions about the company. Also, don't forget to write a thank-you letter!

Figure 6-2 contains a list of questions that were compiled by the University of San Francisco's career center, based on questions developed by Martha Stoodley which you can find in her book, Information Interviewing: How to Tap Your Hidden Job Market. Use these questions as you prepare for your information interview.

Adopt a Mentor. A mentor—an advisor of experience with connections within a company or industry chosen to help a relatively new person or one of less experience—is invaluable in every profession today for many reasons. For instance, a mentor can show you the "ropes" of a company or industry. Learning more about corporate culture can be a long and sometimes painful process. If you have someone who will help you out, and who can be a loyal friend and confidant, it can help you through that process. Some companies have mentoring programs, while others are more informal. Don't wait to be working for a company to find a mentor, though. Having a teacher, guide, coach, and role model at any time can be invaluable. Through a mentoring program, you can learn company cultures, develop technical and professional skills by example, receive guidance in career decisions, increase visibility in your chosen profession, and develop your network even further.

Rama Moorthy had a female mentor who helped her obtain technical expertise as well as savvy to handle the male world of engineering. Rama communicated with her mentor in more of a direct fashion rather than just by observation. "She was approachable and enthusiastic. I could ask her anything and I would get a straight answer. I think because she was closer to my age, I didn't feel intimated to ask her any type of question." Rama highly recommends the mentoring experience.

Check with your school—there may be a formal mentoring program already in place. Another way to get a mentor is through professional organizations in fields of your main interests. There may be formal mentoring programs there, or just people in the profession whom you can meet.

FIGURE 6-2	QUESTIONS FOR INFORMATION INTERVIEW

1) In the position you now hold, what do you do on a typical day?

2) What are the most interesting/challenging/frustrating aspects of your job?

3) What part of your work do you consider dull or repetitious? What percentage of your time do you devote to those activities?

4) What were the jobs that led you to this one?

5) How long does it usually take to move from one step to the next in this career path?

6) What is the step above the one you have now?

7) Given your present position and experience, what position do you see yourself in five years from now?

8) What is the top job you can have in this career?

9) Are there other areas of this field to which people in it may be transferred?

10) What are the prerequisites for jobs in this field?

11) Are there any specific courses I might take that would be particularly beneficial?

12) What types of training do companies give to persons entering this field?

13) What are the salary ranges for various levels in this field?

14) What aspects of a career in this field do you consider particularly good? Bad?

15) What special advice would you give a young person/career changer entering this field?

16) Is there a demand for people in this field?

17) What are the growth prospects for this field in the future?

18) What other fields/jobs would you suggest I investigate before I make a final decision?

19) How do you see the jobs in this field changing over the next two years? How can I prepare myself for these changes?

20) What is the best way to obtain a position that will start me on a career in this field?

Source: Martha Stoodley, Information Interviewing: How to Tap Your Hidden Job Market (Chicago, Ill., J.G. Ferguson Publishing, 1997), pp. 139–43; University of San Francisco.

Keep Current and Active. Don't just join groups to build up your resume. Participate too! By attending monthly luncheons, reading newsletters, or heading up committees, you'll be more visible, you'll have more opportunities for networking, and—perhaps above all else—you'll be gaining invaluable knowledge about the fields you like! The more you know, the more effective your networking can be and the more likely it is that you will have something to offer in exchange for someone's help.

You may hesitate to join a lot of professional organizations that won't be useful to you. If your time and/or funds are limited, you may want to explore which organizations are best for you in the field (or fields) that you've chosen. Ask around—what do professionals in your field recommend? Also, the *Princeton Review of Occupations* (mentioned in Chapter 3) has a list of professional organizations that may be helpful.

The main idea, however, is to keep yourself active and connected. Not only will you increase your networking opportunities, but you will also have a lot more fun!

SUMMARY

Networking is a very valuable resource that can be used for many different needs, including achieving career success. Use the forms and ideas of this chapter to start your networking database. Before you know it, you will have a huge file and a number of new acquaintances, associates, and friends whom you can contact. Whether they are helping you or vice versa, you are building a family of contacts that can stay with you for a long time.

ASKING QUESTIONS AND GETTING ANSWERS

1. **Recognizing Your Networking Skills.** This chapter discusses networking in the context of career goals. We already know how to network, however. Have you ever set someone up on a blind date? Successful or unsuccessful—that's networking! As another example, Sarah knew that her brother was looking for an accountant to help set up a small business. She didn't know any accountants in the town where he was living, but she had a good friend that she knew would have good information, so she told her brother to call her friend. The call was successful, and Sarah's brother was able to find the exact kind of accountant he was seeking.

    Now it's your turn. Write an example of networking that you have done recently.

    _____

    _____

    _____

    _____

    _____

    _____

    _____

2. **Writing a Speech.** As outlined in the discussion on recognizing the perspective of others, one good way to be efficient with the time of the person you're contacting is to write down what you want to say ahead of time. Let's practice! Choose one person from your list in Table 6-1 that you don't know very well and who may be limited on time when you call. In the space provided, write down what you could say to that person so that you efficiently share what you are seeking.

    _____

    _____

    _____

    _____

    _____

    _____

    _____

COLLABORATIVE LEARNING AND TEAM-BUILDING SKILLS

Helping Each Other Organize. In groups of two, pretend that you are making a telephone call to a "friend of a friend" who may have a good job opportunity for you. Select the job that you think this acquaintance can help you get, then make the telephone call (with the other person in your group acting as the "friend of the friend"). Then switch roles. Critique each other's work. Was your phone call too long? Too short? Did you adequately explain the purpose of the call and what the "friend of a friend" can do to help? Did you give options of how your new friend could help? What could be changed for the better?

LONG-TERM PLANNING: KEY TO YOUR PERSONAL PORTFOLIO

1. **Making a List.** Start using your networking contacts and locations. Make a list of places that you will attend and the people that you will contact each month. Although you can list as many or as few as you would like, you should set up this list so that you can achieve the goals you set for yourself. For instance, Jill knows that her busy schedule will allow her to devote only a little time for networking. However, she is at a point in her career where networking is very important. Thus, she will choose three places to go and three people to contact every month.

MONTH	PLACES	PEOPLE
	1.	1.
	2.	2.
	3.	3.
	1.	1.
	2.	2.
	3.	3.
	1.	1.
	2.	2.
	3.	3.

2. Setting a Long-Term Goal. Think about what you would like to achieve over the next six months through your career networking. In the space provided, write down that goal (or goals). Check back periodically throughout the semester to see if you're attaining that goal—or if your long-term goal has changed. Who are the most important people you need to meet?

_____

_____

_____

_____

_____

_____

_____

STUDENT QUESTION

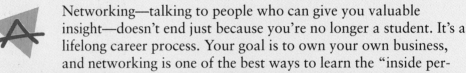

Afrika Higgins, junior at Virginia State University

Afrika chose to major in marketing because she likes to promote things. She wants to own her own business that plans and promotes different events, for example, for a city or whoever would need the event. She is a member of the American Marketing Association at Virginia State University, which recently organized a conference called Building Bridges Through Networking. The Association members wanted to focus on this issue because they know it's vital to the business world. A lot of people asked questions at the conference such as, What's the best way to contact people—should you approach them through someone else or by yourself? When you meet someone, how long should you wait before you give them a call? Many people wanted to know how to make connections, too. Her question:

How should I go about starting my own business? How do I get backing and get others to invest in my *business? I don't think I'll begin with my own business, but I need to plan ahead.*

Networking—talking to people who can give you valuable insight—doesn't end just because you're no longer a student. It's a lifelong career process. Your goal is to own your own business, and networking is one of the best ways to learn the "inside perspectives" on what it is like to be a business owner. Talk to people who are small business owners. What were their greatest challenges? What has been the most rewarding aspect? What has surprised them the most? How did they prepare to become a "jack of all trades" so that they can master all the business functions—sales, marketing, management, planning, accounting, and budgeting? How did they get their financing? How many years did it take them to turn a profit?

You may also want to join an association of small business owners while you are still working for a larger company. You will meet all kinds of people in different types of businesses who can help give you guidance to make the wisest decisions. I think you are smart to work for a company first. You may even decide that instead of running your own business, you want to become an entrepreneur—someone who has a new business idea within a larger, established company. There are many options. Networking with people who have done—and thought about—what you are considering will help you to find the most appropriate path for yourself.

CAREER PROFILE

SHIRLEY KISER As executive director of Lifeskills, Inc., in Tucson, Arizona, Shirley Kiser has her hands full with matching programs with people. Lifeskills, Inc.'s purpose is to help better prepare high school students for the work force by bringing business, community members, and parents into the schools to provide programs that focus on the skills, knowledge, and attitudes students need to find and keep jobs. By giving students greater exposure to community and business leaders and accurate, up-to-date information about the realities of the workplace, Shirley and her organization help students learn that there are alternatives to dropping out, to choosing gang or criminal activities, to going on to college (for which they may not yet be ready) or to becoming anesthetized in dead-end jobs they neither succeed at nor enjoy.

When Shirley began as executive director in 1993, Lifeskills, Inc., had 53 speakers from the business community in Tucson with 1,226 students involved. By 1996, Shirley's work had increased that number to 266, with double the number of students participating! Lifeskills, Inc., began as a way to implement the ideas found in the book *Majoring in the Rest of Your Life* and relied on the topics in that book as a springboard for programs. Shirley and her staff have molded the programs so that often these programs are individually designed with each classroom teacher to best suit what that teacher is looking for. For instance, Shirley and her staff will coordinate having human resource managers come to high school classes to go through and help improve resumes and applications. They bring in teams of professionals (such as an accountant and an assistant) to classes taught on a specific subject (such as accounting) to help show the students the relationship between what they are learning in class and what they would do in the workplace. Most recently, Lifeskills, Inc., created a program called Teachers in the Workplace, which placed teachers in internships during the summer in the local business community so that they have a fuller understanding of what types of environments their students will find in the workplace.

Shirley explains that Lifeskills, Inc., could not have grown so successfully in three short years without networking—that is, reaching out to and relying on business and community leaders. Shirley is an expert in this area, which she calls simply "building relationships." Shirley encourages students to build relationships with others. "It will increase the likelihood of getting a job by using that technique heavily, rather than heavily relying on newspapers, ads, and so on. It's a far better method, albeit slower." She acknowledges that networking is not always easy. "We're all reluctant to call on friends or acquaintances of the family. I think that's a mistake. You have to swallow hard and do that. Also, you have to be prepared for a long haul. You just don't know what people will bring you to a job." Shirley knows from her own experiences both in obtaining employment and in using networking as part of the job that you shouldn't give up. Other advice: "Whenever you're using *any* contact, prepare ahead of time, to make the best impression. Know the company, have questions prepared. Make it easy for them to give you information that you want. This is really critical," she emphasizes. Shirley definitely knows, since she networks—*builds relationships*—every day for Lifeskills, Inc. Finally, Shirley points out that lifelong networking allows you to have "assorted, diverse people" in your life. Being involved in a number of activities and volunteer experiences leads you into other relationships that are just plain fun and probably useful to building toward your career goals.

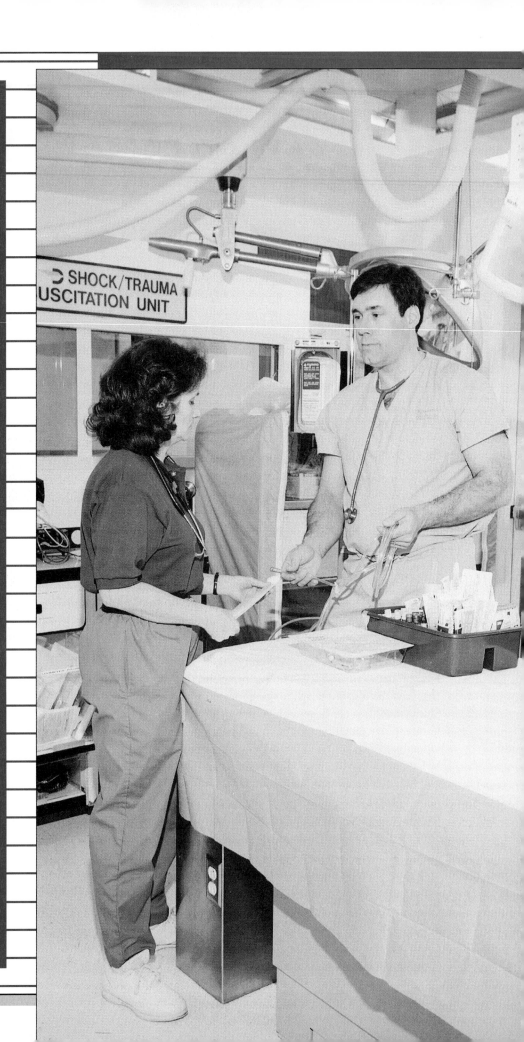

Practical Experience:

Internships, Co-Ops, and Part-Time Jobs

> EXPERIENCE ISN'T INTERESTING UNTIL IT BEGINS TO REPEAT ITSELF—IN FACT, UNTIL IT DOES THAT IT HARDLY *IS* EXPERIENCE.
>
> —ELIZABETH BOWEN

Sometimes it feels unfair that we can't get the job we want because we don't have experience, and we can't get the experience because we don't have the job we want! But there is a time and place for everything. Think of an emergency room doctor, running around barking orders and organizing an emergency team to take care of the people injured in a five-car pileup. There's no time for hesitation or procedural uncertainty. The doctor is too busy making diagnoses, deciding who needs to be treated first, and keeping an eye on all the patients to be wondering, "Now, what did that textbook say about procedures in the emergency room?" If you were one of those injured in the pileup and were now lying in the operating room, waiting to be treated, wouldn't you prefer that the doctor in charge had a lot of practical experience— not only in medicine but in leadership, communication, and organizational skills? So do the hospitals—especially the teaching hospitals, where the doctors of the future are learning from the doctors in charge. The more practical experience a doctor has (not only in medicine but life in general), the more likely the doctor will be sought as an employee. That's why a candidate for an ER job—and for so many other types of careers—will have a step up if he or she has some *practical* experience in working. Whether that experience comes in the form of a part-time job, an internship, a co-op, or extracurricular activities, you make yourself more marketable and you give yourself more confidence if you are developing skills along the way to reaching your ultimate career goal.

This chapter will show you how practical experience not only fits in the "big picture" but how it may be essential to building toward your career goals. Many students have part-time jobs to help meet their living expenses, while others work or have internships just to get some experience outside of school. In either case, the students are gathering information necessary to show a potential future employer that they have "what it takes" to succeed in that employer's company, even if their current work may not be directly related to the job they get out of school. As outlined in Chapter 2, certain skills are necessary to virtually every job. These are the skills that you want to observe your boss and colleagues demonstrate, acquire for yourself, and master.

Therefore, even if you consider the position you hold as mundane, there are lessons to be learned that will help you secure your first position after college. For example, Patricia Farmer really wanted to get a job as a news reporter. She already had a bachelor's degree in English and felt that she would do a great job as a reporter if someone would just give her a chance. She visited the editor of her small town newspaper once a week, looking for work. "I'd go to see her, and she'd tell me she still didn't have any openings." Then one day the editor called. She needed a proofreader. "I thought 'yuck. How boring.' But *some* job in the newsroom was better than none." Patricia decided to try it out. To her amazement, her proofreading job taught her an incredible amount about writing for a newspaper. Her work required that she review everyone's stories, so she got used to the style of newspaper writing. She also learned about how to write headlines, and soon she was helping design the newspaper's layout. She learned how national stories came through the computer system and how they got updated periodically. On a more basic level, she took the opportunity to improve her typing skills. She worked hard, trying to let the editor know that she could take on whatever she gave her. Two months later, when the editor created a position for an education reporter, Patricia got the job. Like Patricia, you too may already be acquiring valuable experience toward your career success.

IS THERE A MAGIC FORMULA I SHOULD KNOW ABOUT?

Because the traditional college students do not have an extensive work history, most companies create a new college graduate hiring formula—a point system for rating and ranking applicants—by which to judge their ability to perform the job they are seeking. In this formula, they list certain qualities they wish to see in their employees. The formula will contain such topics as (1) job-related experience, (2) non-job-related experience, (3) co-op experience, (4) internships, (5) extra curricular activities, (6) offices held in college organizations, and (7) grade point average, to name a few. Obtaining experience in any of these areas will help you in your job applications because you will be able to supply experience in areas that employers have identified.

How Can Practical Experience Help Me?

You can look at your part-time job or internship as busy work, or you can evaluate the experience that you obtain from these activities. First, identify the transferable skills you are learning. These are specific abilities like leadership (ability for someone to get others to abandon their own ideas or position and follow new ones), organizational skills (working in an orderly or structured fashion), discipline (strict mental or moral training), interpersonal skills (ability to work and communicate effectively with others), and initiative (energy for completing an important task, readiness to take action, introducing new ideas) that work for every endeavor in life whether it is in the job market, a volunteer program, or just keeping chaos out of the home. They are valuable attributes that potential employers will view as an asset in an applicant.

Second, realize that your work outside of the classroom is quite an achievement. Even though your job at the local fast-food restaurant does not directly apply to your computer science career, for example, the fact that you're successfully taking care of many different obligations is impressive. Recruiters look for recent graduates who can, among other things, juggle many different tasks without dropping one. So if you're working while going to college, it is essential that you can inform recruiters and prospective employers that you maintained your GPA while working at a part-time or even full-time job. It is extremely important that employees be able to manage more than one project at a time at work, their personal life, and their health so they will always be at work. It is equally important that the person interviewing you know that you have accomplished multifaceted tasks. If you omit this important information from your resume or from the job interview, you may be sabotaging yourself. Don't sell yourself short. You may be a better candidate than you think.

Third, recognize the importance of seeing the real world in action. No matter how much we learn in a classroom, the classroom is no substitute for working in the real world. Back in 1983, Thom Taylor thought he wanted to teach English as a second language in Japan after graduation, so he took a course on the subject. As part of the course requirement, he had to find a teaching internship for ten hours a week, so he volunteered at the local ESL classroom. The work was intimidating because he had never taught before; the ESL teacher didn't know how to let him help her teach; he wasn't in the classroom often enough to get to know the students well; and he found it difficult to communicate with people who knew very little English. Still, his observations taught him a lot about the real world of teaching people who speak no English. He also had the advantage of putting the internship on his resume when he applied for teaching positions in Japan.

HOW DOES MY PART-TIME JOB GIVE ME AN ADVANTAGE?

Almost any job you have during college can benefit you in ways other than financial. Obviously, some jobs are better than others, and you're better off spending some time evaluating the kinds of jobs available and their benefits rather than taking the first job you apply for. Still, there are skills that you can learn in any job, and you actually may be getting some valuable work experience in a part-time job that seems insignificant to you. Do you have responsibility for guiding or supervising other people? Do you have responsibility for money? Do you have a key to the office or store? Are you responsible for opening the store in the morning or closing it at night? Do you have customer service responsibility? Believe it or not, these are all examples of valuable work experience.

When Janice Lewis began her summer job as a housecleaner for conventions held at her school campus, she figured that her only benefit was a relatively good salary. To Janice's surprise, however, she got a lot more out of her summer job than she expected. She learned how to keep a rigid schedule and how to work well under pressure (since there was very little time between conventions to get her job done). She learned that doing her job well meant paying attention — especially since dirt and dust accumulated in places she never realized before. In addition, Janice got to know other housecleaning students who she otherwise would not have met, which broadened her network of contacts for the coming semester and allowed her to brainstorm with new friends about career choices. She also learned that she could learn from others. In this case, she learned to respect and take advice from the older, permanent employees who knew a lot more than she did about running the business of housecleaning. She grew to appreciate the work that the permanent employees did to keep everything running smoothly year-round. By the end of the summer, Janice realized that her newfound communication and organizational skills would be useful in any prospective job in the future.

Pat Duncan, an accountant for Security Pacific Housing Services, learned a lot about leadership and teamwork through her very first job as a telephone operator. "They taught us to manage multiple projects or projects that overlapped. One of the components is to be able to train someone to assist you in your work." At an early stage, then, Pat was learning that she was quite capable of giving instructions and monitoring the work of others. Her accounting work only benefits.

Examine the kinds of "on-the-job" experiences *you're* getting:

➤ **Supervisory Experience.** Most companies look for personnel who can demonstrate leadership. Thus, any supervisory or management experience that you have in your current job may earmark you in a new job for certain tasks or even promotions that require supervisory experience. What if you are currently a shift lead at Disney World? A title that seems insignificant to you may give recruiters a cue that you have developed the skill in a previous position to supervise your peers. It is not just "tooting your own horn" when you let others know of this experience; it may mean the difference between getting an entry-level job or being put on a training program. It even may make a difference in your starting salary. Don't over-look anything when you are preparing yourself for your career success.

In fact, even if your current job title doesn't reflect supervisory experience, think about the ways that you *do* supervise others and add that to your resume. Maybe you train new employees; maybe you organize shift changes. Be creative and opti-mistic about the way you view your job duties.

➤ **Responsibilities.** So, you are a cashier. How will that help you in your quest for a good first professional position? Employers are in the business to make money, so if your current employer trusts you with his money, that says he believes you are a responsible employee that he can trust with his business. The same is true with other types of responsibilities. If you are asked to open or close the business, and your employer gives you the keys to the store, that practice alone says that you are trustworthy, that you are thought of as being responsible, and that you can be trusted not only with the keys but with the entire inventory and/or furnishings. This is a management responsibility and should be presented as such. If you choose to downplay the circumstances of a part-time job, your past experience and management responsibility will most likely also be downplayed. Think through and identi-fy your other responsibilities in this same positive light—and don't minimize your accomplishments!

➤ **Communication Skills.** Your ability to communicate effective-ly with all different types of people could be the deciding fac-tor in whether you get a job you want. Think about how you communicate on the job: do you interface with customers? Get along with coworkers? Represent the company positively? For instance, if you do well with your customer service or cus-tomer satisfaction duties, that says a lot for your ability to work with other people—a real plus and even a necessity in most environments. Where would the business be without customers? Closed! Let your future employers know that you possess these communication qualities. If you don't, they may choose someone else who does.

➤ **Teamwork Skills.** One of the most important skills you can possess in the workplace today is that of teamwork. Industry and business alike have discovered that teams bring more expertise to the problem-solving arena than the individual. The team creates synergism—cooperative or joint action that achieves an end that independent action could not achieve. By working together, pooling ideas and resources, a team can emerge with a consensus that will be better than any other individual's independent contribution. Consequently, it is in your best interest to tell your interviewer about successful team efforts in which you have played a part.

WHAT IS A CO-OP JOB AND HOW CAN IT HELP ME?

If you really want to do yourself a career success favor, you will seek and conquer a co-op job, where the employee divides his time equally between college and work. Co-op jobs are divided differently according to the arrangements made between the college or university and the company providing the work. Some co-op jobs are a semester on/off where the student goes to school full time a semester then works full time the next semester. This is a win-win situation since the student gets valuable, career plan work experience while the company gets a full-time employee for four months.

Even if you're not sure what you want to do, or if you don't get the co-op that you really want, you should still pursue the experience because of how much you can learn.

In a half-day on/half-day off co-op job, the student goes to school for one-half of a day and works for one-half of a day. In another co-op job style, the half-week on/half-week off co-op, the student goes to school for one half of the week and works the other half of the week.

Your co-op job may be in the career of your choice and may net you a job in your chosen field, since many companies will offer full-time jobs to their co-op students after graduation (provided their work was satisfactory). Think about it: if you are a newly hired computer programmer who does not need a buddy or guide (someone assigned to you to show you your way around for your first few months in a new job), you automatically become more valuable. Just by hiring you, the company has just eliminated the need for the buddy system, freeing up a person that would have had to spend part of his time looking after the "new guy."

Even if a permanent offer is not made because of some business environmental reason, you still get real-world experience on your resume through a co-op job, which helps tremendously in a job search. There are also higher points on the New College Graduate Hiring Formula we mentioned previously for co-op experience. This fact gives the applicants with co-op experience a distinct advantage over most other candidates. It also gives recruiters and prospective employers another company to contact to check on your work ethics and actual professional experience. The applicants with co-op experience in the same profession as their career choice will get preferential treatment from the very beginning of the hiring process and may get the job they want because of the experience.

For more information about co-ops, the Cooperative Education Association issues a publication listing the colleges with official programs.

WHAT ABOUT INTERNSHIPS?

Another applicant who gets immediate attention from recruiters and prospective employers is someone who has worked as an intern or apprentice learning a trade or skill while working under an experienced employee or craftsman. There are paid and unpaid internships, as well as graduate and summer internships.

Rob Tokar's career in comics came directly from an internship that he found on his own. Rob was a comic fiend growing up, creating his own comic books into the wee hours of the night. As an undergraduate in college, Rob majored in communications. He had heard that getting an internship was a good idea, but he hadn't spent much time looking for one. Only after he heard from alumni about the importance of an internship did Rob start to look for one. At the time, he worked for the Chairman of Communication's office and was tallying the results of an alumni survey. "One question was, 'If you had any advice to give to students today, what would it be?' Everyone said, 'Get experience *before* you graduate.' It was an overwhelming landslide. All the communications graduates were saying it," Rob remembers. He started investigating possible internships. "Locally, I could get newsmen coffee," but he was really seeking an internship that would give him more experience. Then he read a bulletin in one of his comic books where "they said what people were doing. They said they had a party with their freelancers, editors, interns...And I thought, 'Interns?' Now I know, they have interns *everywhere*, but at the time, I didn't know."

He pointed out the bulletin to his advisor who told him to call. "I got the impression he didn't think I was going to, but I did. I went to my house, I got the number from directory assistance, I called them up, and I got an interview!" For his interview he got all dressed up. "I looked like an idiot. I showed up in my brother's suit and they were all in jeans and ratty T-shirts. They thought I was an accountant. They looked through my portfolio and asked if I could take directions." From that point on, he was hired.

An internship can have the added benefit of giving students experience at a lower level that will springboard them into a professional position without further training. In addition, just as with co-ops, students who work as interns at a particular company can be more valuable to that company because they're not new to the environment. In Rob's case, his internship gave him the experience he needed to work in the comics industry, and his success at his work got him a full-time job at that company as an assistant editor as soon as he graduated from college. Rob's example shows that internships can be just the ticket you need to get started in a career that you really want.

➤ Summer Internships. Summer interns can work full time since they most likely are between school semesters. The benefit to a summer internship is that the students obtain concentrated work experience in an area that they may want to choose as a career path. That concentrated experience may show you that you *don't* want to enter that particular field, like Mark Kirschner decided after he spent a summer in a medical lab (see Chapter 3, Career Profile), or it may solidify your decision that you've chosen a career path that's fulfilling to you.

Kathy Shannon's summer internship at the UN's Department of Information proved to be a valuable learning experience. Her project was to develop a pamphlet from a global perspective on various materials used for substance abuse. "The project provided a window to the world. In 1987, the Cold War was still going on and the only opportunity that I had to learn about life in the Soviet Union and other Eastern bloc countries was through my interviews with the various press delegates from these countries," Kathy remembers. In developing the materials, she gained the perspective that common problems that affect all countries can be solved by cooperative, global efforts. Kathy incorporates this experience into her current job as a television reporter for the NBC affiliate in Portland, Maine. "When I report a story today, I automatically focus on the big picture. I try to connect the human element to the world. Every story has an effect on our lives, no matter where it happens."

➤ Winter Internships. Many companies and firms have programs for students during the winter semester break. During his junior year at NYU, Marcus McPherson had a full-time four-week internship during January with Save the Children Foundation in Westport, Connecticut. Marcus worked with other volunteers to help design promotional packages to sell the art and crafts of South American Indians in national store chains in the United States. He also was able to interpret some documents from Spanish to English, thus practicing his language skills. Although he wasn't paid, Marcus felt the internship was invaluable. He learned about other cultures that had never been completely at the forefront of his mind, and he provided much needed labor to a shorthanded organization.

➤ Internships after Graduation. Think about internships after college. Jamie Turner had a degree in business administration and was looking for a permanent job in her chosen field. She decided to volunteer as a claims adjuster at a local insurance company that was quite shorthanded. She learned a lot working closely with the handful of experienced claims adjusters who were there. One of the adjusters taught her how to go out in the real world and do evaluations of claims that looked fraudulent. Jamie loved the work. Ultimately, this claims adjuster learned of an opening in another office and recommended Jamie for the job. Jamie knows that she would not have her new job without her newfound experience and connections at her after-graduation internship.

> Graduate Internships. There are some degrees such as medicine and construction that require the students to acquire and work in their graduating field a specific amount of time as an intern before they will receive their diploma. The employees must work under a proven professional and demonstrate their ability to do the job as a condition of graduation. Usually the intern will be paid a minimal salary while in the intern status and will be raised to the professional level upon completion of the internship. In some professions like the theater, there are students who will work in an internship or student teaching under a known professional without pay in order to gain the experience or certificate needed to enter the work force in their chosen field.

It just makes sense that if you must work part time, during summer, during winter breaks, or even full time, you should position yourself to make that job count toward securing your first professional position while reaching your career success. You can also intern during the semester for credit at most schools. This may be important to remember for those of you who cannot afford to intern full time (given the low or nonexistent pay of internships).

Be creative with the way you think about internships, and don't discount the possibility that the right internship exists for you. For more detailed information, you can look to *Internships 1996: On the Job Training Opportunities for Today's Market*, which lists more than 1500 organizations in all sectors that offer internships. Also, check with your college's career office for valuable information about internships both on and off campus.

SUMMARY

Now that you know that you have hidden, maybe never-thought-of-before value, you need to take a closer look at yourself and the life experiences you have had. Evaluate the experiences you have had at work and other organizations and functions or activities and give those experiences consideration as lessons learned. Now compare those lessons learned to the attributes we discussed earlier and put them in their proper perspective—job skills.

When you are searching for a part-time or even full-time job to sustain yourself through college, consider a co-op position or an internship. If you are going to work anyway, you should make the most of that valuable time and secure a job that will prove to aid you in your eventual professional job search.

ASKING QUESTIONS AND GETTING ANSWERS

1. **Identifying Skills from Your Present Work.** As discussed in this chapter, there are many skills that you may be getting from your current job, internship, co-op or extracurricular activity. For example, Gerald worked as a laminator in his part-time job, laminating menus, work schedules, and other things for customers. He demonstrated *leadership* because he trained one of the new workers at his business. He showed *assertiveness* when he suggested a new advertising technique to his boss. He showed *presentation skills* when he convinced a potential customer that her menus would look better laminated in a certain way. He demonstrated *professionalism* when he listened carefully and intently to an irate customer and offered to redo part of a large project because the laminating on some of the paper had become discolored, and he showed *ingenuity* when he built special shelves to accommodate their work in progress.

Now it's your turn. Fill out the chart below to identify some of the skills you have gotten from your current work experience. Then fill out the section about coworkers.

SKILLS OR ATTRIBUTES THAT VALUED EMPLOYEES POSSESS	EXAMPLES OF HOW YOU USE THIS SKILL OR ATTRIBUTE IN YOUR CURRENT JOB/ACTIVITIES
Leadership	
Assertiveness	
Presentation Skills	
Professionalism	
Communication	
Teamwork	
Loyalty	
Positive Attitude	
Ingenuity	

2. **Exploring Internships.** One way to get direct experience in a field that interests you is by obtaining an internship in that particular field. Certainly other work experience will give you skills and experiences that can be *transferred* to and useful in the field of your choice, but it can be quite helpful to have an internship specifically in the area that you like. Think about the career choices and goals that you have made already. What are three internships that will allow you to explore the field that currently holds your interest? List them below; then list companies and/or organizations where you can get such an internship. For instance, Charles wanted an internship in San Diego doing marine biology laboratory work. He identified two places where he could try to get such an internship: Scripps Institute and a for-profit laboratory doing research for the city on jellyfish.

a.   Type Of Internship:_____

   Organization #1:_____

   Organization #2:_____

b.   Type Of Internship:_____

   Organization #1:_____

   Organization #2:_____

c.   Type Of Internship:_____

   Organization #1:_____

   Organization #2:_____

COLLABORATIVE LEARNING AND TEAM-BUILDING SKILLS

1. **Obtaining the Internship.** In groups of three or four, practice interviewing for one of the internships listed above. Think of this internship as the one activity that will get you a job that's perfect for you, and that this is a stepping stone that you can't pass up. Spend some time before the interview preparing for it. What skills do you have to offer this internship? What skills are transferable from your other experiences? What questions do you have about the tasks you'll need to accomplish at this internship? Be prepared with those questions. Conduct the interview so that one person is the interviewer, one is the interviewee, and one or two of you are observers. Critique the performance of both the interviewer and interviewee. What could they each do differently? In the space provided, write down three things that you have learned from this interview process, either through the critique of your own interview or the critique of

others. Do you think you'll get the internship? If possible, try taping the interview. Seeing yourself on video can be very helpful.

What I Learned #1:_____

What I Learned #2:_____

What I Learned #3:_____

Will I Get the Internship I'm Seeking, Based on My Interview?

Yes   No

2. **Dealing with the Difficult Customer.** Many, many jobs require contact with the public, and we all need to learn how to deal with the public both in our work and in our private lives. For instance, in many jobs we run into difficult customers. They are unclear about what they want, they are hostile or arrogant in their conversation style, they refuse the help that we offer, they act as if they own the store, or all of the above. Learning how to communicate with *all* people (whether they are difficult or not) is a skill that can be an asset in any job.

In groups of three or four, role-play what to do when dealing with a difficult customer. One person should play a clerk at the return counter at an appliance store, another should act as the customer returning an appliance purchased there a long time ago, and the remaining people in your group should analyze your performance. Fill in the critique of your performance.

Did I Identify the Customer's Problem?_____

Did I Solve the Problem?_____

Did I Think About Solutions Creatively?_____

Did I Continue to Be Pleasant Throughout the Contact?_____

Did I Rely Too Heavily on "Store Policy" and Not Enough on Common Sense?_____

LONG-TERM PLANNING: KEY TO YOUR PERSONAL PORTFOLIO

Choosing an Activity that Will Advance My Career Goals. Think of an activity that you can join that can help you develop yourself in an area related to your ultimate career choice. This may involve getting a part-time job or internship, volunteering at an organization, or joining a club. Be broad in the way that you think of the activity "helping" you develop in the area of your choice. Remember the transferable skills discussed in Chapter 2. In addition, if you can't think of an activity *directly* related to your field, think of how the activity that you *do* choose will look to prospective employers on your resume. For instance, you may not want to be an architect, but volunteering with Habitat for Humanity (a nonprofit organization that builds houses for poor people) is a worthy endeavor and is a quick and easy way to show employers that you are a multifaceted individual. If you can't think of an activity that you would enjoy, contact your career counseling center for ideas.

Once you have chosen your activity, write it down below. Organize your time over the next few weeks so that you can devote at least ten hours to your chosen activity. When you have completed your ten-hour commitment, write "yes" in the space provided and put the activity on your resume.

Chosen Activity: _____

I Have Completed My Ten-Hour Commitment_____

STUDENT QUESTION

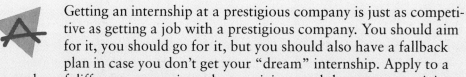

Jeff Ellison, Texas student majoring in electrical engineering

Jeff has been looking for an internship but he hasn't found the right match. He has a possibility of one at Dallas–Ft. Worth airport. He has a few concerns regarding the number of hours and the pay for that internship, however, since he has to balance his tuition expenses with a part-time job right now. He is interested in getting an internship that will let him develop name recognition on his resume. He thinks it is important to have something that will catch the eye of a future employer, so he wants to intern at a company where people know the name.

How do I get an internship at a prestigious company like Texas Instruments? Also, how do I get the most from an internship so I don't waste my time being a gopher?

Getting an internship at a prestigious company is just as competitive as getting a job with a prestigious company. You should aim for it, you should go for it, but you should also have a fallback plan in case you don't get your "dream" internship. Apply to a number of different companies—the prestigious and the not so prestigious. Sometimes you learn a lot more at the smaller company, while larger companies may have you do more "gopher" (i.e., errand-type) work. Whether your internship is filled with a lot of responsibility or more administrative tasks like xeroxing or running errands, you will learn volumes about the company, the people, how things get done behind the scenes and what you believe about the company, the nature of the work and the industry.

No matter what your internship responsibilities, make yourself stand out by taking your job seriously, learning as much as you can about the company, demonstrating a genuine interest in people at all levels within the organization and by offering to do far more than what is expected. If you finish your assigned tasks, ask your mentor or supervisor how you can take on more responsibility with another project. What you will learn is that your internship—like the job you will get out of school—is as much as you will make of it. If you dedicate yourself to learning, to growing, to thinking and to doing, you will be making a demonstrable, quantifiable contribution.

CAREER PROFILE

MICHAEL FULTON Michael Fulton knows a lot about internships, since he works as a staff specialist at INROADS/Northern New Jersey, Inc., a career development organization that matches minorities with companies in the students' area of interest. Michael spends his day working with 42 students and 14 companies to sponsor, match, and manage the work experience of African-American, Hispanic, and Native American college students. Hundreds of students apply to the organization but only a few are selected. "The key to the success of this program is if the student can learn to self-manage."

Michael's knowledge of internships is on a practical level as well. As a high school student, Michael had no plans to attend college. He changed his mind after being recruited to participate in a minority internship program with IBM. The exposure to a corporate environment was an influential experience for him in many ways. First, it taught him what he didn't want to do. Even though he felt fortunate because he was paid well for his work as a computer operator (making more money than his girlfriend's parents), he didn't feel that he fit into the conservative mold of the corporate world. Second, and perhaps more important, the internship taught him that he had options. In fact, because of the internship he decided to go to college since he figured out that, without college, his computer operator position was probably the best work he was going to get in his hometown.

Michael's career has followed a path of helping people help themselves. While earning his college degree, Michael did a work-study program at a residential treatment center. Michael was trained by Paul, one of the most senior staff members. Michael reflects on the expertise of his internship mentor: "Paul was exceptional at his job. I knew that I was being taught by the best. I valued the advice and attention that I got from him because I knew it was at a different level than any of my colleagues received." Michael used Paul as an example when Michael began supervising his own interns.

With his experience as a minority intern and as an internship manager, it makes sense that Michael made a path to his current position. As with his other work, Michael feels that he is making a difference. At INROADS, Michael supports several students in their career development. The biggest challenge that most of the interns express is fear and intimidation. "Up to this point they have been the best and the brightest. Now they see that someone else has more knowledge." Michael thinks that this reality check is good for students because it teaches them to grow up and not to focus completely on themselves.

Michael can sympathize with his students' fears. He knows how uncomfortable he was when he started his internship with IBM. Michael remembers feeling odd about dressing in the conservative shirt and tie. His friends didn't know what to make of him. He felt like he looked "corny." His father was a truck driver and never wore business clothes, so the whole experience at IBM was a new and disquieting one for him in the beginning. But Michael really values what he learned at IBM. It taught him a marketable job skill (computer operations), and it gave him training in commonsense guidelines for the office. "The people at IBM were nervous about what these kids would do 'on the floor.' They didn't want us to fall into our traditional stereotypes; they didn't want us to embarrass them," so they gave the interns "classes on all this commonsense type of information" like communication skills, business acumen, goal setting, how to behave in a meeting, and even what type of IBM style clothing to wear. They helped teach Michael to adjust to whatever world he happened to be in.

Michael believes that INROADS does the same for minority students all over the country. He explains that minority internship organizations open doors to both students and companies where they may have overlooked valuable resources before. INROADS provides students with the opportunity to transition to the professional world with a safety net and helps the company to build a diversified team with quality employees.

PREPARE

Resumes, Cover Letters, and Applications:

A Paper Trail of Achievement

> THE LIMITS OF MY LANGUAGE MEANS THE
> LIMITS OF MY WORLD.
> —LUDWIG WITTGENSTEIN

Imagine getting ready to have a photograph of yourself taken where you want to look your best. Some of us would choose to dress up in a perfectly tailored suit. Others may focus on wearing their favorite color or an unusual outfit that makes a statement about them as an individual. Each of us has ideas about how we want our hair or clothes to look, which side is our best, and so on.

Think of a job application as presenting a prospective employer with a photograph of yourself looking your "best." In making such a presentation, you wouldn't rely on a photograph where you were dressed in torn-up jeans, a paint-covered sweatshirt, and scuffed-up tennis shoes. The same is true about your application. To make the best first impression possible, you want to look your "best" on paper. The purpose of this chapter is to give you some ideas about how to organize your resume, cover letters, and applications.

As you read through this chapter and design your job applications, it may help you to think about who is going to see it. Who will look at your resume, cover letter, or application (along with perhaps hundreds of others)? What are they seeking? When they read your application, what picture are they forming of you in their mind? What opinion are they forming about your skills? Are they looking forward to meeting you? Are they trying to envision how you would do in the position that you applied for? How do other people's applications compare to yours?

Picturing your reviewers may help you understand that the job application process has a final purpose of matching up employers and employees to create the best working environment possible. With that in mind, it's time to put together your applications.

How Can I Design the Perfect Resume?

Your resume is an extremely important part of getting a desired job or position. The resume is not the final decision, nor will it be the final determinant in choosing the best candidate for a job. Even so, the resume does help the applicant get his or her "foot in the door."

There are a number of things you can do to make your resume a great one. This chapter will provide a list of some of those ideas. Keep in mind, however, that there is no "perfect" standard resume—no absolute formula to guarantee success. What will be most important in your resume is the uniqueness that *you* bring to it. Make your resume come alive by having it reflect who you are as much as possible. Remember—the resume is just part of the paper "photograph" of yourself. How can you make this "photograph" reflect yourself in a way that makes a good first impression? The resume should tell employers enough to make them want to talk to you.

Some guidance: most of the current word processing systems have a canned or preprogrammed resume format—a computerized template for making and revising one's resume. This may be useful to get you started. Don't rely exclusively on it, though. Leave your own imprint. Whether you hire someone professionally to do your resume or you do it yourself, you want to have it looking the best it can.

Also, as you are designing your resume, you may want to make more than one for different kinds of jobs. Yes, you may need to make an individualized resume for each employer, or at least for each field in which you are pursuing a position, depending on where you received your lead. In fact, a personalized resume may help you get your ideal job. Use your best judgment in deciding whether you need more than one resume, or a personalized resume for a particular job, since the extra work is time consuming.

There are basically three types of resumes: functional, chronological, and a combination of the two. The chronological resume is actually in reverse chronological order since you insert the most recent employer or educational opportunity first, and so on. This form is probably the most common resume today and is an excellent method if there are no large holes in your resume. However, if you have a large space where you were not employed (for instance, you are someone who stayed home until the kids started school), this type of resume will call attention to the hole (see Figure 8-1).

The functional resume is not as commonly used as the chronology type. It is a great tool for employees who may not have worked in the field sought or who have been unemployed for a period, since it focuses more on skills and talents (see Figure 8-2). However, a resume with no dates raises a red flag for prospective employers and may be screened out of the selection process. The combination of both the chronological and functional resume is a new method that is very useful for job seekers who have extensive experience and also have special skills that make them extremely marketable (see Figure 8-3).

FIGURE 8-1 SAMPLE CHRONOLOGICAL RESUME

ROBERT MC INTYRE, JR.

2104 Rockwood Avenue – Seattle, Washington 87121 – (206) 555-1234

EDUCATION

SEATTLE UNIVERSITY   May 1996
Seattle, Washington
Bachelor of Science in Accounting, 3.7 GPA

    Treasurer of the Student Chapter of the Institute of Management Accountants
    Student Chapter of Toastmasters International
    Co-Captain of the Soccer Team

EXPERIENCE

BOEING SPACE CENTER   October 1994
Seattle, Washington   to present
Internship/Assistant to Senior Accountant

- Assist in conducting general audits by proofreading financial reports and verifying accuracy of calculations.
- Prepare financial statements using Microsoft Word, Lotus 1-2-3, and Lacerte.
- Coordinate interdepartmental and customer communications.
- Reproduce and distribute documents during preparation of annual forecast (includes compiling information from multiple departments within the company and verifying that each department provides timely information).
- Proficient in accounts payable and receivable.

BENEFICIAL ACCOUNTING SERVICES   January 1992
Seattle, Washington   to May 1995
Volunteer Income Tax Assistant

- Prepared taxes for senior citizens.
- Answered tax-related problem calls.
- Led presentations on tax return preparation.
- Analyzed tax returns and led problem-solving teams.

FIGURE 8-2 SAMPLE FUNCTIONAL RESUME

··

KATHLEEN MORRISON
12 Heathcliff Avenue
Bainbridge Island, Washington 99212
206-555-3313

OBJECTIVE

Assistant Buyer position for major department store chain utilizing my skills in sales, customer service, fashion display, and product knowledge to contribute to company profits and provide training in the buying profession.

PROFESSIONAL SKILLS

Summary

Assisted Housewares' buyer in designing displays, handling returns, and preparing promotion markdowns.
Functioned as sales associate in departments with specialties in Men's Fragrances, Housewares, Fine China, and Bridal Registry.

Sales

Awarded Sales Employee of the Year for 1994.
Numerous customer service commendations for **exemplary** assistance.
Consistently increased sales resulting in exceeding sales quotas each year.

Management

Supervised Housewares for one year.
Scheduled, trained, and supervised 12 employees.

Display

Coordinated opening of Housewares Department for new department store.
Arranged merchandise, scheduled and supervised additional staff, and coordinated guest chefs and opening day events.

EXPERIENCE

Sales Associate/Department Manager.   Frederick and Nelson, Seattle, Washington
May 1990 to present
Sales Clerk.   K-Mart Store, Bellevue, Washington
June 1998 to May 1990

EDUCATION

Bachelor of Art-Marketing, May 1997, Seattle University, Seattle, Washington
Associate of Art, August 1990, Bellevue Community College, Bellevue, Washington

FIGURE 8-3 SAMPLE COMBINATION RESUME

MARTA WILLIAMS
1125 Morgenstern
New York, New York 22202
(516) 555-4328

OBJECTIVE: To utilize my customer service, organization, and computer skills to fulfill the duties of an entry-level bank teller in order to contribute to the growth and success of the bank.

QUALIFICATIONS:

- Mastered Claris, Microsoft Office, WordPerfect, and Dazzle through my own initiative.
- Coordinated and performed multiple tasks with ease.
- Assessed and resolved customer complaints.
- Demonstrated eye for detail by keeping appointment books without incident of oversight or omission.
- Possess excellent written and verbal communication skills.
- Function equally well as a member of a team or individually.

EXPERIENCE:

July 1991 to Present

TELECOM INDUSTRIES, New York, New York
Receptionist

- Maintain multiple phone line for large communications firm.
- Track location activities of executive personnel.
- Greet and assist customers and other visitors.
- Coordinate and publish in-house employee communications.

October 1989 to May 1991

SOUTH BEND VETERINARY CLINIC, Phoenix, Arizona
Receptionist

- Greeted pet owners and pets.
- Scheduled appointments for yearly and follow-up exams.
- Arranged payment schedules and collected payments.
- Coordinated room locations for pet exams.
- Distributed medications and educated owners on procedures.

EDUCATION:

TECHNOCROM BUSINESS INSTITUTE—1988 to 1990
Training in dictation, word processing, shorthand, and typing

COMMUNITY SERVICE AND OTHER INTERESTS

Volunteer for SPCA
Local and National Toastmasters Member

Two of the resumes in Figures 8-1 through 8-3 list experience before education. College students or new graduates usually benefit more from starting with education first, however, because that typically will be their most recent "experience."

The following are some ideas for building a great resume, whether it is chronological, functional, or a combination of both:

> **Make Your Resume Brief, Concise, and to the Point.** A one-page resume is best, but for people with years of experience, two pages are acceptable. Three or more are in the trash. Most people will not read more than one page of anything, much less a stranger's assessment of himself or herself. Carol, a seasoned recruiter, says that she spends only about 10 to 30 seconds reading a resume the first time around, so you want to be concise. Your resume tells the prospective employers what you have accomplished that relates to their business, what you can do for them, who you are at this point in time, and what you know. It needs to spark their interest in you and indicate a need for your skills in their company. It should be aimed at convincing them to invite you in for an interview.

> **Make Your Resume Well Organized and Pleasing to the Reader.** You don't have to have it done professionally to look professional. Always print it on a laser or high-quality printer on high-quality bond paper. If you don't have the printer necessary to make a good impression, put your resume on a disk and take it to a quickie printer store and print it on their printer. It could make money for you in the long run. Use 12-point type for the text.

> **Plan Your Resume.** Think through the information you wish to include in your resume; create a plan. Make a list of things that are essential for the prospective employer to know about you.

> **Decide What Comes First.** If you are a recent college graduate, your education and any honors should come first; if you have been in the workplace for at least two years, list your relevant work experience. It should be listed most to least recent experience. Show dates and locations.

> **Decide on the Substance.** Call attention to pertinent skills and responsibilities. Keep in mind that listing tasks and duties is not necessarily the best way to describe responsibilities. Don't overload the resume with tasks but find words that indicate that you were a trustworthy, responsible individual (like "accurately" or "efficiently"). Choose words that reflect your

desire to grow (like "progressed" or "developed"). Emphasize relevant information that might fit into the new job and emphasize less relevant positions. Also, use action verbs to make your resume speak for itself. A few such words are

Achieved	Constructed	Formulated	Launched
Accomplished	Demonstrated	Generated	Managed
Administered	Designed	Headed	Mediated
Analyzed	Developed	Implemented	Provided
Assisted	Directed	Increased	Reorganized
Chaired	Established	Initiated	Solved
Compiled	Executed	Instructed	Streamlined
Created	Facilitated	Integrated	Supervised

Keep in mind that the descriptions of your projects should also include a description of the fruits of your efforts (where applicable). For instance, perhaps you designed a mailing system for your company that resulted in a decrease in costs of 25 percent. In that circumstance, you could explain that you "designed innovative mailing system that resulted in reduced costs of a record 25%." Try to think of a positive net result for each of your activities, and provide that type of description wherever possible.

➤ **Avoid Sentences and Heavy Reading.** Make it easy for a recruiter to pick out pertinent information and buzzwords—skills or attributes that relate to a particular business or industry. Find dynamic, concise words to use instead of going into a lot of detail.

➤ **Point Out the Positive.** Always tell the truth and be positive. If you have something that will look negative in print, try to save it for a face-to-face conversation. For example, think of positive ways to explain a job that you felt was boring; think about the transferable skills you may have gotten from that job. Review lists in Chapters 2, 7, and 10 about skills that can be learned from what otherwise appeared to you to be unexciting. Every employment circumstance has a real-life explanation. Even your sincerity in person can make a difference when you're explaining a negative occurrence.

➤ **Don't List References.** Contacting references is a normal practice in the hiring process, so that listing references up front is not necessary. The prospective employer knows that, as a normal business practice, you will furnish references if asked. Therefore, don't waste valuable space on your resume with references or say "references are available upon request" in your resume unless you are using it to fill up empty space. This is especially true for jobs where you will also be filling out an application, since virtually *all* applications have a space for references.

➤ **Proofread.** *Always* proofread your resume using whatever tools you have at your disposal—a spelling checking system, a grammar checking system, a friend who is good at proofreading, or hiring a professional. No matter which method you choose to use, you are still responsible for the final product, and if there is an error, it will reflect on you.

Remember that the Human Resources Department representatives typically are the first to receive your resume and are probably not technical specialists in your field. Yes, they will have a peripheral or cursory knowledge of the job being sought but not an in-depth knowledge. Therefore, they are looking for certain terms or qualities that the technical manager has given them as essential skills. Hence, pay attention to key terms that are used in telephone conversations, in newspaper ads, by the placement agency, or by your contact on the inside (or by whatever other source you have about the job). If you possess those essential skills, they are a *must* for your resume. Human Resources Department recruiters may spend no more than a minute screening the resume they have for a particular job. The first time they scan for certain essential terms or buzzwords. If the resume doesn't have what they're seeking, they either trash it or (if it contains other skills that are common to their company) they may save it for future reference. The chances of your resume surfacing again are not very good unless there is a desperate need for your particular skills, since very often there are resumes coming in every day to Human Resources Departments for review, and the recruiters most likely will review the resumes right in front of them. Make your first impression stick!

Figures 8-4 and 8-5 are sample resumes that come from a variety of sources. Look them over—do you see things that you want to use? Are there things that don't work for you?

Also, become familiar with producing "scannable" resumes—resumes that can be scanned into the computer in response to Internet job offerings. Resumix (http://www.resumix.com) has developed tips for writing an effective scannable resume. These are listed in Table 8-1.

What Is the Purpose of the Cover Letter?

One of the best ways to bring attention to your resume is to have an effective cover letter accompanying it. Student career counselor Stacey Cloutier believes that the cover letter is an "overlooked" tool in the job search communication process. According to Stacey, using a standard format is the same as missing a great opportunity to show your uniqueness. "Students need to move away from the standard third paragraph regarding, for example, 'I have the following qualifications that you are seeking.' This general type of statement should be replaced with a specific illustration of experience and how it relates to the company's current needs," Stacey says.

The cover letter sends a message of confidence and organization if it is well done; but it sends a message of disorder if it is not. *Always* send a

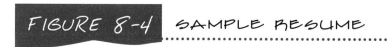

FIGURE 8-4 SAMPLE RESUME

JANE SMITH
1234 N.W. Main Street
San Francisco, CA 94344
(415) 555-1100

WRITER – PUBLIC RELATIONS – REPORTER

EXPERIENCE

ASSISTANT PUBLIC RELATIONS DIRECTOR

American Federation of Teachers—June 1993 to present
Assisted in managing public relations for national non-profit organization representing teachers.

PRODUCE MONTHLY NEWSLETTER

- Wrote articles on issues pertinent for today's elementary and secondary school teachers.
- Edited articles of guest authors.
- Designed newsletter layout via computer program.
- Won award in 1994 for article on increases in wages for teachers.

ASSIST IN INCREASING ORGANIZATION'S MEMBERSHIP

- Supervised two employees during annual membership drive.
- Conducted membership surveys to better address members' needs.
- Increased membership by 20% over three years.

ADMINISTERED SEMINARS

- Compiled materials for several seminars annually.
- Chair committee on location decisions.

NEWS REPORTER

SAN FRANCISCO COMMUNITY COLLEGE NEWSPAPER—August 1992 to May 1993

- Wrote about human interest issues of the times.
- Assisted in drafting advertisements.

EDUCATION/TRAINING

Associate in Arts—Communication, San Francisco Community College–May 1993
Three-day Effective Newsletter Editing workshop at Northwestern University

FIGURE 8-5 SAMPLE RESUME

JUSTIN HERALD
4321 NW Main Street
San Francisco, California 94344
(415) 555-1100

EDUCATION

CARLTON COLLEGE, Wisconsin, Bachelor of Arts Degree
Business Administration and Economics, May 1990–GPA 3.0.

CAREER-RELATED EXPERIENCE

DIRECTOR OF CONFERENCE SERVICES, Regency Hotel, San Jose, California, 1994 to present.

- Coordinated state and national conferences, exhibitions, and meetings up to 700 people.
- Facilitated house arrangements, including convention bureaus.
- Participated in state and national trade shows.
- Initiated sales proposals to different market segments.
- Solicited accounts generating $700,000 and above annually.
- Established and implemented marketing strategies to expand current sales volume in the department with a $100,000 increase the first year.
- Anticipated needs, forecasted results, and analyzed and controlled departmental work process as well as developing internal training programs.
- Developed computerized system for tracking revenues and expenditures.

CATERING MANAGER, Regency Hotel, San Jose, California, April 1994 to July 1994.

- Solicited conferences and meetings from local, corporate, and association markets.
- Increased profits in food and beverage.
- Prepared monthly and year-end budget reports for the catering department.

SALES ADMINISTRATIVE ASSISTANT, Holidy Inn, San Francisco, California, March 1992 to March 1994.

- Developed and implemented data-based management system for group's room control.
- Assisted sales personnel in coordinating promotional materials.
- Prepared market share analysis report on a monthly basis.

ASSOCIATIONS

Active participation in the California Society of Association Executives, National Association of Catering Executives, and Meeting Planners International

TABLE 8-1 TIPS FOR WRITING AN EFFECTIVE SCANNABLE RESUME

- Use white, 8 1/2-x 11-inch paper.

- Multiple pages are okay, but do not fold or staple.

- Provide a laser printer original.

- Use standard typefaces such as Helvetica, Futura, Optima, Univers, Times, or Courier.

- Use a font size of 10 to 14 points (avoid Times 10 point).

- Avoid italics, underlining, shadows, and reverse type.

- Avoid vertical and horizontal lines, graphics, and boxes.

- Avoid two-column format which looks like newspaper.

- Center your name, address, and phone number at the top of the page.

- Use jargon and acronyms specific to your industry.

- Increase your list of key words by including specifics. For example, list the names of software such as Lotus 1-2-3, Microsoft Word, and Powerpoint.

resume with a cover letter emphasizing your strengths. Typically, a resume without a cover letter is bad form. In addition, by not providing a cover letter, you have missed an opportunity to explain your characteristics, skills, or traits that cannot be placed on the resume.

A cover letter is also a place where you can express positively how you feel about working for the company in question. It gives you an opportunity to express what you personally can contribute to make the company's business more successful. Don't miss this opportunity to talk about yourself without being labeled a braggart. Figure 8-6 sets up the basic cover letter format while Figures 8-7(a), (b), and (c) are sample cover letters. Be sure you prove to your prospective employer that you know how to put the icing on the cake or the finishing touches to your resume. Use these figures to help you create a great cover letter to help you reach your career success.

FIGURE 8-6 COVER LETTER FORMAT

Address
City, State, Zip
Date

Contact Person, Title
Company Name
Address
City, State, Zip

Salutation: (Dear Mr. or Ms._____:)

This paragraph is your introduction; tell how you know about the position, whether through an ad (indicate periodical, date, and ad number if appropriate), personal referral (by whom), or other referring organization (name the agency or organization). Then tell what job you are requesting and why you are the best candidate for the position.

The second paragraph should show your qualifications, what specifically you can do for the company other candidates may not be able to do, and your experience. Be sure to restate any qualifiers from the ad in relation to your own experience and/or qualifications. Make it brief but impressive.

Thirdly, indicate that your resume is attached, and tell how you will follow up.

Sincerely,

Your First and Last Name—
Be Sure to Sign the Cover Letter

Enc: (indicates an enclosure)

FIGURE 8-7(A) SAMPLE COVER LETTER

Robert McIntyre, Jr.

2104 Rockwood Avenue • Seattle, WA 98121 • (206) 555-1234

September 5, 1996

Fred Storm
Human Resources
Ernst & Able Public Accounting
Seattle, WA 98121

Dear Mr. Storm,

I have followed the success of Ernst & Able during the merger this past year. The CPA Journal of Accounting says you are recognized nationally as a leader in the industry and provide exceptional on-going training programs for your junior accountants.

Last May, I graduated with a B.S. in Accounting from Seattle University. I am currently seeking employment in a company that offers the chance to train for my CPA license and grow as a professional. If you have an opening for an employee who is dedicated, analytical and an excellent problem-solver, I would be interested in meeting with you.

I have taken the liberty to enclose my resume. My experience as an apprentice at Boeing and my volunteer tax services should prove to be assets for your company.

Sincerely,

Robert McIntyre, Jr.

Robert McIntyre, Jr.

RMJ
enclosure

FIGURE 8-7(B)   SAMPLE COVER LETTER
···

Kathleen Morrison
12 Heathcliff Avenue
Bainbridge Island, Washington 99212
(206) 555-3313

September 30, 1996

Tom Skuggs
Personnel Director
Nordstrom Stores
Seattle, Washington 99210

Dear Mr. Skuggs,

I was recently speaking with Joanne Stewart, a manager with your store. Because she is familiar with my work, she strongly advised me to send a copy of my resume to your office regarding the opening as an assistant buyer in your buying department.

I feel confident that after reviewing my resume, you will see that I am a worthy candidate. Besides having a strong background in sales, I have worked closely with buyers for many years. Not only do I have skill in fashion display, customer service and managing employees, I understand the demands of the fashion and retail industry as a whole. Because of this, there will be no surprises to the dedication it takes to work in retail.

The opportunity to work with you is appealing. I look forward to your response and hope we can meet soon to discuss my resume and work history further. Thank you for your consideration.

Sincerely,

Kathleen Morrison

Kathleen Morrison

KM
enclosure

FIGURE 8-7(C) SAMPLE COVER LETTER

Marta Williams

1125 Morgenstern
New York, NY 22202
(516) 555 - 4328

December 4, 1996

Susan West
Loan Officer
Old Town Bank
New York, NY 12345

Dear Ms. West,

In response to your ad of December 2nd, please consider my resume in your search for a Bank Teller.

My experience as a receptionist supports the requirements for the available position. I am able to handle multiple tasks with ease which would allow me to serve the bank's customers with proficiency and excellence. In addition, I am comfortable responding to customers' needs with professionalism and friendliness.

I believe the Old Town Bank would provide a wonderful working environment and offer the chance to grow in the exciting industry of financial services.

I look forward to hearing from you, Ms. West, and anticipate the opportunity of working with you.

Sincerely,

Marta Williams

Marta Williams

MW
enclosure

Following are the essential elements of a good cover letter to get your first position in your quest for your career success:

Cosmetics

➤ **Length.** Keep the letter one page long—usually no more than three or four short paragraphs. If the letter is longer than a page, chances are that no one will read it completely.

➤ **Size and Color.** Use regular 8 1/2- x 11-inch white or ivory bond (20-pound is sufficient). Most recruiters are looking at content, neatness, and appropriateness. If you try to dazzle them with expensive colored paper, it is probably a waste of money. Typically, a muted tone is the preferred choice. Use the same stationery for your resume, cover letter, and envelope.

➤ **Word Processing and Printing.** Use a word processor and print on a letter-quality printer. If you don't have one, as with the resume, go to a local printer store and use theirs. It looks significantly better and may make a difference in getting you an interview.

Format

➤ **Return Address.** Set this address in the upper right-hand corner with the date under the address (left justified) or under the name at the bottom of the page with the date in the upper right corner. Write the month out; don't use the abbreviation or the number for the month.

➤ **Inside Address.** Call the company (anonymously if necessary) and do everything you can to get the name of the person who should receive your resume so that you can address your cover letter to that person. The first line of the addressee is for the name and title; the next line is for the company name; and the third and fourth lines are for the address, city, state, and zip code.

If you can't find out who should receive the letter, address it to the title of the person who will most likely be reviewing the application. For instance, you could send the letter to "Human Resources Director."

➤ **Salutation Line.** Skip two lines after the address for the salutation. It should be "Dear Mr. Last Name" or "Dear Ms. Last Name" followed by a colon (:). If you are answering a blind ad, you may have to use a generic salutation like "Dear Human Resources Manager" or "To whom it may concern." Do not use a male-oriented term like "Dear Sir"—especially since the person doing the hiring may very well be a woman.

➤ **The First Paragraph.** State in clear, concise language the purpose of the cover letter and your qualifications. Be sure to reference where you got the referral or, if an ad, where it appeared. This paragraph should begin one single-spaced line down from the salutation line, and can be either indented or not—it's up to you.

➤ **The Body of the Letter.** Indicates what you can contribute to the company and why they should hire you. One useful technique is to make a bulleted list of your achievements. The paragraph or paragraphs should be spaced like the first paragraph, and indented (or not indented) the same way.

➤ **The Final Paragraph.** Request an interview and/or tell them to expect a telephone call from you and when. You should try to end the letter in such a way that allows you to make the next move. For instance, you can say, "I look forward to speaking with you soon," which leaves you the option of calling them first. You could also end by saying something like, "If I don't hear from you, I will call you October 7." This lets the employer know how serious you are about your application. Use the same spacing and indenting guidelines as above.

➤ **The Closing.** Place the closing two lines under the last paragraph and in line with the address. Keep the closing short and simple like "Sincerely," "Yours Truly," or "Sincerely Yours."

➤ **The Enclosure Line.** (if you are enclosing a resume). Set this line flush left two lines below the signature line.

HOW DO I FILL OUT APPLICATIONS?

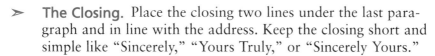

Many jobs have their own application—a paper form to be completed by a person applying for a particular job or position—for you to fill out. Filling out applications may appear to be an insignificant task (especially if you have already given the company your resume), but it is a test of your neatness, truthfulness, attention to detail, and ability to communicate in writing. If it appears that you didn't take it seriously, it could cost you the job.

Warning: Many companies will terminate an employee who falsifies information on his or her application, whether intentionally or just by mistake. It is extremely important for a job seeker to put accurate information on the application. The application becomes a permanent part of your personnel file which will never be discarded. If in the future, an error (intentional or unintentional) is discovered, you could have to suffer serious consequences. So be your best proofreader!

Many companies use preformatted applications; an example of this type of application is shown in Figure 8-8. Others design and print their own version. The main concern companies face in designing their own application is to ensure that they do not violate any employment laws. For example, employers are not permitted to ask questions that do not relate to an applicant's ability to do the job in question. Larger companies have legal departments to review and approve an original design, whereas many smaller companies choose to use a preformatted application to save the money and avoid the possibility of a mistake.

FIGURE 8-8(A) SHORT APPLICATION FORM

Application for Employment

PLEASE PRINT

Equal access to programs, services and employment is available to all persons. Those applicants requiring reasonable accommodation to the application and/or interview process should notify a representative of the Human Resources Department.

Position(s) applied for _____ Date of application ___/___/___

Name_____
           LAST   FIRST   MIDDLE

Address _____
           STREET   CITY   STATE   ZIP CODE

Telephone # (___) _____ Mobile/Beeper/Other Phone # (___) _____ Social Security #_____

If you are under 18, and it is required, can you furnish a work permit? .... ☐ Yes ☐ No

If no, please explain_____

Have you ever been employed here before?.. ☐ Yes ☐ No

Are you legally eligible for employment in this country?... ☐ Yes ☐ No

Date available for work .... ___/___/___

Type of employment desired ☐ Full-Time   ☐ Part-Time   ☐ Temporary   ☐ Seasonal   ☐ Educational Co-Op

Are you able to meet the attendance requirements of the position?.. ☐ Yes ☐ No

Have you been convicted of a crime in the last seven (7) years?.. ☐ Yes ☐ No

If yes, please explain _____
CONVICTION WILL NOT NECESSARILY BE A BAR TO EMPLOYMENT. EACH INSTANCE AND EXPLANATION WILL BE CONSIDERED IN RELATION TO THE POSITION FOR WHICH YOU ARE APPLYING.

Driver's license number if driving is an essential job function_____ State _____

Employment History

Provide the following information for your past four (4) employers, assignments or volunteer activities, starting with the most recent.

FROM	TO	EMPLOYER	TELEPHONE ( )
JOB TITLE		ADDRESS	
IMMEDIATE SUPERVISOR AND TITLE		SUMMARIZE THE NATURE OF WORK PERFORMED AND JOB RESPONSIBILITIES	
REASON FOR LEAVING		HOURLY RATE/SALARY START $_____ PER _____ FINAL $_____ PER _____	
FROM	TO	EMPLOYER	TELEPHONE ( )
JOB TITLE		ADDRESS	
IMMEDIATE SUPERVISOR AND TITLE		SUMMARIZE THE NATURE OF WORK PERFORMED AND JOB RESPONSIBILITIES	
REASON FOR LEAVING		HOURLY RATE/SALARY START $_____ PER _____ FINAL $_____ PER _____	
FROM	TO	EMPLOYER	TELEPHONE ( )
JOB TITLE		ADDRESS	
IMMEDIATE SUPERVISOR AND TITLE		SUMMARIZE THE NATURE OF WORK PERFORMED AND JOB RESPONSIBILITIES	
REASON FOR LEAVING		HOURLY RATE/SALARY START $_____ PER _____ FINAL $_____ PER _____	
FROM	TO	EMPLOYER	TELEPHONE ( )
JOB TITLE		ADDRESS	
IMMEDIATE SUPERVISOR AND TITLE		SUMMARIZE THE NATURE OF WORK PERFORMED AND JOB RESPONSIBILITIES	
REASON FOR LEAVING		HOURLY RATE/SALARY START $_____ PER _____ FINAL $_____ PER _____	

AN EQUAL OPPORTUNITY EMPLOYER

FIGURE 8-8(A) SHORT APPLICATION FORM (CONTINUED)

Skills and Qualifications

Summarize any training, skills, licenses, and/or certificates that may qualify you as being able to perform job-related functions in the position for which you are applying.

Educational Background IF JOB-RELATED

	NAME AND LOCATION	YEARS COMPLETED	DID YOU GRADUATE?		COURSE OF STUDY
HIGH SCHOOL					
COLLEGE			MAJOR	DEGREE	
OTHER					

References

NAME	TELEPHONE	YEARS KNOWN
	( )	
	( )	
	( )	

I UNDERSTAND THAT IF I AM EMPLOYED, ANY MISREPRESENTATION OR MATERIAL OMISSION MADE BY ME ON THIS APPLICATION WILL BE SUFFICIENT CAUSE FOR CANCELLATION OF THIS APPLICATION OR IMMEDIATE DISCHARGE FROM THE EMPLOYER'S SERVICE, WHENEVER IT IS DISCOVERED.

I GIVE THE EMPLOYER THE RIGHT TO CONTACT AND OBTAIN INFORMATION FROM ALL REFERENCES, EMPLOYERS, EDUCATIONAL INSTITUTIONS AND TO OTHERWISE VERIFY THE ACCURACY OF THE INFORMATION CONTAINED IN THIS APPLICATION. I HEREBY RELEASE FROM LIABILITY THE EMPLOYER AND ITS REPRESENTATIVES FOR SEEKING, GATHERING AND USING SUCH INFORMATION AND ALL OTHER PERSONS, CORPORATIONS OR ORGANIZATIONS FOR FURNISHING SUCH INFORMATION.

THE EMPLOYER DOES NOT UNLAWFULLY DISCRIMINATE IN EMPLOYMENT AND NO QUESTION ON THIS APPLICATION IS USED FOR THE PURPOSE OF LIMITING OR EXCUSING ANY APPLICANT FROM CONSIDERATION FOR EMPLOYMENT ON A BASIS PROHIBITED BY LOCAL, STATE OR FEDERAL LAW.

THIS APPLICATION IS CURRENT FOR ONLY 60 DAYS. AT THE CONCLUSION OF THIS TIME, IF I HAVE NOT HEARD FROM THE EMPLOYER AND STILL WISH TO BE CONSIDERED FOR EMPLOYMENT, IT WILL BE NECESSARY TO FILL OUT A NEW APPLICATION.

IF I AM HIRED, I UNDERSTAND THAT I AM FREE TO RESIGN AT ANY TIME, WITH OR WITHOUT CAUSE AND WITHOUT PRIOR NOTICE, AND THE EMPLOYER RESERVES THE SAME RIGHT TO TERMINATE MY EMPLOYMENT AT ANY TIME, WITH OR WITHOUT CAUSE AND WITHOUT PRIOR NOTICE, EXCEPT AS MAY BE REQUIRED BY LAW. THIS APPLICATION DOES NOT CONSTITUTE AN AGREEMENT OR CONTRACT FOR EMPLOYMENT FOR ANY SPECIFIED PERIOD OR DEFINITE DURATION. I UNDERSTAND THAT NO REPRESENTATIVE OF THE EMPLOYER, OTHER THAN AN AUTHORIZED OFFICER, HAS THE AUTHORITY TO MAKE ANY ASSURANCES TO THE CONTRARY. I FURTHER UNDERSTAND THAT ANY SUCH ASSURANCES MUST BE IN WRITING AND SIGNED BY AN AUTHORIZED OFFICER.

I UNDERSTAND IT IS THIS COMPANY'S POLICY NOT TO REFUSE TO HIRE A QUALIFIED INDIVIDUAL WITH A DISABILITY BECAUSE OF THAT PERSON'S NEED FOR A REASONABLE ACCOMMODATION AS REQUIRED BY THE ADA.

I ALSO UNDERSTAND THAT IF I AM HIRED, I WILL BE REQUIRED TO PROVIDE PROOF OF IDENTITY AND LEGAL WORK AUTHORIZATION.

I represent and warrant that I have read and fully understand the foregoing and seek employment under these conditions.

Signature of Applicant _____   Date ____/____/____

Call toll free 1-800-999-9111 to reorder Application for Employment (Short Form) #R5A-0502 D
© 1992 G. Neil Companies, P.O. Box 450939, Sunrise, FL 33345-0939. Printed in U.S.A. (1/95)
G. Neil Companies assumes no responsibility for the employer's use of this form or any decision the employer makes which may violate local, state or federal law. By selling this form, G. Neil Companies is not giving legal advice.

Recycled Paper
Our commitment to protecting the environment

FIGURE 8-8(B) LONG APPLICATION FORM

Application for Employment

PLEASE PRINT

Equal access to programs, services and employment is available to all persons. Those applicants requiring reasonable accommodation to the application and/or interview process should notify a representative of the Human Resources Department.

Position(s) applied for _____ Date of application ___ / ___ / ___

Referral Source   ☐ Advertisement   ☐ Employee   ☐ Relative   ☐ Government Employment Agency

☐ Walk-in   ☐ Private Employment Agency   ☐ Other _____

Name of source (if applicable) _____

Name _____
LAST   FIRST   MIDDLE

Address _____
STREET   CITY   STATE   ZIP CODE

Telephone # (___) _____ Mobile/Beeper/Other Phone # (___) _____ Social Security # _____

If necessary, best time to call you at home is .... ___ : ___ AM/PM

May we contact you at work? .... ☐ Yes ☐ No

If yes, work number and best time to call .... (___) _____ ___ : ___ AM/PM

If you are under 18 and it is required, can you furnish a work permit? .... ☐ Yes ☐ No

If no, please explain _____

Have you submitted an application here before? .... ☐ Yes ☐ No

If yes, give date(s) .... ___ / ___ / ___

Have you ever been employed here before? .... ☐ Yes ☐ No

If yes, give dates .... From ___ / ___ / ___ To ___ / ___ / ___

Are you legally eligible for employment in this country? .... ☐ Yes ☐ No

Date available for work .... ___ / ___ / ___

Type of employment desired   ☐ Full-Time   ☐ Part-Time   ☐ Temporary   ☐ Seasonal   ☐ Educational Co-Op

Will you relocate if job requires it? .... ☐ Yes ☐ No   Will you travel if job requires it? .... ☐ Yes ☐ No

Are you able to meet the attendance requirements of the position? .... ☐ Yes ☐ No

Will you work overtime if required? .... ☐ Yes ☐ No

If no, please explain _____

Have you ever been bonded? .... ☐ Yes ☐ No

Have you been convicted of a crime in the last seven (7) years? .... ☐ Yes ☐ No

If yes, please explain _____
CONVICTION WILL NOT NECESSARILY BE A BAR TO EMPLOYMENT. EACH INSTANCE AND EXPLANATION WILL BE CONSIDERED IN RELATION TO THE POSITION FOR WHICH YOU ARE APPLYING.

Driver's license number if driving is an essential job function _____ State _____

AN EQUAL OPPORTUNITY EMPLOYER

FIGURE 8-8(B) LONG APPLICATION FORM (CONTINUED)

Educational Background IF JOB-RELATED

A. List last three (3) schools attended, starting with most recent. **B.** List number of years completed. **C.** Indicate degree or diploma earned, if any. **D.** Grade Point Average or Class Rank. **E.** Major field of study. **F.** Minor field of study (if applicable).

A. SCHOOL	B. YEARS COMPLETED	C. DEGREE DIPLOMA	D. GPA CLASS RANK	E. MAJOR	F. MINOR

References

List name and telephone number of three business/work references who are *not* related to you and are *not* previous supervisors. If not applicable, list three school or personal references who are not related to you.

NAME	TELEPHONE	YEARS KNOWN
	( )	
	( )	
	( )	

Additional Information

List professional, trade, business, or civic associations and any offices held.
EXCLUDE MEMBERSHIPS WHICH WOULD REVEAL SEX, RACE, RELIGION, NATIONAL ORIGIN, AGE, COLOR, DISABILITY OR ANY OTHER SIMILARLY PROTECTED STATUS.

ORGANIZATION	OFFICES HELD

List special accomplishments, publications, awards, etc.
EXCLUDE INFORMATION WHICH WOULD REVEAL SEX, RACE, RELIGION, NATIONAL ORIGIN, AGE, COLOR, DISABILITY OR OTHER PROTECTED STATUS. _____

_____

_____

_____

_____

List any additional information you would like us to consider. _____

_____

_____

_____

_____

_____

_____

FIGURE 8-8(B) LONG APPLICATION FORM (CONTINUED)

Affirmative Action Voluntary Information

COMPLETION OF INFORMATION BELOW IS VOLUNTARY

We consider all applicants for positions without regard to race, color, religion, sex, national origin, age, mental or physical disabilities, veteran/reserve/national guard or any other similarly protected status.

To be completed by applicant on a voluntary basis. Not for interview purposes. To be filed separately from application.

In an effort to comply with requirements regarding government recordkeeping, reporting and other legal obligations which may apply, we invite you to complete this applicant data survey. Providing this information is **STRICTLY VOLUNTARY**. Failure to provide it will not subject you to any adverse personnel decision or action. Your cooperation is appreciated.

Please be advised that this survey is _not_ a part of your official application for employment. It will not be used in any hiring decision. The information will be used and kept confidential in accordance with applicable laws and regulations.

PLEASE PRINT

Position(s) applied for _____ Date ___ / ___ / ___

Referral Source

☐ Walk-in ☐ Government Employment Agency ☐ Private Employment Agency
☐ Employee ☐ Relative ☐ School
☐ Advertisement - Source_____ ☐ Other _____

Name of person who referred you IF APPLICABLE _____

Applicant Information

Name_____ Telephone (____) _____
       LAST   FIRST   MIDDLE

Address _____
          STREET   CITY   STATE   ZIP CODE
☐ Male ☐ Female

Please check one of the following Equal Employment Opportunity Identification Groups:

☐ White (not of Hispanic origin) ☐ Black (not of Hispanic origin) ☐ Hispanic
☐ American Indian/Alaskan Native ☐ Asian/Pacific Islander

For Administrative Use Only

Position(s) applied for ☐ Available ☐ Not Available
Other positions considered for _____

_____

Hired ☐ Yes ☐ No
Position hired for _____ Date of hire ___ / ___ / ___

From the EEO job classifications listed below, which one best describes the position filled?
☐ Officials and Managers ☐ Sales Workers ☐ Operatives (semi-skilled)
☐ Professionals ☐ Office and Clerical Workers ☐ Laborers (unskilled)
☐ Technicians ☐ Craft Workers (skilled) ☐ Service Workers

Notes _____

_____

Completed by _____ Date ___ / ___ / ___

FRIENDLY FORMS ® Call toll free 800-999-9111 to reorder Application for Employment (Long Form) #R5A-0501 D
© 1992 G. Neil Companies, P.O. Box 450939, Sunrise, FL 33345-0939. Printed in U.S.A. (1/95)
G. Neil Companies assumes no responsibility for the employer's use of this form or any decision the employer makes
which may violate local, state or federal law. By selling this form, G. Neil Companies is not giving legal advice.

FIGURE 8-8(B) LONG APPLICATION FORM (CONTINUED)

Employment History

Provide the following information for your past and current employers, assignments or volunteer activities, starting with the most recent (use additional sheets if necessary). Explain any gaps in employment in comments section below.

EMPLOYER	TELEPHONE ( )	DATES EMPLOYED		SUMMARIZE THE TYPE OF WORK PERFORMED AND JOB RESPONSIBILITIES
		FROM	TO	
ADDRESS				
JOB TITLE		HOURLY RATE/SALARY STARTING		
IMMEDIATE SUPERVISOR AND TITLE		$	PER	
REASON FOR LEAVING		HOURLY RATE/SALARY FINAL		
MAY WE CONTACT FOR REFERENCE? ☐ YES ☐ NO ☐ LATER		$	PER	
EMPLOYER	TELEPHONE ( )	DATES EMPLOYED		SUMMARIZE THE TYPE OF WORK PERFORMED AND JOB RESPONSIBILITIES
		FROM	TO	
ADDRESS				
JOB TITLE		HOURLY RATE/SALARY STARTING		
IMMEDIATE SUPERVISOR AND TITLE		$	PER	
REASON FOR LEAVING		HOURLY RATE/SALARY FINAL		
MAY WE CONTACT FOR REFERENCE? ☐ YES ☐ NO ☐ LATER		$	PER	
EMPLOYER	TELEPHONE ( )	DATES EMPLOYED		SUMMARIZE THE TYPE OF WORK PERFORMED AND JOB RESPONSIBILITIES
		FROM	TO	
ADDRESS				
JOB TITLE		HOURLY RATE/SALARY STARTING		
IMMEDIATE SUPERVISOR AND TITLE		$	PER	
REASON FOR LEAVING		HOURLY RATE/SALARY FINAL		
MAY WE CONTACT FOR REFERENCE? ☐ YES ☐ NO ☐ LATER		$	PER	
EMPLOYER	TELEPHONE ( )	DATES EMPLOYED		SUMMARIZE THE TYPE OF WORK PERFORMED AND JOB RESPONSIBILITIES
		FROM	TO	
ADDRESS				
JOB TITLE		HOURLY RATE/SALARY STARTING		
IMMEDIATE SUPERVISOR AND TITLE		$	PER	
REASON FOR LEAVING		HOURLY RATE/SALARY FINAL		
MAY WE CONTACT FOR REFERENCE? ☐ YES ☐ NO ☐ LATER		$	PER	

Comments INCLUDING EXPLANATION OF ANY GAPS IN EMPLOYMENT _____

_____

Skills and Qualifications - Summarize any special training, skills, licenses and/or certificates that may qualify you as being able to perform job-related functions in the position for which you are applying.

_____

_____

_____

FIGURE 8-8(B) LONG APPLICATION FORM (CONTINUED)

I understand that if I am employed, any misrepresentation or material omission made by me on this application will be sufficient cause for cancellation of this application or immediate discharge from the employer's service, whenever it is discovered.

I give the employer the right to contact and obtain information from all references, employers, educational institutions and to otherwise verify the accuracy of the information contained in this application. I hereby release from liability the employer and its representatives for seeking, gathering and using such information and all other persons, corporations or organizations for furnishing such information.

The employer does not unlawfully discriminate in employment and no question on this application is used for the purpose of limiting or excusing any applicant from consideration for employment on a basis prohibited by local, state or federal law.

This application is current for only 60 days. At the conclusion of this time, if I have not heard from the employer and still wish to be considered for employment, it will be necessary to fill out a new application.

If I am hired, I understand that I am free to resign at any time, with or without cause and without prior notice, and the employer reserves the same right to terminate my employment at any time, with or without cause and without prior notice, except as may be required by law. This application does not constitute an agreement or contract for employment for any specified period or definite duration. I understand that no representative of the employer, other than an authorized officer, has the authority to make any assurances to the contrary. I further understand that any such assurances must be in writing and signed by an authorized officer.

I understand it is this company's policy not to refuse to hire a qualified individual with a disability because of that person's need for a reasonable accommodation as required by the ADA.

I also understand that if I am hired, I will be required to provide proof of identity and legal work authorization.

I represent and warrant that I have read and fully understand the foregoing and seek employment under these conditions.

Signature of Applicant _____ Date _____ / _____ / _____

Guidelines for completing an application are the following:

➤   Complete the application in ink or on the typewriter. Neatly print everything except your signature. Sign it legibly; it may be the only writing sample they have from you, and they expect it to be your best work. If you find it necessary to change something on your application, draw one line through the old word(s) and initial the change. Do not use white out or scratch it out so much that you can't read the information you are replacing. In fact, it may be worth starting the application over again. Sometimes you can ask for two applications, filling out the first one for practice. If you can't get two copies, make a copy of the one you receive and fill it out first.

➤   Answer every question. If you do not know the answer or if it does not apply to you, print "N/A" or not applicable in the space provided or draw a line. This will indicate to the reviewer that the space was intentionally left blank.

➤   If dates or salaries from previous jobs are requested and you do not remember, say "approximately" next to the amount you write in (or "unknown" if you can't remember at all) in the space provided. That way, the person reviewing the application will know that it was not an oversight or attempt to conceal information. It will also buy you time to get more detailed information if necessary. Get the information as soon as possible.

➤   Furnish complete addresses and phone numbers, including area code and zip codes, for yourself, former employers, and/or references that you might list. If not, the application could be returned to you as incomplete and could delay your interview or start-to-work date. It also could affect the prospective employer's opinion of you, who may choose to locate another job seeker who is more detail oriented.

➤   Have a specific job title or classification for "Desired Position." The employer knows if the company has another position that you are qualified to take and will probably be able to offer it to you in the event that the company does not have the position available for which you are applying. Even if you will accept any job that the employer offers you, "anything" is not a very good answer to "employment desired." If you are concerned that the employer not view your application too narrowly, write "preferred" before the specific job title or classification that you write down.

➤   Keep a prepared list of former employers, references, or any other address you might need to list. It will not only enable you to complete the application properly, it will also send a clear message that you are well organized and serious about their company (two qualities that interviewers are always seeking). Often you will need to fill out the application on the spot. If you have the information handy, you are at an advantage. Keep a sample, completed application in your portfolio to use as a reference.

Speaking of references, a credible reference is one that the company can trust to tell the truth, has nothing to gain by giving you a good report, is not a relative, has a good reputation, and is easily accessible, such as a:

➤ Former instructor or teacher

➤ Former employer or coworker who knows your knowledge and work ethics

➤ Person who is known in the community or known for having an expertise in your particular field

➤ Friend who is already in business

➤ Person who has known you for many years who is not related to you

One of the reasons to develop a rapport with your employers and/or instructors is because they will be writing letters on your behalf. Help them out by letting them get to know you personally and understand your strengths. An example of an excellent letter of reference is Figure 8-9.

HOW DO I PUT THE PACKAGE TOGETHER?

Prepare for all contingencies. Do you have someone who has written you a reference letter? Make that letter accessible at the drop of a hat. Do you have your resume on disk? Do you have a sample cover letter ready? Each of these plan-ahead tasks can make your job simpler when it comes time to apply for an internship or job that interests you a great deal.

Jennifer Moe, a student editor applicant, prepared her application quickly and efficiently. In Figure 8-10, we show you her entire package—cover letter, resume, and a letter of reference.

HOW SHOULD I APPLY FOR POSITIONS?

Now that you have the information in your mind and on paper that belongs in your resume, cover letters, and applications, think about ways to send out what you have:

➤ **Personal Referrals.** If you have contacts inside the company, interview them before the company interviews you. Ask them about the company culture and exactly what skills are important to them. There are many buzzwords that are helpful in generating an interview if you put them in your resume.

....

GONZAGA UNIVERSITY

COMMUNICATION ARTS DEPARTMENT

November 13, 1996

To Whom It May Concern:

I am pleased to write an extremely enthusiastic letter for Raymona Baldwin. Raymona worked for me in the Communication Arts Department for two years. She was also a student in two of my communication classes—Speech 101 and Interpersonal and Small Group Communication.

Raymona is an extremely bright, dedicated young lady who excels at whatever she does. Three of us were completing a textbook on Interpersonal Communication. Raymona was a tremendous help as she copy-edited galley proofs for the book. She was a most conscientious editor.

I am aware she is a journalism major and know that she is an excellent writer herself. She loves journalism and everything associated with it.

Raymona is very mature and responsible. I could give her any job with the assurance that it would get done with thoroughness and skill. I never had to worry about her completing assignments.

Finally, she has excellent communication skills. She establishes a warm rapport with everyone she meets. She is also a very good listener. Raymona may come across at first as somewhat shy, but I can assure you she is excellent with people.

In summary then, I can give Raymona Baldwin the highest endorsement. I am confident she will do very well in any job she is hired for.

Sincerely,

Harry Hazel

Harry Hazel, Professor
Communication Arts
Gonzaga University

SPOKANE, WASHINGTON 99258-0001 • (509) 328-4220

....

FIGURE 8-10(A) ....

Beth M. Bollinger
505 West Riverside, Suite 500
Spokane, WA 99201

Jennifer Anne Moe
N. 1104 Dakota
Spokane, Washington. 99202

December 2, 1996

Ms. Bollinger:

I received notice of your student intern position via a flyer distributed to all the members of the student news publication of Gonzaga University, the <u>Gonzaga Bulletin</u>. As paid internships are doubly valuable for both their experience and provision of funds, I am doubly interested in the position you are offering.

I have included a copy of a story I wrote for the latest issue of Code magazine. Code magazine was founded the summer of 1995 in an overpriced New York apartment by lead man Lou R. Maxon, III and his cohort Stephen E. Schottman. Mr. Maxon, a former fellow staff member of the Gonzaga Bulletin, introduced me to his brain child fall semester 1996. Since that time, I have been an avid reader of Code and became a contributor and editor with the publication of issue #5 last August.

In my spare time last summer, I held an internship position with the Rocky Mountain Elk Foundation (RMEF) at its world headquarters in Missoula, Montana. Along with acquiring a proficiency in envelope stuffing, filing, and copy making, I had the opportunity to edit manuscripts, contribute three articles to <u>Wapiti</u>—the RMEF's quarterly member newspaper—and write a nationally distributed news release. I have enclosed a copy of a manuscript I edited along with the reply letter I wrote that critiques the author's submission.

I hope these materials will allow you to see the wide range of writing and editing skills I have acquired over the years and determine whether or not they are skills adequate for the position you have open.

Please feel free to contact me at 509.555.1234, ext. 4247 if you would like additional information on anything contained herein.

Cordially,

Jennifer Anne Moe

<u>Career objective:</u>
to use my writing and editing skills to provide the public with views of the world

....

FIGURE 8-10(B)

Jennifer Anne Moe

N. 1104 Dakota
Spokane, Washington. 99202
509.555.1234, ext. 4247

<u>Education:</u>

Aug. 1994-present
- *Gonzaga University; Spokane, Washington*
pursuing a degree in Journalism complemented by an English minor; diploma will be conferred May 1998 or earlier

<u>Experience:</u>

Nov. 1996-present
- *Senior Editor, <u>Code Magazine</u>;*
submit articles and photography for publication, organize <u>Code</u> distribution in Mont. and Spokane, Wash., discover new writers, edit new writer submissions, assist as needed in editing new submissions for webzine <u>Printed Matter</u>

Fall 1996-present
- *Features Editor, <u>Gonzaga Bulletin</u>;*
create story ideas, discover new writers, review submissions, edit submissions for print, write articles for Features and other sections of the <u>Bulletin</u>, design and layout features pages

Summer 1996-Nov.1996
- *Managing Editor, <u>Code Magazine</u>;*
contributed article for Sassy issue #6, managed <u>Code</u> distribution in Mont., discovered new writers, edited submissions, promoted <u>Code</u> in Mont. distribution area

- *Work study/intern, Rocky Mountain Elk Foundation; stuffed envelopes, filed, reorganized magazine library, wrote a news release, edited copy for <u>Bugle</u> and <u>Wapiti</u>, contributed three articles published in the fall issue of <u>Wapiti</u>, contributed to department evaluation and made recommendations for its future, edited website for content and design*

Spring 1996
- *Executive West Coast Editor, <u>Code Magazine</u>; contributed article for Job issue #5, set up <u>Code</u> distribution in Missoula, Mont., promoted <u>Code</u> through radio spots and submission for review*

- *Art direction, <u>The Blue Marble</u>, fifth edition; created publication templates, taught fellow students the basics of layout and design using QuarkXPress, designed cover and table of contents, set style guidelines, aided in production as needed*

- *Assistant Opinion Editor, <u>Gonzaga Bulletin</u>; solicited opinion writers, reviewed submissions, edited selections, laid out letters to the editor, fought to keep opinions from being censored, contributed opinion as a member of the staff editorial board*

Fall 1995
- *Opinion Columnist, <u>Gonzaga Bulletin</u>; submitted opinions for print almost every week mainly on topics of social justice or responsibility*

<u>Computer Skills:</u>
- *QuarkXPress*
- *Microsoft Word 5.1*

- *ClarisWorks 3.0*
- *Word Perfect 5.1, 6.0*

- *Pagemaker 5.0*

<u>Career objective:</u>
*to use my writing and editing skills
to provide the public
with views of the world
they may not normally see,
experience, or realize.*

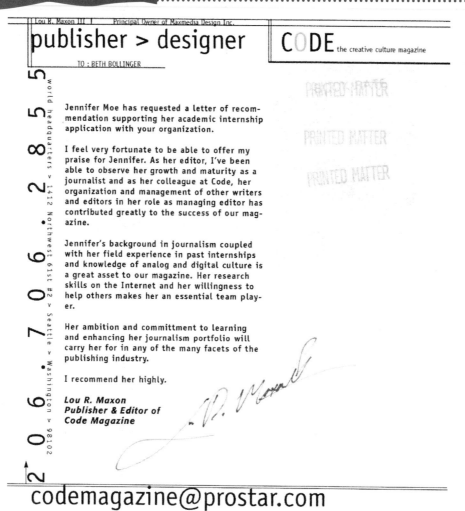

FIGURE 8-10(C)

Lou R. Maxon III   Principal Owner of Maxmedia Design Inc.

publisher > designer

CODE the creative culture magazine

TO : BETH BOLLINGER

Jennifer Moe has requested a letter of recommendation supporting her academic internship application with your organization.

I feel very fortunate to be able to offer my praise for Jennifer. As her editor, I've been able to observe her growth and maturity as a journalist and as her colleague at Code, her organization and management of other writers and editors in her role as managing editor has contributed greatly to the success of our magazine.

Jennifer's background in journalism coupled with her field experience in past internships and knowledge of analog and digital culture is a great asset to our magazine. Her research skills on the Internet and her willingness to help others makes her an essential team player.

Her ambition and committment to learning and enhancing her journalism portfolio will carry her for in any of the many facets of the publishing industry.

I recommend her highly.

Lou R. Maxon
Publisher & Editor of
Code Magazine

world headquarters v 1412 Northwest 61st #2 v Seattle v Washington v 98102

2 0 6 . 7 0 6 . 2 8 5 5

PRINTED MATTER

PRINTED MATTER

PRINTED MATTER

codemagazine@prostar.com

> **Newspaper or Trade Magazine Ads.** The hiring companies will put certain characteristics in their ads that are important to them. They put them in the ad to attract a certain type of applicant. If you have any of the special technical words that are in the ad, be sure to emphasize them in your resume or cover letter. It may be the difference in getting a "come in and interview call" or not. Check out the sample ads on the next page.

> **Professional Recruiter.** If you go through placement agencies, make up questions for your interview with them. Ask them specific questions relating to what the company or corporation that has hired them to find candidates is seeking. They have a specific job posting from the Human Resources Department with qualities listed. Ask what those qualities are and what unique skills the last person they placed possessed. Remember, if they don't place someone with the company,

they don't get a commission. In other words, it is to their advantage if you make a good impression.

➤ Cold Calls. These are risky. If you walk into companies cold without knowing if they are hiring or not, you are taking a chance that you will be categorized before you have an opportunity to create that specialized resume just for them. One idea: talk to the receptionist about the kinds of positions they have been hiring. Ask if there is a job posting and if you may see it. Even if it is an internal job posting for employees only, it will give you an idea of the skills for which the company is searching. If you can start up a friendly conversation, the receptionist may not know what skills the Human Resources Department is looking for but will probably be aware of the new hires and their job titles. That little piece of information could be an advantage to you over other applicants. If nothing else works, put your best foot forward and emphasize the most unique, impressive, hardest-to-find skill you possess on your resume. What makes you special?

Using the telephone in the job-seeking process is important, however. It's just not as effective when your telephone calling is done without any contacts to the company or specific individual you're calling. Go back to Chapter 6 on networking for ideas on how to make your telephone contacts work for you.

SUMMARY

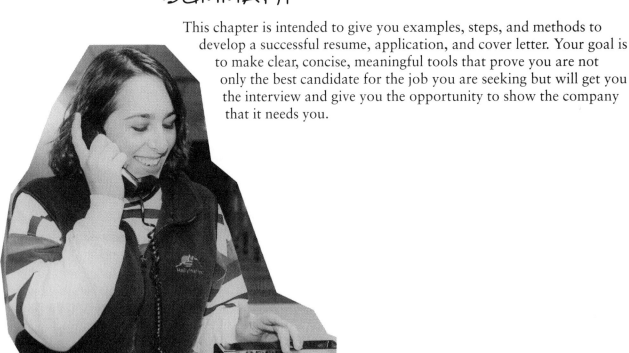

This chapter is intended to give you examples, steps, and methods to develop a successful resume, application, and cover letter. Your goal is to make clear, concise, meaningful tools that prove you are not only the best candidate for the job you are seeking but will get you the interview and give you the opportunity to show the company that it needs you.

ASKING QUESTIONS AND GETTING ANSWERS

1. **Planning Your Resume.** You need to think through the information that will help attract a prospective employer. As you think about your resume, jot down the following information in outline form. Later you can rearrange it into a proper format. Use this as your plan, and it will write itself.

RESUME INFORMATION

I. Personal Information

A. Name_____

B. Address_____

_____

C. Home Phone_____

D. Message Phone _____

II. Objective (Whether professional, technical, administrative, managerial, or special title, don't leave your intention to guesswork.)

Objective:_____

_____

_____

III. Summary of Qualities (What are your top three strengths? Your top three skills?)

Strength #1_____

Strength #2_____

Strength #3_____

Skill #1_____

Skill #2_____

Skill #3_____

IV. Education

University or college _____

City/State _____

Degree Received _____

Years Attended or Graduation Date (if not degreed) _____

_____

"Specialty" Skills and/or Courses Taken_____

_____

Hardware/Software Computer Skills_____

_____

Activities _____

_____

Honors Received _____

_____

V. Experience (Chronology of your work experience—remember if you gained valuable knowledge in a non-relevant position, highlight the specific knowledge or experience gained.)

Most Recent Job

Name of Company _____

City/State Location_____

Dates of Employment (Month/Year to Month/Year)_____

Job Title _____

Describe What You Did/Do _____

_____

Accomplishments _____

_____

Advancements or promotions _____

_____

Job Prior to Your Most Recent Job

Name of Company _____

City/State Location _____

Dates of Employment (Month/Year to Month/Year)_____

Job Title _____

Describe What You Did _____

_____

Accomplishments _____

_____

Advancements or promotions _____

_____

VI. Military

Starting Rank _____

Ending Rank _____

Awards/Commendations _____

VII. Professional Associations or Clubs, Extracurricular Activities, Community Involvement, Publications

_____

_____

VIII. Certifications

_____

_____

IX. Other Comments or Accomplishments

_____

_____

2. **Drafting Your Cover Letter.** Put together your own sample cover letter. Get an ad or other printed job description to work from. What skills do you have that will help you perform well in that job? Does your resume reflect the skills you need? Draft a letter that emphasizes your strengths for that position. It may be that your practical skills do not match the job description. If that's the case, then look

back to your *transferable skills*—your ability to communicate, be a leader, be a team member, and so on—and emphasize those. In drafting your letter, refer back to the sample letter shown in Figure 8-7.

_____

_____

_____

_____

_____

_____

_____

_____

_____

_____

COLLABORATIVE LEARNING AND TEAM-BUILDING SKILLS

Building a Resume Together. In groups of three, imagine that you run a small business and are looking for a new office manager who can do everything from answer telephones to balance the business accounts. What will you be looking for in evaluating resumes, cover letters and applications? Why?

_____

_____

_____

_____

_____

_____

_____

_____

LONG-TERM PLANNING: KEY TO YOUR PERSONAL PORTFOLIO

Drafting the Resume. Now that you have filled out the sections regarding your background, it's time to actually design your resume. Put together two different resumes that best fit you. Look at the samples in the chapter for guidance. Print out the resumes and show them to three friends for feedback. Make changes as necessary.

STUDENT QUESTION

Nicole Bauer, student at Washington State University in Pullman, Washington

Nicole is majoring in the very competitive profession of broadcast communications. She doesn't have a lot of experience in this area, and she won't have her internship until next summer. She is going to take a Spanish class and spend a semester in Costa Rica to learn Spanish, but she feels like her resume looks pretty bland. She has had to take jobs to earn money, like waitressing during the summer, that she feels won't help her on her resume. She went to a seminar on job hunting for broadcast journalists, and they told the students that employers in that field don't want to see regular resumes. They even told the students *not* to send regular resumes. They said that they wanted something that "catches the eye." Her question:

What can I do to have my resume stand out? What are they looking for? What's too outlandish? Do they want me to put my athletics on there? Computer skills? Things I did in high school? I'm concerned because I feel that I'm just not going to look exciting enough on paper. I'm looking forward to my internship, and I think it's going to be at a news station in a big market, so that will help. Even still, I don't know what employers want in the way of resumes.

Think about what makes you interesting, unique, and special. Don't focus on the physical aspect of the resume; whether it is white or buff colored paper is irrelevant. Employers are looking for what you have to offer, what you have done in the past that makes you who you are today, and what visions you have of yourself for the future. They want to know that you have a track record of success and that you are well-rounded academically, workwise, and personally. What you select to put on your resume should show some balance in these areas. If you don't have the balance you ideally want today, go have some additional experiences which will round you out as a person. If you have done some volunteer work, it is a big plus because it says that you care about more than your own needs and have the ability to focus on larger societal problems which need to be solved. Your Costa Rica experience sounds wonderful. Not only will you learn Spanish, but you will learn so much about different people and cultures. That makes you stand out. Employers want to know that the people they hire have a diverse mind and that they value learning about others who are different from them.

Your resume should state in one page that you have intelligence, experience and a sense of challenge. Your "intelligence" can be demonstrated by your academic record or your career progression/promotion track; your experience can come from jobs you have had like waitressing or working in fast food because of transferable skills you learned (outlined in Chapter 7); your sense of challenge can come from athletics, foreign travel, or hobbies like chess or photography. When writing your resume, ask the question: Have I described what is special about myself on this piece of paper so that a prospective employer will know how unique I am and what I have to offer?

CAREER PROFILE

JOHN BRINGMAN As senior executive recruiter with Aim Executive, John Bringman has gotten where he is in his career through the same process that he recommends to the executives he recruits—hard work, self-awareness, network development, and a dash of good fortune.

Although John has been at his job for 14 years, life has not always been secure or defined. When Bringman started college he thought he would become a dentist. After his first year of school, his father had a heart attack and it required John to change schools so he could be closer to home. He attended classes part time and worked the graveyard shift at a bank as a computer operator to pay for his tuition. It took him five and a half years to earn his degree in computer science. Instead of pursuing a computer programmer position with the bank, he changed his intended career path to a sales position.

Through a network contact, he received an offer from an executive search firm as an information systems recruiter. John had no formal sales training or experience, but his father was a salesman, and over the dinner table John had learned how to persuade, present, and promote. Although not his ideal job, John saw this new position as a stepping stone. He started in personnel placement at an "agency" search firm. "My job was to find jobs for my clients. I used a shotgun approach and mass marketed people to every company I knew; it wasn't very satisfying."

John started to look for another job after 18 months because he was unhappy and wanted a more strategic environment. While on vacation visiting his family, John learned through a friend of a recruiting position in his hometown. At the time he did not intend to pursue a career in recruiting, but to start his career in computer programming. He decided to interview for the position as a way to determine if his problem with recruiting was the job or the company. He did well in the interview and received an offer for a senior executive recruiter position; he's been there for the last 14 years and is quite satisfied. He finds his work challenging and rewarding. "You never know when your network is going to pay off, but it always pays to be prepared."

As a recruiter, John has a lot of advice for job seekers. He recommends that, with all the corporate downsizing that occurs, you should always be prepared for seeking that next job. John thinks we should view the job search as a continuous process. "Keep everything up to date: your skills, your network, and your resume." Because of the software that search firms and large employers use to sort for possible candidates, John thinks that it is imperative to update your resume with current industry vocabulary, skills, and terms. "When you're starting a new search, develop your resume from scratch. Don't just add your most recent job." John thinks that this approach allows a resume to sound fresh, and it is easier to incorporate the "hot phrases and acronyms" that will bring your resume to the top of the headhunter's pile.

Interviewing:
Preparation and Outcomes

Watch an expert interviewer like Katie Couric on NBC's *Today* Show. She has a set of questions already planned. She works to make her guest feel at ease but is unafraid to ask the tough questions in the more controversial interviews. She also is not afraid to ask the same question twice if the interviewee ducked the tough question the first time.

Now think of the expert interviewees that Katie Couric and other journalists interview all the time. They seem to be anticipating the questions. They probably are, since they know the types of things they'll be asked. But they do more than just anticipate the questions; they also give answers that they seem to have thought through, even before hearing the question. The best interviewees are those who are able to make their "rehearsed" answers seem natural.

Unlike Katie Couric, most employers do not conduct interviews as a way of life. Thus, of all the various selection criteria available to employers, interviewing is probably the least effective but most highly used technique. Interviewing is extremely subjective, and the interviewers may overlook all other more scientific methods because they may like to go with their gut instincts. Their instincts may not serve them well since they may not have gotten to the heart of the matter during the interview. Nevertheless, the interview ends up being key.

You, on the other hand, can choose to be the expert interviewee. If you, as a job seeker, are well prepared, then you will not only be ready for the interview, but you will also make a good impression on the interviewer and increase your chances of being selected. Preparation is the key to successful interviewing. Therefore, get prepared. Then get psyched. Figure out the questions that are likely to be asked and the answers that need to be given, and get ready to ensure success during the interview process.

Sometimes you may feel like just a number in the process, so it's up to you to make the most out of the process. Cindy Parker, who now works for a large advertising agency on the West Coast, remembers her interview process to get a job. She thought it was a "phenomenal" experience to have so many interviews, and she believes she benefited from the experience. It made her identify who she was and what she had to offer. Cindy had a strategy for the interviews: "Write down a huge list of questions—general, specific, and random questions—and then write the answers down. Think about what things cause concern on your resume and what things attract interest."

She thinks that it was important for her to be herself and to be completely comfortable—and to do that, she had to be fully prepared.

You can be prepared for your interviews like Cindy was. The three steps to preparing for an interview are: first, make a plan; second, follow through with the plan and make a positive impression; and third, follow up after the interview.

STEP ONE: HOW DO I MAKE A PLAN?

Preparing for an interview is just like any other assignment you have had at school, in your job, or in your personal life. First, sit down and prepare a plan of attack. If you stumble into the interview haphazardly, your results will be the same. Break your interview process into small, manageable pieces and get started. If you can have a few days advance notice before your interview, it will certainly help; however, in the event you don't have any time between that telephone call asking you to come in for an interview and the actual interview appointment, make as many preparations in advance as possible. Use Figure 9-1 to organize your planning.

Getting to Know the Prospective Employer

There are many excellent resource books in the library that can help you find the information for Figure 9-1 and much more. If you want to consider positions all over the United States, a periodical you might want to purchase is *The Wall Street Journal*. *Standard & Poor's* is a good resource for financial information about a particular company. *Fortune* comes out annually with the top 500 and 1000 companies in the United States. Most companies have sites on the Web that can be great sources of information. You may try simply typing the company's name into a search engine and see

FIGURE 9-1	ADVANCED PLANNING FOR INTERVIEWING

Know the Prospective Employer

- Financial stability, recent track record, projects
- Locations (cities, states, international, etc.)
- Corporate culture
  - Current and future projects/plans
  - Career paths—opportunity to grow in skill or rank
- Rules about
  - Dress codes
  - Flex time/overtime/on call/pager
  - Nepotism
  - Other
- Officers, alumni of what college/university, degrees, experience
- Benefits/holidays/sick leave/vacations, etc.

Prepare Your Physical Appearance

- What to wear?
  - Does your interview outfit still fit? (Instead of wearing it to work, keep interview suit or dress in reserve so it can be ready.)
  - Is it appropriately styled for the corporate culture?
  - Is it clean? (Keep it clean in a garment bag in the closet; check for loose buttons.)
  - Are shoes polished?
- Hair cut/set
- Grooming: facial hair, nails, eyes, breath
- Appropriate jewelry and watch
- Briefcase/portfolio up to the task? (If you don't have one, borrow one.)
  - Have a nice gold, silver, or black pen (not plastic).

Mental Planning

- Do you have a list of what *you* want to find out/accomplish during the interview?
  1.
  2.
  3.
- Have you prepared—and practiced saying out loud—a list of answers to anticipated questions? (Check Table 9-1.)
  1.
  2.
  3.
- Have you prepared a list of questions? (Check Table 9-2.)

- Can you talk about the company? (List important facts and questions you might want to ask.)
  1.
  2.
  3.
- Do you have a positive, winning mental attitude?
  1.
  2.
  3.
- Have you made a practice run on how to get to the interview? (Be no more than 10 or 15 minutes early, and *definitely* don't be late.)

what turns up! Also, revisiting Chapter 5 of this book will give you good ideas on how to obtain the information you're looking for here.

Another great resource for finding out about a prospective employer is a current employee. By talking to an employee, you will gather information concerning employee satisfaction, whether the company is employee oriented, and whether it is perceived to be a stable, profitable, or growing company. Most people love to talk about their company and their position within the company; therefore, they will be eager to talk to you and give you formal as well as informal information about the company.

Physical Appearance

The old saying "You only get one chance to make a first impression" is even more important during the interview process. If you make a bad first impression during the interview, you will probably not get another chance

to redeem yourself. Additionally, it is the perception of interviewers that prospects will be on their best behavior and look their best during the interview. Hence, you need to be impeccably groomed and dressed for your interview. If you come to the interview disheveled, it is a clear message that you will come to work that way if hired.

You need to prepare for an impeccable appearance well in advance of the actual interview. Because you want to look crisp, your interview suit should be fresh from the cleaners. When you know an interview is coming up, have the suit cleaned and pressed and hang it in the closet in the cleaning bag until the interview. That way there are no mistakes. Make sure you have a recent but not brand new hair cut or set. Make sure your shoes are polished the night before. Don't wait for the morning of the interview because you don't want polish to stain your hands or nails.

If you wear jewelry, make sure it is simple and discreet. Any watch that you wear should be a dress watch (not a sports watch or digital or plastic—no Mickey Mouse watches for a job interview unless you are interviewing with Disney World). Leave your jeweled or diamond watches at home in the safe. They are too ornate for the office, much less the interview. And take all those fancy earrings out of your ears and nose!

A worn briefcase might show character and hard work, but you do not want all the attention to go to the briefcase instead of what you have to say. Therefore, if your briefcase has too much character, is plastic instead of leather, or is fabric, either get a new one that is leather and simple or if that is not practical at this time, borrow one from a friend for the interview. A thin briefcase or portfolio is all that is needed. Women should put their billfold and whatever identification they may need in their briefcase in order to keep from lugging around both a briefcase and a purse. Also, black, brown, charcoal gray, and maroon are the only briefcase colors that yell "hire me." The others either don't shout at all or they shout "look at me," which is not your intention.

Mental Planning

Now that you have researched the company thoroughly and look wonderful, it is time to positively prepare mentally for the interview.

> ➤ **Company Data.** You have read everything you could find about the company and know almost as much about the company as the interviewer; the next task is to develop a list of pertinent, positive information about the company that you can discuss.

Note: If you know of negative information or publicity regarding the company, you may not want to bring it up during your interview—especially during an initial interview. As important as the "real" story may be to you, putting an interviewer on the spot in the middle of the interview may just be too awkward. Think of alternatives to dealing with your questions: do you have a friend who works at the company who may be able to help you answer your questions confidentially? Is there research you can conduct that can get to the heart of the matter? Also, you may find that a company with negative publicity often will voluntarily raise the issue at some time during the interview process. Patience could bring just rewards. Blurting out your concerns too soon, however, can result in some awkward moments and most likely will result in a notation on your interview file.

> ➤ **Anticipated Questions.** Compile a list of questions that you are likely to be asked. Add to that list the questions that you were asked on your last interview. Ask your friends and professional recruiters, if you are using one, questions that they have been asked before.

Your purpose during the interview is to sell yourself to the prospective employer and be able to answer questions that are asked of you in a short, concise manner that will evoke further questions. In this manner, your answer can guide the interviewer to the topics that you can answer most comfortably. When responding to a question, think about what the interviewer is really trying to discover about you.

Sometimes the anticipated question is an open-ended one about who you are or why you applied for this job. Be ready to answer that open-ended question by preparing a description of yourself, your skills, and your abilities ahead of time. This description can last anywhere from one to five minutes, depending on the time that the interviewer has available.

By preparing for anticipated questions ahead of time, you can insert your own agenda into the interview process. Think through what key pieces of information you would like the interviewer to have about you. For instance, if you have a talent for public speaking, think of how you can tell the interviewer about it.

There are several questions that you can expect to hear in an interview no matter what position you are seeking and who the interviewer is. These questions are not only revealing, effective data-gathering questions, they are tricky, and you should prepare answers in advance in order not to look stumped. Table 9-1 gives some of these standard questions and some possible answers. Of course, every answer will be different according to the background of the individual; however, some thought needs to be given to these questions, and answers for each need to be developed. Even though the answers will not be the same as someone else's, they will force you to think of what is true for you and how you should answer the question if it is asked. Remember, formulate short, concise answers.

TABLE 9-1   POSSIBLE INTERVIEW QUESTIONS AND ANSWERS

POSSIBLE DIFFICULT QUESTIONS	ISSUE INTERVIEWER IS TRYING TO ADDRESS	POSSIBLE ANSWERS
"Why did you leave your last job?"	Trying to determine if there were any problems and understand your motivations in your career path.	Want more challenge; moved; downsizing; no room for advancement.
"What are your strengths?"	This actually can be the interviewer's way of trying to give you a chance to shine.	Seize the moment. Answer this with a skill that can be used in the job you're seeking, including a "transferable" skill like problem-solving, etc.
"What are your weaknesses?"	Trying to get an idea of what you think of yourself; who better will know your weaknesses than you? Trying to determine if you have a realistic sense of who you are.	Try to turn this into a positive like "I sometimes get so involved I lose track of time." Or bring up a skill that does not involve this job, like "I type with two fingers only." Or identify a weakness which you are correcting into a strength: "I don't consider myself to be the world's greatest speaker, but I recently joined Toastmasters and the six speeches I've made have increased my confidence a lot."
"What are your strengths and weaknesses?"	Again, do you have self-knowledge? Can you maximize your strengths and minimize your weaknesses?	Often our strengths are also our weaknesses, and we can phrase them that way. For instance, "My strength of perseverance is also my weakness because I can sometimes get too single-minded." (For "and" questions, be sure you answer both parts of the question.)

TABLE 9-1   POSSIBLE INTERVIEW QUESTIONS AND ANSWERS (CONTINUED)

POSSIBLE DIFFICULT QUESTIONS	ISSUE INTERVIEWER IS TRYING TO ADDRESS	POSSIBLE ANSWERS
"Tell me about a time when your boss was dissatisfied with the job you did."	Trying to learn more about weaknesses and how you deal with pressure and criticism. This is a good question because it allows for storytelling without value judgments on your part.	Describe a time when you had a bad experience but you have since corrected the incident—a learning experience. Try to use an incident that you turned around.
"What is your ideal job?"	Trying to get an idea of where and how you want to grow in your career; your answer should also reflect your strengths and weaknesses.	Discuss jobs that use talents and skills related to the job you're interviewing for. Make your answer task-oriented rather than benefit-oriented. Be honest—what is your ideal job, anyway?
"Why should I hire you?"	This sounds like a no-win, set up question. Prove yourself! Actually, it can just be an honest inquiry: what makes you different? What makes you *you*?	Everyone will be willing to do the job so give an answer relating to what makes you special. Talk about positive qualities like tireless energy, self-starter, team-player, etc. Be prepared to give believable examples.
"How do you feel about detail?"	Exploring a skill that is necessary in virtually every job—important but not the glorious part of work.	Talk about the detail you have used in setting up a project or job that you have been assigned. You don't have to say whether you hate it or love it; just give an instance of using it.
"What if you have to work overtime or another shift on occasion?"	They are questioning your flexibility and reliability; your team player mentality.	Talk about being a team player and wanting to do what you can to get the job done. If you can work the overtime, tell them that. If you have a shift preference, indicate it.
"What is special about you?"	Do you have a unique vision for yourself?	Think of what makes you special and say something straightforward: "I am creative, dedicated, and determined to make a difference on my team in your company." Be prepared to give believable examples.
"How is your attendance—any problems?"	Anticipating where trouble may lie with a new employee who otherwise appears to be responsible.	If you have had a problem, try to present a solution to that problem or a good reason (like surgery or illness). Let them know that it's behind you.

TABLE 9-1 POSSIBLE INTERVIEW QUESTIONS AND ANSWERS (CONTINUED)

POSSIBLE DIFFICULT QUESTIONS	ISSUE INTERVIEWER IS TRYING TO ADDRESS	POSSIBLE ANSWERS
"Name something you didn't like about your last boss."	Trying to identify conflicts with authority.	Try not to complain about your old boss. Did he or she have a bad habit (like smoking) that you can talk about? Be honest, but also emphasize that you had a good working relationship with your old boss.
"How would your coworkers describe you?"	Identifying skills again, as well as personality traits. Are you easy or difficult to get along with?	If you are widely known for a positive work trait, use that trait; otherwise say something about good work ethics, hard-working team player, etc. Ask your coworkers how they would describe you for some good insights.
"Tell me a difficult problem you've had at work."	Looking for how you identify problems as well as how you solve them.	Think of a work-related problem and how you solved it. If possible, stay away from problems with a boss or coworker that might indicate personality problems.
"What contribution or accomplishment are you most proud of? Why?"	Again, trying to identify skills and abilities to complete projects. In many ways, trying to let you shine. What is the magnitude of your contribution?	Think through one or two answers to this question. Why did your accomplishment make you proud? What did you learn?
"What do you do in your spare time?"	Trying to get to know you personally. Are you an interesting/inspiring person? Do you have a sense of balance in your life?	Think of your hobbies. Did you record any on your resume? Be honest—don't start talking about bookkeeping if you've never done it because luck will have it that your interviewer will be an expert on it.

➤ Questions for *You* to Ask. At the end of the interview, you are looking the interviewer in the eye, feeling good about the way the day went, when the interviewer asks, "Are there any questions?" You freeze; you knew it was coming, but things have gone so well that you have completely forgotten your list. Don't say, "No, that just about does it" or "I think you've covered everything." You are depriving the interviewer of showing that he or she can answer anything, and it deprives you of the opportunity to show that you have been thinking deeply about this employment opportunity. *Be prepared!* Have a list of questions prepared in advance tucked away in your portfolio. Check your list and ask one that you know he will know the answer to and that has not already been answered. See Table 9-2 for ideas.

Note: If you are interviewed by a series of people, they will all ask this dreaded question, so have enough pertinent questions developed in advance to satisfy each of them. See the end-of-chapter exercises to assist you in creating that list.

Also, remember that you are interviewing the company just as the company is interviewing you. If you get—and take—this job, you will be working with these people in this location for the majority of your waking hours, potentially for a long period of time. What do you want to know about the company to help you decide whether you want to make that kind of commitment?

TABLE 9-2   PERTINENT QUESTIONS TO ASK

- What challenges might I encounter in this position?

- Will this job be a team effort or will I be working alone?

- What are the goals of the group over the next year; in the future?

- What about the company? What are the immediate goals? What are the long-term goals?

- What about training and employee improvement? How do you feel about employees keeping up with new trends and skills?

- Who will I be leading in this position? Who will I be reporting to?

- Who is the competition for your company, and what are your strengths compared to that competition? Do you see room for improvement?

- Any new business on the horizon?

- What is your formal reporting structure? Is there a formal chain of command or communication?

- Reference any recent newspaper article you might have seen, and if it was positive, ask about it.

- What are the qualities which made the most successful person who has ever had this job excel?

- What makes this place a good place for you to work?

- If you could change anything here, what would you change?

➤ **Illegal Questions.** There is no easy answer to dealing with the illegal question. Realize that if someone *does* ask you an illegal question, it is probably by accident. In today's workplace, no one wants to risk a lawsuit to find out how old you are, inquire if you are pregnant, or ask any other personal question. If you want the job, you might want to answer the question and then, after you are hired and start to work, tell the Human Resources Department and let them handle it. You might want to make a nonthreatening joke about the question itself as a way to let the interviewer know that this is illegal ground. Of course, you also have the right to tell the interviewer that the question is illegal. The choice is yours, but keep in mind that the interviewer *probably* did not mean to tread on illegal ground. If you are interested in the job, you might want to delay being "right" until after you start to work.

STEP TWO: HOW DO I FOLLOW THROUGH WITH MY PLAN AND MAKE A POSITIVE IMPRESSION?

It is the night before the interview, you have completed your research, your clothes are ready, and your answers are completed. You have done everything that needs to be done. Don't forget to follow through.

➤ **Review Your Appearance.** Check out your clothes (open that garment bag and make sure a new crease has not materialized where it didn't belong); your shirt (if it's new, you will want to iron out the folds); and your shoes (can you see your face in the shine? Just a joke, but are they polished to the caliber of the rest of your clothes?).

➤ **Check Your Briefcase or Portfolio.** Does it have the complete package that you need for your interview—your notes, your application (if applicable), an extra copy of your resume, pens, breath mints, or anything that might keep your confidence up to its peak level? Be sure to put in your briefcase or portfolio a complete list of references (with their addresses and telephone numbers), military papers, proof of employability (such as your passport or birth certificate), and a transcript.

What? You think you will remember most of this information and don't need to write it down? Wrong! You may know the information, and you may be able to discuss it freely and openly, but you are not under the amount of pressure presently that you will be during the interview. Put your notes, the answers to your questions, and your prepared questions tucked neatly away in one part of your briefcase or portfolio. You may review and/or rearrange the information during breaks and other times you are alone to keep the appropriate information visible to you. It's okay to keep the portfolio open during the interview for note taking, so you can glance over the papers on the left-hand side from time to time. It could keep you focused and help you not get your data confused. This will be your insurance that all that important information you gathered will not be wasted by getting it mixed up or momentarily forgetting it. *Write it down!*

When they ask about questions, don't be afraid to take out your prepared list. The employer will be impressed that you were so thorough and that this job was so important to you that you went to this much trouble.

➤ **Set Your Own Agenda.** Remember that this interview is a two-way street—the company is trying to learn about you, and you are trying to learn about the company. What do you need to know when you leave the office? Be sure to ask the questions that matter to you. Also, be sure to answer issues that they may have regarding your employment, even if they do not raise the issues themselves. Perhaps they need to know that you can speak Spanish, but they don't think to ask you that. Volunteer!

➤ **Be Concise.** Just like with the resume and cover letter, you should try to be concise in your interview. Try to use action words when describing yourself. Michael Fulton trains his interns to use the S.A.R. method of interview question response. "You need to listen to each question and you respond by structuring your answer by 'S'—identifying the situation; 'A'—explaining the action you took; and 'R'—the result of the action," he says.

➤ **Let Them Know about Your Transferable Skills.** For every job, there are specific skills that you will need to have. Likewise, there are "transferable skills"—skills used in virtually every job such as leadership, teamwork, communication, and decision making—that you have. Be sure and let the employer know about your "transferable" skills. These skills are just as important in figuring out how you will fit into the company.

➤ **Be Positive AND Be Yourself.** Try to be as comfortable with yourself as possible. The purpose of the interview is to determine whether both your *skills* and your *personality* will be a fit for this office, so try to show who you are as honestly as possible. Of course, you will be nervous, especially at first. You might even mention your nervousness if you think that will help the prospective employer understand you a little better. Above all, though, think of yourself just the way you are—a worthwhile, special person who may just be the perfect person for the job being advertised.

➤ **Deal with Bad News Honestly.** Maybe you were let go from your previous job; maybe you have important child care issues that affect your availability to travel or work odd shifts. Try to be up front and positive at the same time about these difficult issues. If you get the job, you will be working with these people, and you want your relationship with them to be built on a solid foundation. Think through some answers to some of these more difficult questions so that you're not caught flat-footed and so that you can place your answers in the best light possible. Be prepared for the worst question that you think you might be asked.

➤ **DON'T Ask about Money or Benefits**, at least at the first interview. Those issues are usually handled through the Human Resources Department anyway, so a discussion of those benefits with the interviewer probably will not be fruitful. Focus on the job itself. Money and benefits will come later.

If anyone asks you what salary you expect, recruiter John Bringman recommends a number of nonspecific answers, such as

➤ What is the salary range for this position?

➤ I'm sure whatever offer your company makes will be fair for the responsibilities of the job.

➤ I'm not comfortable answering that question until I know more about the job. Salary is just one part for me to consider.

➤ I would like to discuss salary after I know what the responsibilities and challenges are.

If the employer wants more specifics, be more specific —as long as you have an idea in your mind about what would be fair and reasonable in this position. John Bringman suggests that you can answer with a range rather than a specific number.

STEP THREE: WHAT SHOULD I DO TO FOLLOW UP AFTER INTERVIEWS?

Immediately after the job interview, you should send a follow-up letter to say "Thank you for taking the time to talk to me" and reiterate your strengths and other unique qualifications for the position. If you still want the job, be clear about your interest. Don't let them think that you are not interested but just being polite. The follow-up is very important because it may mean the difference between you and all the other candidates. The follow-up letter indicates to the company that you are interested, and you have an eye for detail. See Figure 9-2, Sample Thank-You Letter. Follow-up calls also are a good idea. Send your letter after you make the call.

FIGURE 9-2   SAMPLE THANK-YOU LETTER

1234 Anystreet
Anywhere, State, Zip
(000) 777-7777

January 2, 1996

Ms. Janice Jones, Human Resources Manager
Hiring Corporation
1111 Main Street
Anywhere, State, Zip

Dear Ms. Jones:

Thank you for the opportunity to meet with you yesterday to discuss the Specific Title position. Our meeting was enjoyable and quite informative. I particularly was interested in learning about the Hiring Corporation's five-year plan.

I was very impressed with your company and am extremely interested in joining Hiring Corporation. I am confident that my experience and education are a fit with your organization, and that I could make a significant contribution to the further growth of Hiring Corporation.

Thank you again for your time and consideration.

Sincerely,

Eager Applicant

Even if you are no longer interested in the position, or you feel that the interview did not go well, a follow-up letter is a good thing to do. Think back to Chapter 6, on networking. You may decide at a later date that some of the people you met at the interview are good connections for the future. Also, you may find yourself working in the same industry as these folks, and you want them to remember you positively (even if you don't take a job with them). Finally, it's simply good manners to recognize the effort taken to interview you by following up with a thank-you note.

If you interview with a number of people, you may want to send a thank-you note to just one person—perhaps the Human Resources person, the head of the office, or the most senior person who interviewed you. If you only interviewed with two or three people, it may be worth your effort to write a thank-you note to each of them. Try to personalize the letter—what did you talk about that was especially interesting or helpful? Take the opportunity in the middle of the letter to reemphasize your strengths, state something that you feel was omitted during the interview, or emphasize something that was not discussed fully in your interview. Also, offer to be available for follow-up questions.

Summary

As you prepare to make a great impression on the people who interview you, remember your three-step approach: First, make a plan. Next, follow through with your plan and make a positive impression. Third, follow up after interviews with thank-you letters expressing your interest. If you follow this plan, you will no doubt feel prepared and ready to take on the interview—and the job.

ASKING QUESTIONS AND GETTING ANSWERS

1. **Describing Yourself.** As discussed in the chapter, often a prospective employer will begin an interview by asking you to describe yourself or describe why you want the job. In the first space below, design a one-minute speech in which you describe yourself, your skills, and your interests, and why you want this job. In the second space below, design a three-minute speech with those same goals in mind.

ONE-MINUTE DESCRIPTION

_____

_____

_____

_____

_____

THREE-MINUTE DESCRIPTION

_____

_____

_____

_____

_____

_____

2. **Designing Questions and Answers for Your Interview.** As Table 9-1 demonstrates, there are many questions that you will need to anticipate when getting ready for a job interview. You should also think ahead about the questions that may arise regarding the specific work done by the particular company where you're interviewing. Choose a company where you will be interviewing or where you would like to interview. Design five questions that you think you will be asked that are specific to that company. Next, write down what your answers would be to those questions.

Sample Question #1:_____

_____

Sample Answer #1:_____

_____

Sample Question #2:_____

_____

Sample Answer #2:_____

_____

Sample Question #3:_____

_____

Sample Answer #3:_____

_____

Sample Question #4:_____

_____

Sample Answer #4:_____

_____

Sample Question #5:_____

_____

Sample Answer #5:_____

3. **Preparing Your Own Questions.** For this same interview, prepare three questions that you want to ask. Be careful in selecting the questions. For instance, try to think of questions that the interviewer will know the answer to and that seem to seek information important to the job.

1. _____

_____

2. _____

_____

3. _____

_____

COLLABORATIVE LEARNING AND TEAM-BUILDING SKILLS

1. **Designing the Perfect Employee.** Get together with two other classmates in groups of three. Suppose you are getting ready to interview prospective employees to take over the position as supervisor in your pillow factory. The past supervisor was a tough person, unable to deal with sensitive employee issues, and as a consequence, a number of your employees quit. What qualities are you seeking in your next supervisor? What questions are you going to ask in the interview to figure out whether you've found the right person for the job?

   Qualities:_____

   _____

   Questions:_____

   _____

2. **Dealing with the Inappropriate Question.** In the same groups of three as above, think of questions that are inappropriate or illegal for an interview. Think of ways to answer those questions in a positive way. Imagine that this particular job is the one you really want and you don't want to have this exchange "blow" it for you. Brainstorm why it's a sensitive issue for you. For instance, if someone asks you if you have any children, the answer to that question can be uncomfortable for different reasons, depending on the person. A 35-year-old female with no children is concerned that she may not get the job because the employer thinks she is getting ready to get pregnant and take maternity leave. A 25-year-old female with three small children is afraid that the employer thinks she will be asking for a lot of time off to care for her children.

   a. Sensitive/Illegal Question:_____

      Why is it sensitive for you?_____

      What diplomatic answer can you give?_____

      _____

   b. Sensitive/Illegal Question:_____

      Why is it sensitive for you?_____

      What diplomatic answer can you give?_____

      _____

c. Sensitive/Illegal Question:_____

Why is it sensitive for you?_____

What diplomatic answer can you give?_____

_____

3. **Interview Day.** In groups of three, practice interviewing from the questions that are listed in Table 9-1 and designed above. One person should be the interviewee, one person should be the interviewer, and the third person should be the observer. Keep rotating until everyone has played each role. Before beginning the exercise, the interviewee should inform the other two about details of the company where the "interview" is taking place. If possible, plan this exercise ahead so that each person can come dressed for the interview. Below, fill in any notes you have for each of the three interviews.

· ·
NOTES AS INTERVIEWER
══

a. What did you like about the interviewee's responses?_____

_____

What suggestions for improvement do you have?_____

_____

b. What did you like about the interviewee's appearance?_____

_____

What suggestions for improvement do you have?_____

_____

c. What did you like about the interviewee's manner?_____

_____

What suggestions for improvement do you have?_____

_____

d. What did you like about the interviewee's questions of the

interviewer?_____

_____

What suggestions for improvement do you have?_____

_____

e. How did the interview go overall?_____

_____

What suggestions for improvement do you have overall?_____

_____

f. What did you learn about the interviewee's character?_____

_____

NOTES AS OBSERVER

a. What did you like about the interviewee's responses?_____

_____

What suggestions for improvement do you have?_____

_____

b. What did you like about the interviewee's appearance?_____

_____

What suggestions for improvement do you have?_____

_____

c. What did you like about the interviewee's manner?_____

_____

What suggestions for improvement do you have?_____

_____

d. What did you like about the interviewee's questions of the

interviewer?_____

_____

What suggestions for improvement do you have?_____

_____

e. How did the interview go overall?_____

_____

What suggestions for improvement do you have overall?_____

_____

f. What did you learn about the interviewee's character?_____

_____

· ·

NOTES AS INTERVIEWEE

a. What did you like about your responses?_____

_____

What would you do differently next time?_____

_____

b. What did you like about your appearance?_____

_____

_____

What would you do differently next time?_____

_____

c. What did you like about your manner?_____

_____

What would you do differently next time?_____

_____

d. What was the most effective question that you asked of the interviewer?_____

_____

What other questions might you ask next time?_____

_____

e. How did you feel about the interview overall?_____

_____

What would you do differently next time?_____

_____

f. Do you think you showed the interviewer important things about

your character?_____

_____

What else would you want to emphasize next time?_____

_____

LONG-TERM PLANNING: KEY TO YOUR PERSONAL PORTFOLIO

1. **Interview Day Again!** Before tackling the interviews of your future, try practicing an interview with a friend in business. Call a friend or family acquaintance who you know in the business world and ask that person to interview you. Try to choose someone who has experience interviewing people. Perhaps someone from your list of supporters in Chapter 4 or your networking list in Chapter 6 would be willing to help you out. Treat the interview seriously. Do all the research necessary to be prepared. In short, treat this interview as if it were for your dream job. If you have trouble finding someone to do the interview, ask a teacher, minister, or other person for help in finding someone to interview you. After the interview, ask the interviewer to fill out the list below:

a. What did you like about the interviewee's responses?_____

_____

What suggestions for improvement do you have?_____

_____

b. What did you like about the interviewee's appearance?_____

_____

What suggestions for improvement do you have?_____

_____

    c.   What did you like about the interviewee's manner?_____

_____

         What suggestions for improvement do you have?_____

_____

    d.   What did you like about the interviewee's questions of the interviewer?_____

_____

         What suggestions for improvement do you have?_____

_____

    e.   How did the interview go overall?_____

_____

    f.   What suggestions for improvement do you have overall?_____

_____

2. **Driving Your Own Agenda.** Think of things that you want to get across that the interviewer may not ask about, or may be too uncomfortable asking about. For instance, Patience went on a number of interviews lately in her sister's hometown. It dawned on her that the interviewers were surprised that she was looking for a job far away from her current residence, but that they were not inquiring into her personal reasons for seeking a change. She decided to explain her circumstances so that they would feel more comfortable with the idea that she could make a long-term commitment to their company.

    a.   What do you want to explain?_____

         How will you explain it?_____

_____

    b.   What do you want to explain?_____

         How will you explain it?_____

_____

STUDENT QUESTION

Brad Bauer, student at University of Alaska at Anchorage in Anchorage, Alaska

Brad plans to be a teacher. Right now, he is taking classes for that profession, and he is also training to ski in the 2002 Olympics. He worries about how to prepare for interviews for teaching jobs when he hasn't had any experience teaching yet. He is only going to student teach for one semester, so that won't give him a lot of experience in the classroom. He has thought about substitute teaching to get some experience, but he's afraid if he makes one mistake at a school, the other teachers will blacklist him for a job. He has one friend who can't get out of substitute teaching because of that. Plus, Brad's free time in college is limited because of his athletic training. He has heard that, in interviews for teaching jobs, the interviewers ask you questions about impromptu situations—like how to solve a fight between two students. Without the actual experience, Brad isn't sure what his answer should be. He wants to prepare for those kinds of questions, but he also wants his answer to be honest, not just rehearsed or plastic. His question:

What can I do to prepare and make a good impression for these interviews?

Have you ever taught skiing? Although this isn't the "classroom" experience, you will still be drawing on the same skills which are required from the best teachers: patience, a sense of being demanding and supportive, guidance, and encouragement. Sometimes our life experiences require some of the same skills that our future jobs require because we are drawn to things we enjoy.

Substitute teaching is a great idea. You will learn about other teachers, their classroom styles, likes and dislikes, and the firsthand realities of the classroom. Don't be afraid because you haven't done it before. It is just like going down a steep ski slope you've never skied before. Sure it is a challenge, but it is a fun challenge for which you are fully prepared.

The most important part of the interview process is that you come across as genuine and prepared. So you have to be *genuine and prepared*. Think about the questions they will ask, the expectations they have of the job, and why you would be terrific as a teacher. Envision yourself in a variety of classroom situations. How would you handle the apathetic students? The slow learners? The hostile parents? The students who need to be challenged most? How would you make every class interesting and dynamic for students? How would you be exemplary and stand out from other teachers? What would your students say about you five years after they had your class?

CAREER PROFILE

KATHY KARPAN   Some people say it's in the blood. However the political bug bit Kathy Karpan, it appears as though she's destined to be involved in politics throughout her life. From press secretary for a U.S. congressman to Wyoming's secretary of state to candidate for the U.S. Senate, Kathy has worked hard to help other people through her work in public office.

Kathy was born a coal miner's daughter in Rock Springs, Wyoming. She lost her mother at age 12 and made a commitment with her father that she would help raise her younger brother and sister so that the children would not be split up or sent to an orphanage. "This is a really critical thing," Kathy says. "If I were making a movie of my life, this would really be a big scene, if not maybe even an opening scene. My dad and I made a pact. Well, we all did...The terms were, 'Dad, if you'll keep us together and not ship us off, then I will cooperate in raising us and not cause any trouble and do what you say. And he said, 'Okay. We'll do it on our own.' Kathy went "from the monkey bars to the laundromat, from being a child to being a very grown-up person."

In spite of the difficulties, Kathy went on to college at the University of Wyoming. She ultimately majored in journalism. After heading a student organization for a congressional candidate, she was offered a job to work in Washington, D.C., as his press secretary. She went to law school after working as a news reporter and editor and ultimately returned to politics as Wyoming's secretary of state—an impressive feat since she is a Democrat in a historically Republican state. As Secretary of State, Kathy proposed innovative business regulations to encourage regional and national companies to relocate to Wyoming. The laws (passed by bipartisan votes) have created a lot of opportunity for the state.

Kathy's experience with interviews is on both sides. As a journalist, she learned a lot about what types of questions get good answers and what types allow the interviewee to get around delicate issues. As a politician, she knows to expect questions, so much so that she doesn't even pause when the more common ones are asked. She simply is calm and direct. She remembers what she was looking for from her interviewees when she was a journalist and she tries to respond as quickly and thoroughly as she can. Her ability to interview well (and bluntly) has resulted in her quotes landing in *Newsweek* and other national publications.

Kathy's political life has had difficulties in the recent past. She suffered a tough loss in Wyoming in 1996 when she ran an extremely close race for U.S. Senate there. She has gone back to her law practice and is planning her next steps. Even though Kathy didn't succeed at the Senate race, she is sure to keep working to effect the changes that she thinks are important.

Part 3

YOU'RE HIRED

Chapter 10

Becoming Employable and Promotable: Preparing for Change

Chapter 11

Workplace 2000: How to Be Competitive and Still Remain True to Yourself

Becoming Employable and Promotable:

Preparing for Change

Southwest Airlines has been a remarkable airline success story. How did this happen? The company began 26 years ago, when two businessmen (its founders) were sitting in an airport dealing with the inconvenience of flying around the state of Texas. One took a napkin, wrote "Houston, Dallas, San Antonio" in three spots, and drew a triangle connecting the three city names. That triangle was the beginning of building an alternative to conventional air travel that would attract the public in droves. Southwest's owners decided to identify what would set their service apart from other airlines and then began promoting that uniqueness. Southwest takes as a given things like good customer service and on-time arrival and instead focuses on being interesting and down-home. In the process, Southwest has looked to its audience (people interested in flying high frequency between cities and accommodating ever-changing schedules) and designed a business to meet the needs of its customers. Why provide inexpensive flights only for cross-continental travel to the largest cities? Southwest prides itself on "puddle-jumping"—having short flights to cities for economical fares. Why give low prices for round-trip travel only? Southwest instituted the cheap one-way fare. Why limit service to Texas businesspeople? When Southwest realized that its unique approach to air transportation was attractive to all kinds of people all over the country, it expanded its service. Southwest identified a need and filled a void. In short, Southwest made itself special.

You too can know yourself and know what you can do well within the world that you are creating for yourself. Your ability to be unique and a standout can become your trademark as you develop yourself into the best and most productive person you can be.

HOW DO I ACHIEVE MY PERSONAL BEST?

You either already are or soon will be working in jobs that help guide you along your chosen career path. If you choose to be the best you can be each step of the way, you are well on your way to being ready for each new step as it develops. Just as other airlines have followed Southwest's lead by starting to show some personality themselves, you too can be a leader among your colleagues and set the tone for being productive and innovative on the job. Being aware of where you are strong and where you need to improve necessarily makes you a more desirable employee and allows you to grow personally as well. Think of the categories that follow as life skills. Though few people are adept at all of them, becoming good at some of them is a significant accomplishment.

WHAT ARE THE BUSINESS SKILLS THAT I NEED TO HAVE?

No matter where you are or what you choose to do, there are certain skills that will help you do well in virtually any career. The "tools" for business success have been discussed throughout this book and are categorized in the paragraphs that follow. In fact, you may recall that Chapter 7's discussion of part-time jobs gave a preview of some of these universal business success skills. Focus on developing these skills as you progress in the workplace and toward your ultimate career goals. No matter how often you see them written down, you will have the best opportunity to learn their true meaning in the context of real-life situations. As you master these skills, you will have a greater chance of succeeding.

Don't fool yourself into believing that you can wait to develop these kinds of skills until you've found a "real" job—they count every step of the way. Jasper, a young administrative assistant who had just graduated from business school, was unhappy with how little he was paid. He was willing to work hard, but wanted financial reward and recognition. He chose not to attend staff meetings where all the sales managers discussed the newest products because the meetings were held early in the morning and he felt that his low pay didn't justify his making a special effort to attend. Jasper's reluctance to focus on developing basic business success skills had two negative consequences. First, he nearly wasn't hired at the office when a junior sales position finally opened up because the head of the office was afraid he wasn't willing to work hard in general. Perhaps more detrimental for Jasper, however, was his failure to attack all aspects of his administrative assistant position, which left him without the developed business skills that would have helped him immensely in tackling the new sales position with gusto. Ultimately, Jasper developed a positive attitude and was quite successful, but his initial attitude could have been disastrous for his career.

You can avoid making a similar mistake by starting to develop these important business success skills now, even if you aren't in your optimal job yet.

Communication

The ability to articulate your thoughts well both on paper and orally and to speak effectively one-on-one as well as in groups is one of the most important skills for many occupations. Whether you need to be able to communicate with the public, your clients, or your coworkers, effective communication can be key. Included in the skill of communication is having good *interpersonal skills*—the ability to talk openly with others and to put them at ease with you.

Keep in mind that few people are effective communicators in every forum. For instance, some are good writers but not good public speakers, while others are great public speakers without a talent for one-on-one communication. Think about your own communication style. Where do your strengths lie? How you can develop them?

Problem Solving

The ability to identify and analyze problems, determine their causes, and make suggestions for resolving them is an effective way of standing out in any job. Some people complain incessantly about the problems they see on a job; others simply solve the problems. Who would you rather have in your place of employment? "If anything, effective thinking is what you need to learn" to do well in the workplace, RN Kelly Fox says. "Obviously, you need to know the area you're working in. But if you're not learning to problem solve, then you can't do anything with the information you have. In school, you learn a little about everything but not enough about anything. I really learned on the job. But if you can effectively think through and solve problems, then you can tackle anything."

Rama Moorthy also stresses the importance of problem solving. Every time Rama approaches a problem, she makes lists of all the various issues and all the things that could be possible causes or influences. "I review the problems from all angles and perspectives, turning over the information that is under every rock." Rama has incorporated her medical dream into her current career in that she loves to "diagnose problems." She is enthusiastic about the process of discovery when solving a problem and is energized by her experiences with her colleagues.

Pat Duncan, an accountant, has developed a reputation for handling unique business problems. Whenever there's a complex, confusing project that crosses interdepartmental lines in her office, Pat is called to handle it. Her secret formula for successfully managing difficult projects is organization and consistency. "People think accountants only work with numbers, but my job is to determine the process that was followed and to investigate which numbers are there and which numbers shouldn't be there." Because Pat is so organized—beyond just the normal filing system and clean desk—she can approach just about any messy project and make sense out of it for everyone involved. Pat's problem-solving abilities make her an invaluable employee.

Decision Making

The ability to review a variety of options and choose the best one, given the special circumstances at hand, is an extension of problem solving. Some decisions only have two options; others are more complicated. Learning how to recognize the various options is key to learning how to make decisions. In addition, however, learning how to weigh those options is equally important. What are the benefits to this solution? What are the drawbacks?

Kelly Fox recalls that some of the people who did the best in her nursing classes at college did the worst on the job because they were looking for one answer to one question. "You're at a disadvantage if you're unable to break out of that mold," Kelly warns since, in real life, the choices are numerous and there often is not one definitive answer.

Teamwork

The ability to work with others toward a common goal, to be supportive of their ideas, and to focus on the goals of the group cannot be overemphasized. Good team players listen to and respect the opinions of others, clearly and concisely state their own opinions, and focus on the final outcome (or goal of the team) rather than their individual interests.

P. D. Shabay, profiled at the end of this chapter, stresses the importance of teamwork. "One thing that always hits me between the eyes is that the higher I go, the more dependent I am on the people around me, from the managers to the word processors to the janitor. It takes the whole team to turn around a ship this large. You need everyone on the team to be good at their job." Kelly Fox agrees. "I think working as a team is imperative. We do a lot in a hospital. Everyone has roles. It's chaotic. If the team effort doesn't work, it's frustrating, there's no flow, and the patient suffers. Definitely, you have to be a bright person, but there are other qualities just as important—or even more important" at work. One of them is teamwork.

Leadership

The ability to influence others in a positive, motivating way and to command attention and respect, will help you in almost any career, whether you want to flip burgers or be the President of the United States. Leadership skills can keep you in line for promotions to management positions. Leadership means taking charge—taking responsibility—with a group of people to see something through to completion. It often means sticking your neck out and fighting for the cause of the group in the face of numerous obstacles. It can also mean being unpopular because you have to stick to what you believe is right for the group or the situation, not what is going to make everybody happy.

You may not want to be a manager, but developing leadership skills allows you to keep that option open. If you've never been a leader before, think of ways at work or at play where you can develop that skill. Can you volunteer to head up a committee or spearhead a new project? Can you offer to train a new employee? Each of these activities can help you learn about leadership. They give you the opportunity to show your enthusiasm for being a team member, too.

Creativity or Innovativeness

The ability to let your mind wander and to discern larger patterns and relationships, to see the overall as well as the detail-filled picture helps not only in exploring career options (as you did in the beginning of the book) but also in growing and developing within the career that you choose. The closer you are to your skills and interests (explored in Chapter 2), the more likely it is that your creative juices can flow and you can come up with new ideas for the benefit of your company. Just like with communication, different people have different ways of expressing creative ideas. Some people like to sit in a large group and brainstorm. Others like to sit for a period of time, mulling over the issue quietly. Still others would prefer to come up with creative ideas after educating themselves on the topic in question through research. Be aware of your creative strengths and use them.

Tenacity or Perseverance

The ability to work hard and stick to a project that needs to be accomplished, even in the face of opposition, is difficult but important. The more willing you are to "hang in there," develop new ideas, and carry through with plans that may not look like they'll be either successful or easy to accomplish, the more valuable you are to a company that's trying to grow and respond to the needs of its customers. In fact, being a creative thinker often will have no results if you are not also perseverant and willing to take the time to convince others of why your creative ideas should be implemented. Look back to Chapter 6, where we described how Beth used an e-mail system to get a continuance in a sentencing even when it looked like she wasn't going to get the continuance. Beth could have chosen to accept whatever the judge decided without trying to think of ways to influence that decision. Instead, she was not only creative but perseverant in her thinking—and it paid off for her client!

Drive or Energy

The sheer energy to get the most out of your career while balancing your life and activities and the ability to be productive over long hours and to go above and beyond what's required, can be a large part of your perseverance. We can't all be tenacious at all times. Figure out your own strengths in this area and pace yourself.

Common Sense

The ability to know how things work in the "real world" and to know instinctively what to do in different kinds of situations is an important component of each of the foregoing qualities. For instance, although you want to be tenacious, you do not want your tenacity to exceed your good judgments; although you want to work as a team member, you also want to recognize when you're ready to complete a project on your own; although you strive to communicate, you also need to know when to let sleeping dogs lie; and so on.

Your Ethics or Honor Code

Doing what you believe is right, based on your values and morals, will help guide you throughout your career. Don't be afraid to take a stand, even if it appears that you will meet opposition. If your common sense and your honor code tell you that you need to act in a certain way, you'll be happier in the long run if you act in that way. If in doubt, ask yourself some questions: Would others approve of my behavior if they knew about it? Is what I'm doing (or my company doing) right? If not, what can or should I do about it?

You can develop other personal qualities to make yourself successful in the business world. *Independence*—the ability to be unconventional, to take a stand on something that you believe in, but which may be unpopular with a larger group—is scary but important. *Adaptability*—the ability to adjust quickly to any situation, group of people, or environment, to use past experiences to measure new ones and respond nondefensively to criticism—allows you to grow outside of rigid parameters. Other qualities to develop for the workplace and in your life are *initiative* and a *positive attitude*. In sum, the more you develop as a person, the better you become as an employee.

Also, recognize your weaknesses and make sure that your work doesn't suffer because of them. Comic editor Rob Tokar remembers an assistant editor who was better than he at making their freelance writers and illustrators keep to a set schedule. "I would give people too much slack," Rob admits. "I would draw up a schedule but would remake it" if anyone complained about deadlines. "I gave it to my assistant editor. She wanted to try whip cracking. We'd sit down and draw up the schedule, then she would watch the way things were coming in. If someone got behind, she'd call them up." Rob laughs at how much more effective she was at getting their freelance people to respond. "She had a real soft voice…and she had them *jumping* to her word," he remembered. She held onto the scheduling responsibilities. "We both saw that I wasn't doing that well to start with, and then saw how well she did. I gave her as much credit as I could—I was just so relieved."

How Can I Handle Juggling the "Real-World" Workplace?

We all can get discouraged with trying to handle "real-world" challenges in the workplace such as managing conflict, creating quality, conducting effective meetings, keeping our bosses happy, managing time, and overall handling stress. There are no simple answers to meeting these challenges. Each person must tackle these issues in his or her own way.

Developing the business skills listed earlier will help you to take one *big* step to handling problems as they crop up, however. Identify the problem, then look through the list of business skills. Can any one of these skills help you solve your current crisis? For instance, keeping your boss happy may require the use of your communication skills. What can you say to your boss to make sure you're getting the right work done? How often can you check with your boss to figure out how best to work together?

Sheer experience is another great tool for learning to deal with a lot of conflict and stress. The more often you do an activity, the better you will become. That's why we encourage the use of internships or part-time jobs on the road to your career success. Making yourself comfortable with the process will take you a long way.

Also, try discussing specific issues with your friends, family, or other coworkers. Brainstorming specific issues almost always results in solutions. Using others as a sounding board can help you decide whether your frustrations and concerns are commonplace or unique to you.

If you find yourself dealing with a lot of stress, try to take steps to relieve it. Sometimes just taking a deep breath and relaxing your shoulders can do the trick. Other times, it may require changing the structure of your job—or reducing the number of responsibilities that you have. There are many self-help books on how to deal with stress. The more stress you have, the more likely you will benefit from reviewing such books. Whatever you do, try not to get too caught up in stress. Stress is called the "silent killer" and can lead to serious or fatal illnesses like heart diseases, high blood pressure, and ulcers. It's better to deal with today's stress today than bottle it up and have a heart attack tomorrow.

HOW CAN I APPRECIATE AND UNDERSTAND DIVERSITY?

One way that you can become a more productive and promotable employee is by learning to appreciate all the different types of people in the workplace. This is especially true today, when we have a growing number of people from all kinds of backgrounds, ages, and beliefs and when our working world has expanded to include international as well as national sources. In a recent edition of *Lessons in Leadership*, Peter Senge notes, "One of the most important areas that is going to determine success and failure of businesses will be their capacity to nurture deep understandings that transcend cultural boundaries. Americans are probably the least qualified of any advanced industrial society to undertake this because we arguably have the lowest level of cultural sensitivity. This comes from a tremendous lack of experience in dealing with multiple cultures."

Having an openness and appreciation about other cultures and other walks of life helps immensely in dealing in the business world. Ned Smith, a political science major, found that his major was invaluable in that way as he began his leadership development program with Southwestern Bell. "I chose my major because it thrilled me to study it. I saw it as the study of how human beings interact with one another. I had to understand humans' culture, religion, art, politics, history—all the things that influence how nations act. I find it very valuable in my career. When I meet someone international, I will know where his or her country is, and things about it. So much about being successful is not crunching numbers but getting along. When you become friends with someone, and have an easy rapport, you can be most productive. It becomes two people grinding through" a big project, working together, rather than two strangers.

The more you understand the diversity in the world around you, the better you can perform your job. Dr. Becky Parker recently came to value the numerous Spanish classes she took in high school and college when she began her ER residency in El Paso, Texas. "My initial goal with Spanish was not to broaden my horizons but to meet requirements," Becky admits. "I took Spanish in high school because people told me I should have a foreign language." After she began working at the El Paso hospital, "I started to use the language all over again." Knowing Spanish has made it easier for her to practice medicine. "I have more of a perspective on how the culture views health differently here," she says. "Like how they view pain—in English we talk in degrees, but in Spanish they talk more in temperatures, like a burning pain or a freezing pain. Being 'drunk' in Spanish is being dizzy." In addition, although other doctors don't know Spanish and don't have time to learn it, Becky feels she "definitely" has a "big advantage" because of knowing Spanish. "I think my patients trust me more because of it," she says. Becky believes that she can break down barriers with her patients by speaking in Spanish.

Helping others appreciate diversity is rewarding. Lisa Aldisert recalls one class she taught on oral communication skills where people from diverse ethnic backgrounds ultimately were able to understand and appreciate each other. The class was part of a Cornell University program where the class was taught on-site at a company for employees who wanted to get a college degree while working. "Nearly everyone in that class was born in another country," Lisa says. Although the employee-students joined the class separately, they ended with a better understanding of each other. At the end of the class, there was a graduation ceremony. One of her students, Juan, was chosen to be the speaker, but all the students felt "pride, enthusiasm, ownership" about his speech; "that's how much they'd come together as a group." In one part of his speech, Juan spoke of "how they learned to accept and care for each other even though they were from such different backgrounds." Lisa believes that their newfound understanding of each other helped her students in the workplace when dealing with people of different backgrounds.

Being a minority in the working world can be difficult, and it may be up to you to help bridge gaps, no matter what color, race, or culture you come from. Herman Walker, an African-American attorney and entrepreneur in Anchorage, Alaska, knows that "no matter what I do, people first see me as black and then as Herman Walker," but he does not allow other people's perceptions to define him. He has the following advice: "First, know who you are. To me, that's key. And don't let anyone take that away from you, no matter how slight it may be. Second, don't belittle who you are or your culture. If something's not right, speak out against it." Herman also suggests: "Know your history. I come from a strong family history. I was raised to be proud of my culture but also to accept everyone. People are people—it's how you treat them that counts. And know your culture, be proud of your culture. Don't let anyone take your culture away from you. There are many ways—through racist remarks, or systematic ways. Don't let it happen." He says, "It goes back to my universal rule that what you put out in life comes back to you." Herman sees his advice as "very basic, very simple. But people complicate things. People ignore the obvious."

Women, too, can find themselves minorities in male-dominated fields. Lisa Quigley, for example, feels that "wearing a skirt" in different male-dominated fields—like pharmaceuticals, engineering, or marketing/firearms instruction—"has been to my advantage. I didn't get a job because of it, but I know it didn't hurt. It's been an asset. You have to have some women on the payroll, and because I already had the qualifications, being a woman was a help." She acknowledges that there is some sexism, since there are certain men who will be judgmental about having her work in the engineering field. But, Lisa says, engineers are fairly straightforward people, so that what really matters is doing the work right. How should *you* cope with sexism? Lisa gives the following advice: "Set up your behavior and don't vary from it—even one time." Also: "You have to have a sense of humor because you do hear things that could seem like a gender slur or a putdown for women that's not directed at you. Some of it you have to let roll off your back, because you *are* going to hear it." Personally, Lisa tries to dress "more traditionally and businesslike" so that the emphasis is on her abilities and not her appearance. "Nothing foofy," she says. Lisa feels that she has received a lot of support from women that she has met on the job and overall has had a wonderful experience in her line of work. She encourages young women not to hesitate entering into more male-dominated fields if they have an interest in the subject matter.

Even if you are not a minority, you can work toward appreciating and promoting diversity in the workplace. Mike Patterson, the city administrator profiled at the end of Chapter 4, recalls a time when he came to appreciate at least some of the issues that African Americans confront. "When I interned for the Council of University Presidents in Olympia as a student lobbyist" with the Washington state legislature, "I had an African American roommate named Rob (another intern). We were thrown together because we rented the upstairs of a family home. Rob was very strongly connected with his heritage and I learned a lot," Mike recalls. "One of the biggest parts for me was that I thought racism was a thing of the past. That it didn't exist." Mike found that wasn't true. He remembers that he and Rob were treated differently on the job. "It was interesting to see how legislators—it sounds horrible, but mostly Republicans—treated us differently. They patronized Rob. They were real polite, but it was like he was an idiot. Me, they wanted to show me all the things they'd done." In retrospect, Mike believes he "came to appreciate what Rob had to endure, in a way. No one was outwardly racist, but there was always this subtle message of second-class citizen." Mike uses that experience when dealing with issues in his city now, to keep an open mind about what others might be experiencing even if he isn't experiencing it personally.

One way to grow in this area is for companies to develop diversity. Michael Fulton, a staff specialist with a career development organization called INROADS who we profiled in Chapter 7, thinks that most companies will have more success in dealing with cultural issues in the workplace if they groom all types of capable candidates rather than solve problems with "lip service to the idea of diversity." According to Michael, "If a company really wants diversity, then they need to develop it from within. We all have a lot to learn. If you want to grow, you have to go outside of what is safe for you." Michael remembers one of his INROADS candidates was having a difficult time adjusting to her corporate sponsor. She was African American and her sponsor was an older Caucasian man. The woman called Michael daily trying to quit, but Michael persuaded her to continue. The two worked things out over time. "They learned how to work together because they identified the issues, confronted them and worked them out. They had to work together in order to show results."

Rick Benito, vice president and district sales manager for Bank of America, attributes much of his success to his diverse background. He grew up in Guam, attended college in the Midwest, studied in Cambridge, England, and served in the Navy before he started his financial career. The fruits of his multicultural exposure is that "I don't prejudge any situation. I've learned that people are different and that you have to listen carefully so that you don't miss any opportunities." Rick thinks that the abilities to be tolerant and respectful contribute to his success. "I get to know the people who work for me and what trips their trigger. If I appreciate their background, it helps me to communicate with them and motivate them." Rick used this philosophy to motivate the employees of the National City branch that ranked 33rd out of 36 branches and moved it to among the top 10 branches in less than an eight-month period.

A company's sensitivity about diversity gives it a step up in this global economy. P. D. Shabay believes that his company benefits from its international internship program because the program allows the company to develop a culturally diverse work force that has the advantage of better understanding its global customers and competitors. "For years, Bell has been dominated by the traditional white, male work force. The diversity program is one way for us to develop goodwill on a global basis. When the students return home, they have a positive perspective of Bell Helicopter that they share with their families, friends and employers." Bell Helicopter also benefits because "the students are young, eager and in the prime of their learning process. They offer fresh insights." Bell's international program is one way that Bell works to keep a pulse on our global society and keep its competitive edge in the global market.

The examples above show how some people deal with and appreciate diversity in the workplace. You can use their tools and ideas to help create your own ideas on the same subject.

SUMMARY

Developing good business skills and appreciating diversity are just two ways to help you make yourself a valuable employee and grow in your career. The task may not always be easy, but succeeding at it allows you to feel that you are responsible for a job well done.

ASKING QUESTIONS AND GETTING ANSWERS

1. **How Do You Communicate?** No matter how much the future will change our work environment, we still will need to be able to communicate with each other, and one of the most important times to communicate well is when there is a conflict. Think of a recent conflict you had with another person, preferably someone you work with (although it could also be a conflict with a friend, family member, professor, etc.). How did you handle it? How did you use your communication abilities to resolve the problem?

   For instance, Charlene had an important document that needed to get out in the mail by the end of the day. Typically, Charlene does all of her own word processing, but she had fallen behind and intended to give her assistant Janelle handwritten edits to input into the document on the computer throughout the day. Janelle was having a busy day herself, as she is the assistant to three other salespeople. Charlene went with a new set of edits to give to Janelle and discovered that Janelle had left for a late lunch. Charlene was concerned about whether the project would get done in time and left an angry note for Janelle. Janelle (a sensitive perfectionist by nature) didn't realize that Charlene would have more edits and felt hurt that Charlene thought she was doing a bad job. Once the project was finished, Charlene and Janelle sat down to discuss what had happened. They both started out feeling defensive. Instead, however, they used this exercise, identified the other person's frustrations and concerns, and vowed to communicate more clearly in the future about how to solve production problems. Write down the information relevant to your conflict:

   1. Briefly describe the conflict:_____

      _____

      _____

   2. What did the other person do or say that triggered a reaction

      in you (or vice versa)? _____

      _____

      _____

   3. What were your thoughts about the person during the conflict?

      _____

      _____

   4. What were your feelings?_____

      _____

      _____

5. Analyze the other person's position. What do you think they thought about you?_____

_____

_____

6. What were their feelings?_____

_____

_____

7. What were your goals in regard to the conflict?_____

_____

_____

8. What were the other person's goals?_____

_____

_____

9. What did you do to resolve the situation?_____

_____

_____

Was it resolved?_____

10. Did you *communicate* with that person about thoughts, feelings, and goals? _____

_____

_____

11. How did you use (or could you have used) *communication* more effectively to resolve this conflict? _____

_____

_____

12. How did you use (or could you have used) some of the other business skills listed in this chapter?

Problem Solving _____

_____

Creative Thinking_____

_____

Tenacity/Perseverance_____

_____

Common Sense _____

_____

Your Ethics or Honor Code_____

_____

2. **Helping Others Appreciate Their Diversity.** You have been asked to mediate an argument between Roland and Jesus, two administrative assistants at a local real estate office. Jesus is angry because Roland told a joke about the pope. Jesus is very religious, while Roland has been clear with Jesus that he disagrees with Jesus' religious views. Jesus tells you that he is less angry about the joke and more angry about Roland's negative attitude toward him. He feels that the joke is just a very good example of how Roland does not treat him with respect. Roland has told you that he feels bad about telling the joke and has already apologized, but he thinks Jesus is too sensitive in general.

What can you say to Jesus and Roland to help them understand the point of view of the other?

_____

_____

_____

COLLABORATIVE LEARNING AND TEAM-BUILDING SKILLS

1. **Using Your Business Success Skills.** Bud is the manager in a fast-food restaurant, and he has an employee (Jennifer) who is constantly late to work. In addition to being late, Jennifer never calls to let Bud know to expect her to be late. Jennifer has two daughters (Sandy and Terri). When Jennifer is late, it's usually because Terri is sick. Bud is so exasperated by Jennifer's tardiness that he's starting to doubt that Terri gets sick this often. Bud also believes that Terri's sickness should not be an excuse for Jennifer to be late as often as she is.

In groups of four, role play a meeting between Bud and Jennifer where they discuss Jennifer's tardiness with two people playing Bud and Jennifer and two observing. How effective a leader is Bud? How well do they communicate? Do they come up with creative solutions? Write a summary of what went well during the conversation and what could be improved.

_____

_____

_____

Now, switch roles so that the two observers are doing the role-playing. Write comments in the space provided.

_____

_____

_____

3. **Helping Solve Each Other's Problems.** As discussed in the chapter, we often run into on-the-job problems where there are no easy solutions. In groups of two or three, discuss a problem that each of you has had on the job (or in the classroom). It could be a conflict with a coworker, a difficult boss, a problem with managing time or stress, or even a question about how you could have done better on a particular project. Take turns discussing your problems and coming up with ideas of how to improve in the future. Make notes on the problems in the space provided.

_____

_____

_____

_____

_____

LONG-TERM PLANNING: KEY TO YOUR PERSONAL PORTFOLIO

Choosing to Solve Problems. One way to practice problem solving is to solve some of the problems that are in your life currently in a methodical way. First, identify a problem that you have. It could be in your personal or professional life. Next, think of three possible solutions to the problem. What are the benefits to each solution? What are its drawbacks? Choose one of the solutions you have outlined and put it into action. Did it work? Use the following blanks to record what happened.

PROBLEM

_____

_____

POSSIBLE SOLUTION #1

_____

_____

PROS   **CONS**

_____

_____

POSSIBLE SOLUTION #2

_____

_____

PROS   **CONS**

_____

_____

CHOSEN SOLUTION

_____

_____

EVALUATION—DID IT WORK?

_____

_____

STUDENT QUESTION

Q **Lupe Caballero, interpreter for public defender's office**

Lupe is 26 years old and has already reached her original employment goal that she made after college—that is, to become an interpreter. As Lupe says, "It's weird. I see other people who are much older than I am who are struggling and still trying to figure out what they're going to do. Usually your first job or first couple of jobs won't be what you want to do. In my case, I'm still working at my first job." When Lupe started her current job, only half of her duties were interpreting, but that is her full-time job now. It hasn't taken a long time for her to graduate to what she wants to do. She believes that she *does* have direction. Way down the road, she will want to go out on her own. In the meantime, though, she wants to do what she can to keep motivated and not fall into the rut of her job getting too old. Her question:

How do I keep improving my job so it doesn't get to a point that I dread going to work? How can I keep growing where I am, especially since this is training for my long-term goal?

A Life is a series of goals. When you attain one, remember to take some time appreciating and celebrating the achievement of goals. But then get ready to set new goals for yourself so that you continue to grow and avoid becoming stagnant or satisfied with yourself. If your long-term goal is to learn to be in business for yourself, then think about how you can expand your current job to play an even greater leadership role in the job you have now. Ask your boss for constructive ideas on how you can improve. Perhaps there are some additional projects you can spearhead for the office which will stretch you by allowing you to take on new responsibilities. You can also grow a lot outside of work. You can take a class on leadership or entrepreneurship and learn about what it would be like to be your own boss. You'll get fresh ideas from others on how to grow in your current job. You may also want to join an outside business organization which is made up of people with their own companies. The main piece of advice is to push yourself to recreate your job that you have mastered into something more impactive than how people conceive of it today. This ability will help determine if you have the inner drive, vision, and wherewithal to run your own company.

CAREER PROFILE

P. D. SHABAY is one of the oddities of today's business world. He's been with the same company his whole career. But constancy has not made P.D. complacent—far from it. P.D.'s career with Bell Helicopter in Fort Worth, Texas, is marked by creative and farsighted attitudes and goals. He has an eye for developing his company's business through effective management and leadership skills.

P.D. was hired at Bell Helicopter in the summer of 1965 in the paintshop there. By 1968, he was a training instructor; in 1971, he moved to Labor Relations; in 1987, he moved to Industrial Relations; by 1990, he was Vice President of Human Resources; and by 1994, he was Senior Vice President of Operations. In 1997, he assumed the role of Executive Vice President.

P.D.'s experience at every level has taught him a lot about leadership. The P.D. Shabay prescription for effective leadership requires a manager to balance seven elements. According to P. D., the absolute most important trait for a leader is to be a "focused, active leader." P.D. explains that to have this leadership style you have to have first-hand knowledge of the company and remain totally in tune with its everyday workings. He believes that a leader can manage with this type of closeness without micromanaging. "In the past, the farther up you were in the organization, the more out of touch you were. They wouldn't have their hand on the heartbeat of the organization."

The second element to P.D.'s leadership prescription is communication.

"Now everyone, including the leader of the team, must contribute so that the overall team is successful." P.D. believes that this requires excellent communication skills. P.D. has several techniques to feed the desire for communication. He holds an employee breakfast once a month to answer any question that an employee has. P.D. doesn't prepare a formal presentation for this meeting—the purpose is solely to answer questions. Employees attend with questions and notebooks ready, and they jot down the responses so they can share them with their coworkers.

P.D.'s third leadership rule is that a leader must have specific, clearly defined goals that can be measured. "As a manager, if you want an employee to perform to a certain level, you have to explain exactly what that level is. By establishing measurements to the goals, the employee knows the performance that is expected and the manager gets the performance he or she desires." P.D. notes that Bell "establishes goals and stretches goals for the company. The functional groups break off their goals based on the overall company goals; this process continues down the line to every department and team. To truly measure against these goals, every functional department head must report their progress at a monthly meeting. These meetings are open for employees to attend so that anyone can hear the progress. No one wants to come to these month after month and stand up and say that they didn't achieve their goals. When they do reach their goals, you can't get them to shut up. Everyone is accountable and when they're successful they share the spotlight."

The final four leadership prescriptions are (4) trust and integrity ("they go hand in hand," P.D. says), (5) encourage teamwork, (6) "have a passion for what you're doing—show some heart and soul in everything you do," and (7) recognize that you're only as good as the people who work for you. These prescriptions work for P.D., and he recommends them to you.

CHANGE

SALAMANCA
Zamora
Guarda
Avila
SIERRA DE GREDOS
Talavera de la Reina
Toledo
S P A
MONTES DE TOLEDO
Ciudad Real
Almadén
Puertollano
SIERRA MORENA
CORDOBA
Andújar
Linares
Jaén
SEVILLA (SEVILLE)
Ecija
Antequera
GRANADA
MC-1
SUUNTO

Workplace 2000:
How to Be Competitive and Still Remain True to Yourself

As we get ready to begin a whole new century, we can reflect and recognize that the world is getting smaller by the day. With the advent of technology and industry, the increase of exports and imports, and the expansion of so many corporations from one country to the next, there is increasing globalization. Our communities both nationally and internationally seem to be getting smaller and more similar. Only a few years ago, we couldn't imagine the national and international connections that can be made so easily now! We need to grow with these changing times.

CNN, the 24-hour news network based in Atlanta, Georgia, is a perfect example of one of the first truly global businesses that recognized the ever-changing face of the business world. The makers of CNN recognized that we all need each other and that we are all as nations interdependent. By establishing itself internationally and by bringing news from "all around the world" to countries everywhere, CNN has done its part in making the world a smaller place with at least a little better understanding of how we all work. When it was first proposed, people laughed. A 24-hour news program? What's the use of that? But CNN grew in sync with the globalization of society. It started at a perfect time to symbolize our ability and need to communicate and understand each other all around the world.

Just like CNN or any other truly global company, you need to enter the twenty-first century with an open mind toward adjusting to all the changes and nuances of a highly technological world. What things should you be aware of? How can you fit your career into all these changes and still maintain a personal life? What is this new century—this new millennium—bringing your way?

WHAT ELEMENTS OF THE WORLD HAVE CHANGED THE WORKPLACE?

In the 1990s and beyond, there will be more life and work options than at any other time for people of all ages, stages, races, and economic backgrounds. That fact poses opportunities and challenges. For those who are most committed to using their minds and keeping them sharp through continuous learning and hard work, the options will be brighter. For those who get out of school and adopt the "automatic pilot" work mode, prospects may be bleaker. All of us, no matter how well prepared, will have to deal with a shifting and unpredictable work environment. If your skills are sharp and you are committed to finding creative ways to meet business and personal challenges, you will increase your chances of landing on your feet.

Now and in the future, people work in ways not thought possible even 20 years ago. You may have seen the ads of the executive on partial vacation in the Bahamas with computer and modem, cellular phone, and suntan lotion in tow. While some people do spend their vacations this way, the truth is that technology has made it very easy for people to live and do things in places as remote as Priest Lake, Idaho, or Fayetteville, Arkansas, or virtually anywhere else. While jobs a few years ago dictated that these same people live in Chicago, San Francisco, or New York, now they can conduct business not only in small towns and far-away places, they can also do business en route—on planes, trains, automobiles, and yes, even in airports.

Some people may want to work 15 hours a week. Others may work 90. If companies find people whom they value, whose talents are clearly an asset, they may be willing to bend. Take Stacy Wittingham. She and her husband had a child three years ago. She wanted to stay home with her child but she also wanted to work and learn and grow on the job. She proposed a flex-schedule to her manager that would allow her to come into the office three days a week in the morning and work at home the rest of the time. A laptop computer and phone card were all she needed to do the job from her house.

Companies also seem to be looking for alternatives to traditional work environments. No longer are you obligated in every field to work an 8-to-5 schedule, especially when your work spans national or even international boundaries. In addition to working out of the home and having flexible schedules, there are several alternatives to those traditional work hours and attitudes:

Job Sharing

The ability for two or more qualified people to share the same full-time job has become very popular, especially among stay-at-home parents who only want to work part time. Often job sharing occurs when the employer needs someone physically present during certain hours of the day. The job can have either separate, distinct projects or easily transferable projects. The people sharing the job must be great communicators with each other so that there is not a lot of time wasted transferring duties to each other every other day (or whatever other schedule they have designed for the job sharing). They have the benefit of using day care as a learning experience for their children rather than round-the-clock babysitting.

Flextime

Coming to work at hours other than standard allows employees to schedule their workday around the personal tasks they need to accomplish. For instance, someone who wants to have afternoons free could come to work from 6 A.M. to 2:30 P.M., with only a half-hour for lunch. Some companies even allow employees to work longer workdays in exchange for working less than five days a week. This kind of schedule can be more expensive for employers but seems to increase productivity of their employees as well.

Contract Work

Working on short-term projects as the need arises may be perfect for someone who is in transition and is looking for the perfect job. Some contract work can give you immediate experience without a lot of administrative responsibilities at the office. It also can allow you to work independently at your own pace, especially if you are being paid by the hour. Unfortunately, contract employees are typically not given benefits such as health and dental coverage and usually do not have their taxes withheld from their pay, so be sure to set aside enough money to pay taxes throughout the year. On the other hand, contract work can give you a break between projects, which may suit your lifestyle.

Working Out of the Home

With today's technological world, people have the ability to work with a computer out of their home rather than having to be in the office during standard working hours. Employers and employees both are learning to explore more options so that people can save commuting time, live in the areas they want to live, or balance careers with personal life schedules. The limits are not the technology but the courage and imagination of the participants.

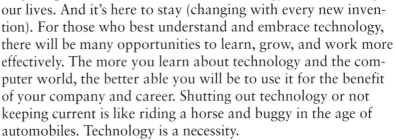

HOW CAN I EMBRACE THE TECHNOLOGICAL WORLD?

Name virtually any career field—entertainment, business, education, law, medicine, transportation—and you'll find technology. In today's world, technology permeates everything. Whether you use e-mail to communicate with your friends around the corner or around the world, reference the World Wide Web to place mail order shopping requests or buy your tickets for your next air flight, or check the balance in your checking and savings account, technology has only begun to impact the way we think, work, and live.

Technology is simultaneously wonderful and difficult. For instance, computers have replaced card catalogs at the library, making the search for a book instantaneous; on the other hand, when the computer is down, no one can find *anything*. For better or for worse, technology also has changed

our lives. And it's here to stay (changing with every new invention). For those who best understand and embrace technology, there will be many opportunities to learn, grow, and work more effectively. The more you learn about technology and the computer world, the better able you will be to use it for the benefit of your company and career. Shutting out technology or not keeping current is like riding a horse and buggy in the age of automobiles. Technology is a necessity.

Mark believes that technology is a must in the workplace today. "I'm stunned when I meet contemporaries of mine who don't turn on a computer all day. Maybe it's because I used to work in the Silicon Valley, and I got used to using technology, but I think it's critical. How a company uses technology shows how sophisticated they are. It reflects a corporate culture."

According to Mark, things are only getting "leaner and faster" so that anyone who is not adept at using technology may get left behind.

You may even choose to join the technological field when you learn more about it. Katherine Minges-Albrecht would love to see more women in technology. "I'm shocked at how few women I see" in the technological entertainment field. She believes that women could add a whole new dimension to this field. "Whenever you get *two* women discussing technology, there's so much synergy. The whole direction of the discussion changes." For instance, Katherine enjoys working with other women in brainstorming about the development of computer games. While the men are discussing "shoot'em up" games, "slaughtering everyone with chain saws," the women tend to emphasize game development that address critical social issues. Katherine believes that, by not involving women, the computer entertainment field is losing "all the community-building that women are so good at. Unless you have women involved at the development stage, you're not going to like the result." According to Katherine, there are no barriers to women getting into this field. "Being a woman should in no way slow you down or stop you." Instead, she sees the problem as one of attracting women to the field in the first place. "It's so utterly male-dominated," she says. Computer technology has been "designed by men, with male themes. Women are just uncomfortable" and are not going to enter the field as readily until "pioneering women make changes" to the entire structure and "open up the field for their gender." She recalls that she personally had been turned off by computer technology until she became active on the Internet and saw the broader spectrum of possibilities. She thinks that there is a whole untapped market of female consumers and encourages women to find their place in this field to develop it with an eye toward meeting these consumers' needs.

At the very least, having knowledge of technology is important. "Technology is becoming more pervasive," says Hewlett-Packard electrical engineer Pat Mealey. "The cost of technology is becoming less of a barrier" at the same time that technology is becoming more and more challenging. The need to have an expertise in this area is increasing. Pure knowledge "is enough that people will want you around. Knowledge is power in this case—it's a rare instance where pure knowledge does you some good."

HOW CAN I GROW THROUGH CONTINUING EDUCATION?

Just because you've landed the job you've been looking for doesn't mean that you will no longer grow and learn within the field that you've chosen. At a minimum, your education and training will continue as you learn from your ever-increasing experience. In addition, however, you will continue to grow from the training that your company may provide and from the courses or seminars that you may decide to take to improve yourself. In fact, continuing your education both formally and informally is an important key for workers in today's global society!

Your continuing education can take many forms. You can stay educated about changes in your field. You can take seminars on basic office skills to improve yourself in new or changing areas. You can take courses on management skills to be a better manager. Rob remembers how seriously he and his colleagues took their management responsibilities. "Our workload had increased dramatically and we were getting upset. We wanted to be good at what we were doing" but there wasn't a lot of time. "Our bosses bought videos about management and organization. *Everyone* was showing up for them. Some of the things were, if you hog all the fun tasks, people working for you might resent it. Also, even if there are tasks that you like to do, you should delegate them to people who also have the ability to do them."

However you choose to continue to grow, be aware of how important growth can be. An employer appreciates an employee who is enthusiastic enough to dedicate time to training and further education. Sometimes the further education can even give you a salary increase or a job promotion. Continuing education also helps to keep you ready for changes within your current job or may help you reach the next level of your career path.

Jacob Stout was able to apply what he learned in seminars directly to his work. As a salesperson, Jacob has attended numerous professional sales seminars. At one such seminar, "they said that 'price is the perceived drawback.' During one of my sales calls to a newspaper in Martinsburg, Virginia, the owner/editor was jumping up and down on his desk because he was upset about the price. I thought back to [that particular seminar] and how this unpleasant demonstration wasn't supposed to be happening, it is only 'perceived,' even though it seemed very real. I calmed down the owner and we went to lunch and everything worked out."

Keep in mind that the world of technology can be one of your greatest assets in continuing in your education. Part of what these alternative learning methods—CD ROM, Web sites, on-line services—will provide is an easier way for you to keep learning without having to always be in the college classroom. Technology and life-long learning go hand in hand and will remain an integral part of our world and our lives.

Other ideas for keeping yourself educated: attend museum and library lectures (usually free and regularly available); join or form a book or writing club; attend free or inexpensive concerts or plays held by your city or at local churches and synagogues; register for weekend seminars; join a professional organization and attend its meetings and seminars; and keep an eye on announcements in your local newspaper for upcoming activities.

For those of you who feel that continuing education seems like more work, we have two suggestions. First, think of your life as an exciting learning experience, where every day allows you to tackle a new challenge and learn more things about yourself, your career, and the world around you. Doesn't that make the idea of a half-day seminar on basic office skills seem a lot more interesting and worthwhile? Second, remember that your most important and unique asset is *you*. The more you develop who you are, the more opportunity you will have to design your own career path. Any skills or ideas you gain because of continuing education just benefit you as you continue on your path.

HOW DO I MANAGE MY FUTURE?

You are the manager of your own career. The clearer and more organized you are about your weekly, monthly, and annual goals on the job and in your career, the better you will feel about the direction your life and career are taking and the more in control you will feel. Rather than be reactive to situations as they arise, try to be proactive and anticipate what you want from your future.

One way to stay organized on the job is to organize your personal records so that you can remember your own track record. Keep a folder with a list of career goals, past achievements, and past and future projects. Place copies in the folder of nice letters from clients praising your work or positive notations from your supervisor on your work. If the compliments come in verbal rather than written form, write a memo to your file to keep track of what was said and by whom.

Keep track of what you do through monthly reports. Break up the report into categories, such as:

➤ Your accomplishments this past month

➤ The biggest impact you made this month

➤ Goals you met this month

➤ Goals you are setting for the next month

Give your monthly report to supervisors for their information and input, or simply put the report in your personal file.

Think of this as your personal portfolio. Keeping a paper trail of your accomplishments is no different from completing the portfolio development exercises at the end of every chapter. Your long-term thinking and planning begins with keeping track of what *you* have accomplished. Don't rely on anyone else to do this for you. Keeping a file of your monthly achievements will help you at salary review time and in the event that you are laid off or terminated. In fact, your paper trail could save your job if your work results are ever called into question.

Alternatively, if you decide to look for a new job, the monthly reports will remind you of your most recent accomplishments that can be put into an updated resume. You may even want to show samples of your work to your prospective employer. It's surprisingly easy to forget the details of your accomplishments if they are not written down. Plus, there is no proof that you have accomplished these things if you can't show your results.

For example, Susy Inahara never kept these kinds of records because she was happy in her job and didn't plan to look for a new one. She saw herself as a dependable, hard-working employee who stayed late, showed leadership, and could think creatively. She never imagined she could lose any job she had—and certainly not her current one.

Unexpectedly, Susy had a new supervisor who decided that Susy was not good enough at keeping up with administrative tasks. Although this was a minor part of her job, Susy and her new supervisor could not agree on how these tasks should be accomplished. When Susy realized that she was being "encouraged" to leave the office because of this problem, she found it difficult to defend herself and her abilities. Had she kept a record of her monthly accomplishments on this job, she would have been in a much better position to challenge her new supervisor's sudden criticism of her abilities.

WHAT SHOULD I DO TO PREPARE FOR A CHANGE?

There are many reasons that people begin looking for a career or job change. Sometimes they feel they are not growing professionally. Other times, they are just unhappy—perhaps they do not fit with their current boss or supervisor; their job responsibilities may not match their skills (either because their skills have grown or because the job has changed in some way). Maybe they are just bored.

Whatever the reason, the key to managing these types of career milestones is to plan for them as much as possible and embrace them as a period of personal growth when they do come along. A person with a self-reliant attitude will have the best success. Here's a top ten list of career management techniques:

1. Keep your skills current.

2. Be proactive—work outside of your job description when you need projects that will develop new skills or experiences.

3. Network, network, network.

4. Develop communication skills—it is imperative that you can write, speak, listen, and get along.

5. Have a positive attitude—you don't have to play all the political games, but know yourself and communicate positively and diplomatically.

6. Examine your industry/occupation for future growth.

7. Review and revisit whether your optimal job design still fits you—are you getting what you want? What changes need to be made to your plan?

8. Keep a balance in your life.

9. Embrace education—advanced degrees, special business or occupational programs, or corporate training will give you an advantage.

10. Always be working on your next step.

How do you know when you've reached a dead end? There can be lots of signs—perhaps you don't feel energized during the day. Or maybe you're too preoccupied with insignificant company politics or personal responsibilities to handle your job duties well. Maybe you're continually passed over or not even considered for a promotion. Sometimes, deciding that you've reached a dead end requires having heart-to-heart talks with family, friends, coworkers, mentors, and managers to verify that your feelings are correct.

Stacey Cloutier received an accounting degree from Notre Dame and went to work as an auditor for Deloitte & Touche. She thought that everything was going along fine when the human resources director made an observation that her talents could be better utilized if she changed her career path to something that had "people" as the end result. She humored the human resources director and spent a summer as a college recruiter. She did very well but decided not to continue because she had worked so hard to earn her accounting degree. After returning to her old job, she was not the same person and needed to make a change. "I realized that I had made a mistake, but I had a difficult time admitting it to myself." She reconnected with the human resources director at a recruiting function and knew instantly that she had to make the change. When he asked her if she was going to come back to work for him, she said yes. She enjoys every minute of her "new" job.

The two difficult tasks in dealing with a career change are first knowing when to make the change and then knowing what to transition to. Sometimes you may find yourself in a situation where your experience is based in an industry that doesn't interest you anymore, and you have the challenge of convincing a new company to take a risk and hire you over someone who has the industry experience.

One way to persuade a hiring manager to give you a chance is to use your novice experience as an advantage—you have a fresh outlook and the enthusiasm to make the transition!

The best way to try on a new career is to find out exactly what that occupation entails. This exercise is very much the same one as when you were *choosing* your career. Look back over the earlier chapters on finding the right career for you and follow those same steps. What are your skills? What careers match those skills? Conduct some information interviews with people who have the types of jobs that you are interested in. Ask them how they got their start, what pieces of experience are crucial to their success, and what attributes they think make a person successful in their line of work. Ask them what they like and what they don't like. Present them with a list of your transferable skills and ask them which ones to highlight in your resume and in interviews.

If you're looking for a change, do some soul searching. What's your motivation? Do you want to change *careers* or just jobs? Sometimes a poor match with a boss or company may mislead you to make a drastic decision. Take some time to determine if the new career path that you're considering actually meets your life-style demands and brings you closer to (or farther away from) your ultimate life goals.

How Can I Prepare for the Unexpected?

These days, it is unusual to stay with the same company for a long time. You have to assess which jobs, opportunities, and career paths are best for you while you build a solid track record in each position you sign on to take. For better or worse, one reality of today's ever-changing work force is that companies' needs change with the changes in society, technology, and communication. A new invention simultaneously can create and eliminate jobs. No matter how hard you work, you can be subject to layoffs or reductions in force.

One way of avoiding this consequence is to plan ahead. "Planning ahead" does *not* mean knowing the future for the next 50 years. Sure, you may be lucky and select a field that will grow throughout your entire working life, but chances of that occurring are slim. In fact, some people entered computer programming 15 years ago specifically because they thought it would always be a growing field, only to find out that the industry's needs have drastically changed and computer programming (as we used to know it) is no longer a growing field. Instead, "planning ahead" means preparing for the unexpected. If your company went bankrupt tomorrow, what options would be available to you? What people do you know who think highly of your work? What options can you develop, either quickly or over a long-term period, to keep your career interesting and to keep yourself working and earning money?

One way to "plan ahead" is to recognize your most valuable resource: you. Rather than placing all your emphasis and identity into your *company*, think about who *you* are and what you've accomplished. Look back to the top ten list for career management. Are you following these steps? Are you being self-reliant or company-dependent?

Tom Peters addresses this very issue in *Lessons in Leadership:*

Who do you see when you look in the mirror? Will I see GE or GM or General Mills or Quaker Oats? What I'm really suggesting these days is that, when people look in the mirror, Tom Peters sees Tom Peters and Joe Jones sees Joe Jones and Doris Smith sees Doris Smith. Americans, in particular, must try to return to the Ralph Waldo Emerson notion of self-reliance. It's your life; it's your career; it's your project; it's your learning experience.

Too many of us have allowed Toyota or Nissan or Hitachi or Semens or General Mills or General Motors to essentially take care of our life, while we behaved in a passive fashion and climbed some mindless career ladder as we used to call it. Those days are gone. As individuals, whether we are American, Japanese, German or Korean, we must get the gumption to try to take charge of our lives.

Rob Tokar appreciates a philosophy that life can be ever changing. When he was laid off from his job as comic book editor, Rob could have panicked. Instead, he assessed his skills and started to explore new avenues. He had prepared for the possibility of a layoff, both by accident (he had entered a contract that provided severance pay) and on purpose (he had put a lot of money away in a savings account). Now he is exploring what to do, given all the skills he has developed so far. "On the one hand, this is one of the greatest opportunities of my life," Rob says. "On the other hand, it's very scary. I suppose when you're exploring new territory, it's always scary. Part of me is saying to do just goofy kinds of things, like work on a cruise ship. Part of me is saying go back to school. Part of me is saying that I always wanted to be an illustrator, so I should give that a shot. I've even thought about doing web page illustrations." Whatever he chooses to do, Rob is at an advantage because he has a unique and portable set of skills, talents, and interests.

Sometimes a job loss can be a blessing in disguise, in that it can force you to change your career course when you may otherwise be too busy or too unfocused to evaluate what you really want to do. Cindy Parker graduated from Northwestern's Kellogg School of Management with an MBA and specialized in marketing. Her first love was advertising, but this industry was downsizing, so she got a job in another area of expertise—software. Deep down, she realized that she was unhappy but was too busy to do anything about that unhappiness. After six months with the company, it started doing poorly and had to lay off 50 percent of its work force. Cindy was glad when she was released from her job. She was ready for the transition and started interviewing immediately. She found a great job working for an advertising agency in San Francisco and hasn't looked back.

Keep up your spirits, even if you lose your job in circumstances more controversial than a reduction in force. Kerry Drake—former editor of *The Wyoming Eagle*—had his life change drastically four years ago when he was fired for refusing to wear an antiunion button during a campaign by nonmanagement members to unionize the newspaper staff. Although it was a devastating time, Kerry made the experience a positive one. Kerry works now as a reporter (not editor) at a competing Wyoming newspaper and believes that he made the right decision not to wear the antiunion button. "I'd still do it again. The decision was right. I've never second-guessed that. You have got to live with yourself. I wouldn't have had any respect for myself" if he had worn the button as ordered. Kerry believes that everything happens for a reason, although "sometimes when it's happening to you, you don't understand it." Kerry reflects that, at the time of his firing, "I had lots of questions about staying in journalism" because of how unhappy he was at his job at the time. Now he realizes it wasn't journalism that made him unhappy but the place where he worked. He respects and likes the people he works for now. Although he is making less money, "that all becomes secondary when it comes down to what happened and basic happiness." Most days with his current job "I look forward to going in. I never felt that way at the old place."

If you do leave a job because you have the misfortune of being fired or laid off, remember always to maintain your professionalism. If you handle the situation with grace, control, and tactful honesty, you will have laid the groundwork for future job searches. The respect you earn by acting in a professional manner will stay with you.

ELEMENTS OF MYSELF IN THE WORLD: HOW CAN I BALANCE LIFE'S PRIORITIES?

Whether you are reading this book at the age of 18 or the age of 81, you will have or have had life goals and priorities that shift with each age and stage of life. At any given point in your life, you can figure out which career path or type of work is best for you. There may be times when you don't have that luxury because you need a paycheck, and for the time being, that is the best you can do. That's okay. Many of us have been in that situation where we plod through with our less than ideal job because we need the money and we know we are working toward something else. The point is to have something else which is better—which will make you happier—for which you are aiming. And in the process be dedicated to whatever job opportunity you have been given, whether it is waiting on tables or answering the telephones. Take pride in each job. Be glad that you have a starting point and that someone has given you that opportunity from which you can go forth and build your future. No matter who you are, no matter what type of lifepath you forge for yourself, think about what qualities are unique to you. How can you give back to your family, friends, or community through your unique abilities? What imprint do you want to leave on the world?

Don't forget, when working through this book, that your career should fit into your life and not the other way around. It's easy to get on the "fast track" and spend all your time worrying about work to the exclusion of enjoying life to its fullest. But you've heard throughout this book about self-improvement, about "following your passion," about trying to make the most out of every situation. This advice all stems from the same theme: live your life to the fullest so that you can enjoy it the best way possible.

SUMMARY

No matter what your situation is, face all new circumstances with a sense of confidence and ease. Tom Peters called one of his books *Managing Chaos*. This is an effective title because it describes the process of becoming comfortable with uncertainty—embracing the unknown and knowing that you have the inner resources to figure things out. You will better be able to navigate the uncharted waters of your job search or your new job if you *believe* that you have the ability to do that successfully. So start now. *Believe* in yourself when the way is not clear, when a professor is not there to tell you what is due when, when an authority figure is not around to offer advice. Be your own best captain.

Asking Questions and Getting Answers

1. **Building a Team: Part I.** In creating a good working environment, you must look not only to people's skills but also to their personalities and goals. Often you can have two or three people who are great individually but who don't work well together. Camille has come to you for advice on who to hire to work at her new camera store. She just purchased the store from John, who has owned and run the place for the past 20 years. The store sells cameras and camera equipment, develops film, and sells little knickknacks. Before selling the store, John had purchased a computer and software to do sophisticated work with photography, but had never learned how to use what he had purchased. Camille is very interested in developing new services through this equipment but isn't sure how to use it herself. She thinks she can afford to hire three full-time employees, although she's concerned that money might be a little tight in the beginning.

Review Camille's choices, write down the three people that you think she should hire, and explain why.

Gina, age 57, average intelligence, has worked in the store for John for 17 years, knows the entire business inside and out, has incredible loyalty to John, is very unhappy that he's sold the store, resists any change to the store, gets along very well with all the customers.

Mike, age 20, above average intelligence, hard worker, son of Camille's best friend, taking night classes in computer technology, recently fired from his last job for smoking marijuana but indicates that he has quit using completely.

Joanna, age 31, extremely bright, master's degree in computer technology with an emphasis on photography, would prefer high salary, probably temporary because she won't get paid enough, previous employer says she's difficult to get along with because she refuses to admit when she's wrong.

Anthony, age 43, bricklayer all his life, obtained his GED six months ago, seems to be very bright and a hard worker, very interested in learning anything new, a little experience in the area of computers.

Cecily, age 23, BA in literature, excellent student, recently moved to area because of husband's military post, easy to talk to, great sense of humor, introduced to you by Gina.

David, 34, level-headed, used to sell computers, single father of two.

Jonah, 28, lived all his life working on father's ranch, has knowledge of computers through father's ranch (where they had accounting programs, charts and projections), recently moved to city, is well liked.

··

YOUR SELECTIONS

a._____   Why?_____

b._____   Why?_____

c._____   Why?_____

2. **Preparing for a Career Change.** Pretend that you get to sit in the interviewer's chair for a moment. What objections would you have to hiring someone with your experience or education deficits? Prepare specific responses to every objection and figure out how to convince "You, the Interviewer" to hire "You, the Career Changer."

Objection:_____

Response:_____

Objection:_____

Response:_____

Objection:_____

Response:_____

COLLABORATIVE LEARNING AND TEAM-BUILDING SKILLS

1. **Building a Team: Part II.** In groups of three or four, review the selections you each made regarding who Camille should hire to work for her in her new camera store. Brainstorm the various possibilities. Come up with a group list of three people that you believe Camille should hire and explain why. Your group must agree on the three choices.

··

GROUP'S SELECTIONS

a._____   Why?_____

b._____   Why?_____

c._____   Why?_____

2. **Designing Your Second Career.** Sometimes you need to keep alternative careers in mind. In groups of two or three, brainstorm with each other to get ideas for second careers. Think about all the things that you liked and didn't like from previous jobs and educational experiences. Categorize all positive experiences into the groupings listed below.

PREVIOUS JOBS

Things I Liked:_____

Things I Didn't Like:_____

POSITIVE EXPERIENCES

Management/administration_____

Research/science_____

Information systems_____

Marketing/advertising/sales/customer service_____

Human resources_____

Operations_____

Accounting/finance_____

This brainstorming process will help you to identify the areas that you like and have been successful at and are the foundation for your transferable skills set.

Next, brainstorm together possible career paths for each of you.

CAREER PATHS

_____

_____

_____

_____

_____

_____

LONG-TERM PLANNING: KEY TO YOUR PERSONAL PORTFOLIO

1. **Exploring the Field of Technology.** What do you know about computers? What more can you learn? Think of a skill that you have wanted to know how to do in connection with the technological world. It could be formatting a computer disk, understanding how airline travel agencies create reservations, making graphs, using color schemes in projects, or creating "wallpaper" for the background on your computer. Select one task related to technology that you will learn in the next month:

   Task:_____

   Make a checkmark in the following space when you have learned

   how to do that task. _____

2. **Planning Ahead for Continuing Education.** Start now keeping yourself up to date and educated in your field. Think of something you can do to educate yourself in a way that you otherwise would not be educated. For instance, Beth has chosen to start attending a weekly writers' group to gather ideas from them about how to write well.

   Educational Activity:_____

   Make a checkmark in the following space when you've completed

   that activity. _____

3. **Expecting the Unexpected.** As discussed in this chapter, rarely can you depend on working at the same company for 20 years. Plan ahead now for what you will be doing and where you want to be working over the next year, 3 years, 5 years, 10 years, 20 years. Do you plan to change careers? When will you make that change?

   Next Year:_____

   _____

   _____

   In 3 Years:_____

   _____

   _____

   In 5 Years:_____

   _____

   _____

In 10 Years:_____

_____

_____

In 20 Years:_____

_____

_____

2. **Envisioning Your Future.** Close your eyes and take a moment to think about what you want in your future ten years from now. What job do you want? How much money are you earning? What kind of responsibilities do you have? What is your work week like? How about your personal life? What kind of house do you want? Do you want to marry? How many children? What kind of vacations will you take? What hobbies do you have?

Imagine that you are getting up on a typical workday. Describe that day in the space provided.

_____

_____

_____

_____

_____

_____

_____

_____

_____

_____

_____

Now look back to the final exercise in Chapter 1, where the same exercise is given. What did your perfect day look like there? Have your goals changed over the course of this book? Did they change because of ideas that you have gotten through this book or through completing the chapter exercises?

STUDENT QUESTION

Sabrina Pabilonia, Ph.D. candidate in Economics

Sabrina's biggest question right now is how to juggle her career with her husband's career. She has done her class work for her Ph.D., and all she has left is writing her dissertation. She specializes in environmental economics, and she hopes to end up in academics. Her husband just took a job in Oregon, however, and she is trying to decide what to do. She will move there now if she and her husband can afford not to have her teaching the microeconomics course that she is currently scheduled to teach. But she is concerned about the long run. She has to think about whether she should narrow her job search to where her husband is living now (there are approximately three colleges in the area) or whether she should do an all-out search. She really does want to be in academics because she likes teaching and because she thinks there's a lot less freedom to do what you want in the private sector. But now she is thinking that she should conduct a search for a job with private companies too. Also, if she *does* get a teaching job outside of her current region of the country, it may just be a one-year position rather than a guaranteed tenure track position. Her questions:

Is it a good idea to disrupt my husband's career for a one-year teaching position that may not even become tenured? And I wonder about when we should have children—while I'm still in graduate school? After I get a teaching job? What should I do about all these options—or lack of options?

I would postpone the children until you are both in a solid position jobwise. It is hard to incur multiple stresses at once—moving, changing jobs, adjusting to a new environment, and the like.

Often, these multiple stresses are unavoidable. They just happen. You may want to come to terms first with your short-and long-term career goals. What type of job will give you the most satisfaction and the best options while raising a family? Do you want to teach at the college level only or consider a community college or high school teaching position? What are the trade-offs and benefits to working now for a larger company outside of academia? The best way to answer these questions is to make a personal needs list for your goals in the short term and the long term. Then weigh what you know of each of these options against that list. That is the mind method of evaluation. In addition to your rational thoughts, you must decide what your heart most wants also. The best decisions combine both head and heart.

CAREER PROFILE

MICHELLE LARSON is a group manager for a large toy company, a board member of the national Down Syndrome Association, and the mother of a two-year-old boy with Down Syndrome named Ethan. Michelle didn't start out her career with this outcome in mind. By balancing life and career priorities, however, Michelle has learned that the best-laid plans may not ultimately fit your best interests down the line. By staying flexible and creative, Michelle has opened more avenues for herself than she ever imagined.

Michelle always had a sense of style, fashion, and design. She earned a two-year interior design degree from the Fashion Institute of Design and Merchandising. Her studies included coursework in Los Angeles and San Diego. Her first job as a sales representative was with the 100-year-old fabric company, Schumacher. She assisted designers and their clients with fabric selections for home and furniture remodeling.

When Michelle's son, Ethan, was born two years ago, she struggled to make a decision about her career. Because Ethan was born with Down Syndrome, he required more care—not because he was a difficult baby, but because of the number of doctor and therapy appointments that were required. "While I was on maternity leave, I decided that I was not comfortable leaving him. He was so vulnerable and had so many demands. I needed a job to work around my schedule."

Thus began the complete metamorphosis of Michelle's career. Michelle had learned of an educational toy company, Discovery Toys, that distributes its products through personal representatives. Initially she wasn't interested in a sales position with the company, but the more she learned about the products, the more she thought that she should investigate the possibilities. Michelle's first toy demonstration with a group of friends earned her $100 for two hours of work. She then saw a connection between her past work experience in sales, her concerns as a mother of a child with special needs, the educational benefits of the toys, and her demanding schedule and began her new career as a Discovery Toys distributor. In the last year, she has developed a successful part-time business. Currently, she manages a group of 45 sales representatives in the San Diego area and has her sights on this style of job as being her career.

To be a group sales manager requires Michelle to step out of her comfort zone. She describes herself as being reserved and shy, not the typical gregarious personality type associated with salespeople. Rather than feeling at a disadvantage, however, Michelle has learned to use her personality strengths to excel in the sales environment. "People who are calm and reserved tend to gravitate toward me. I don't intimidate them with a pushy sales attitude." Michelle's position requires her to conduct sales demonstrations, mentor employees, and develop new sales strategies. One of the reasons that Michelle enjoys her work so much is she respects the products and the company: they have won industry awards from parenting, toy, and education organizations.

"My job is easy because it doesn't seem like work. This job seems to fit naturally with my schedule, my beliefs and my income needs at this time."

To manage her daily routine, Michelle schedules everything. "Children with Down Syndrome need lots of activity and structure; they have a high need for stimulation." Besides medical-related activities, Michelle and Ethan attend several community playgroups, church groups, and parenting organizations. The mixture of work and play is good for both of them. "Ethan enjoys the stimulation, and I double my business. It seems like everywhere I go, people are interested in my products and that creates business opportunities for me."

Michelle is committed to life balance. She plans the days that she works, the times that she will return telephone calls, and the days she leaves open (she calls these days "no commitment" days). "I try to control my time and make the best choices based on my family's needs first." Michelle has been so successful with her career, volunteer work, and family responsibilities that she is ready to take on a new challenge—she was recently nominated to be on the Board of Directors of the Down Syndrome Association. She's nervous but excited about this new venture and plans to tackle it with the same creativity and enthusiasm that she uses to manage the rest of her life.

A

B

C

DO YOU HAVE ADVICE?

We would greatly appreciate your comments on what you did and didn't like about this book. We will use your comments and suggestions as we revise the book in the future.

1. What were the greatest strengths of the book?

   _____

   _____

   _____

2. What were the greatest weaknesses that you could improve on if *you* were the editor or author?

   _____

   _____

   _____

3. If you could have a conversation with the authors, what would you tell them about how to improve this book to make it more effective and inspiring for all students?

   _____

   _____

   _____

4. What other issues are important to you that you think should be covered in a book like this?

   _____

   _____

   _____

5. What were the most important lessons you learned from this book? Break up your decisions into the following:

   What you learned about yourself

   What you learned about your career potential

   What you learned about your abilities to set goals and make them happen

6. What did you learn from the end-of-chapter exercises? How would you improve them so that they could be more effective?

_____

_____

_____

7. Did you have a personal story that you believe other students would learn from? If so, the authors would love to hear from you. Write up your experience as you would a brief essay for your composition class and send it to us.

Thank you for taking the time to complete this survey. Your time and energy will make a difference in the lives of other students who are at a similar point in their own lives. Mail this form (and any personal stories) to:

Carol Carter
Prentice Hall
One Lake Street
Upper Saddle River, NJ 07458

Your name and address: _____

_____

_____

Phone: _____

	YES	NO
Do we have permission to quote you?	_____	_____
Do we have permission to contact you?	_____	_____

USEFUL WEB SITES
FOR CAREER PLANNING
AND JOB LISTINGS

1. TRIPOD.COM
    http://www.tripod.com

2. MONSTER BOARD
    http://www.monster.com

3. AMERICA'S JOB BANK
    http://www.ajb.dmi.us/index.html

4. CAREER MOSAIC
    http://www.careermosaic.com:80/cm/cm1.html

5. THE INTERNET JOB LOCATOR
    http://www.joblocator.com/jobs

6. EMPLOYMENT EDGE
    http://www.employmentedge.com/employment.edge

7. CAREER PATH
    http://www.careerpath.com

8. DR. DAN SPEARING'S JOB HUNT PAGE
    http://www.rescomp.stanford.edu/jobs

For additional web site addresses to help with your career planning, see Chapter 3 and Figure 3-1.

Write down below the additional web addresses that are useful to you:

_____

_____

_____

_____

_____

_____